THE VETERINARIAN'S WIFE

a memoir by
SUSIE BERTA

D1453331

Boll Weevil Press

2022

Published by Boll Weevil Press, bollweevilpress.com

Library of Congress CIP data
Berta, Susie
Veterinarian's Wife, The / Susie Berta.
1. Veterinarians — Spouses — Biography
921 — dc22

ISBN: 9781733467056

Also available from Boll Weevil Press
    Another Farewell to the Theatre, Marc Honea
    Lichtenbergianism: procrastination as a creative strategy, Dale Lyles
    Flies at the Well: The Trial of the Killer John Wallace, Jim Halliday/W.
        Jeff Bishop
    Personality Matters, Mr. Personality

The Veterinarian's Wife was designed by Dale Lyles. Front cover design by Susie Berta.

For my love, Rick, who was and always will be worth fighting for.

The world is violent and mercurial. It will have its way with you. We are saved only by love—love for each other and the love that we pour into the art we feel compelled to share: being a parent; being a writer; being a painter; being a friend. We live in a perpetually burning building, and what we must save from it, all the time, is love.

— Tennessee Williams

The Veterinarian's Wife

a memoir by
Susie Berta

CONTENTS

PREFACE

I begged my husband—for years—to write a book about all the stories of his experiences during his forty-six-year veterinary career. Then, because I concluded he was not now, nor would he ever be writing said book, I decided I would tackle it myself.

It was then I realized I had some things to say too. Of course, I would include animal stories and Rick's veterinary adventures, but I would also describe what it's like to be a veterinarian's wife—and not just any veterinarian or any wife but Rick Berta and me, specifically. I would share how we've acknowledged and hung on to our own identities in the process.

I've included essays of my personal reflections on our lives, and observations about life in general as it applies to us. There are stories about me, Rick, and us as a couple. There are stories about what it's like to navigate a life and marriage with so many spinning plates, how we dropped a few and broke them, and the way we put them back together despite being so different individually. It's totally a "his, mine, and ours" book.

This is a work of nonfiction, although some names have been changed. All the stories are true to the best of Rick's and my recollection. I am faithful about writing his version of what happened when I wasn't present. Some of what I share isn't pretty, especially the very personal accounts, but it's a story we both agreed to tell. Our hope is that it will resonate with others who run into challenges. Consider it a testament to how Rick and I not only recovered but now thrive in all new and wonderful ways.

My writing doesn't follow the strict confines of a through-line, chronological memoir as dictated by most publishers, but I have written my heart out and I am blessed with a publisher who believes in me. My undying thanks goes to Jeff Bishop of Boll Weevil Press for taking my book under his wing. Thanks also to Dale Lyles for his help with formatting and assistance with Scrivener—a program which, even though I consider myself to be fairly computer savvy, has been a huge pain in my ass.

Many thanks to my editors Brooke Bohinc and Peyton Heidman for their expert advice and assistance.

Also, inestimable thanks to all who have encouraged and supported me, have listened to me, read my work, made suggestions, and who don't blow smoke up my skirt. I can/could count on them always to tell me the truth:

My best and worst critic—my mother—who, despite her relentless red pen, contributed encouragement too.

Friends and family—Rick, Scotty, Nick, Leanne, Larry, Ellen.

Members of my writing group, "Three Hearts Writers"—Meredith, Liz, Trahlyta, Elsa, Martha Ann, Patti, Maureen, and Rivka.

Members of my book club, "Carpé Diem!"—Gina, Glenda, Lauren, and Carol.

All the teachers who encouraged me to write from elementary school forward: Mrs. Cheeseman, Lovett School, seventh grade English; Northside High teachers Rosemary Lockhard, Creative Writing and Herb Meyer, English; Atlanta College of Art professors Harriette Grissom, Contemporary Lit, who wrote on one of my papers, "If this art thing doesn't work out, please go into writing;" Dr. Dan Zins, World Cultures I and III, who was so enthusiastic about my writing he often gave me A+++++ on my essays; Carl Parrish, English Composition; Rick Lovell, Drawing and Sketchbook essays; Cynthia Kristen-Graham, World Cultures II; Dinah McClintock, Art History II. Phantom thanks to the literature professor at Stephens College whose name I don't recall but who wrote on my paper he was angry with me for leaving because I was a really good writer and wished me well.

Thanks to my local newspaper publishers at *The Newnan Times-Herald*—Clay and Beth Neely—who gave me the space to write and grow as a writer while establishing myself as a published one.

Thanks to all our friends—many of whom are/were Rick's large-animal and small-animal clients in our small southern town of Newnan, Georgia and others who are great, supportive, loving people who have encouraged me, expressed their pleasure over reading my articles and columns in the local newspaper and elsewhere and have promised to get a copy of my book. I have faith they were/are serious about that.

Saving the best for last, I am eternally grateful for and indebted to my darling Rick, who has been the love of my life, and the incredibly interesting, funny, wonderful person he has always been and continues to be. Even in the hard times when we were both pains in each other's asses. Even then.

Love and blessings,
Susie Berta

GETTING TO KNOW ME
IN THE MOST RANDOM WAY

Phoenix was my *birthplace*. I left Arizona in 1957 at the age of seven when my dad moved our family across the country for his new job with *The Atlanta Journal-Constitution*. Atlanta became my *home*.

Even at the tender age of seven, I knew Atlanta was home when I first saw all the beautiful trees and the green, green, green, and felt the humid air that rushed in the car window and cooled us as we drove. I would learn about the pollen from all that green soon enough.

I didn't return to Arizona until fifty-one years later when my husband, Rick, and I took an amazing trip to Phoenix, Sedona, and the Grand Canyon in 2009. I love Sedona, Scottsdale, Jerome, and the Grand Canyon. I *still* do not love Phoenix proper.

That trip made me remember the desert picnics my parents took my brother and me on just outside of Phoenix when we were little. I hated those. It was hot and dry and very dusty. I remember stepping on a small, round cactus and the exquisite pain of a zillion sharp needles my dad had to yank out of my heel with a pair of pliers. Why was I even wearing open-heeled sandals with socks in the desert? There is a photo somewhere of Larry and me perching on some random piece of driftwood, or whatever fallen things deserts have, and I am wearing overalls with a Dutch-boy haircut and looking dour. I am Tatum O'Neal in Paper Moon's evil twin.

I just heard on ABC News that losing weight can improve your memory. I would like that. If it would still allow me to forget some things, that is. Anyway, I'm sticking to my diet, and we'll just see, won't we?

Am I the only naive, babe-in-the-woods old lady in the world who just discovered the word "broccoli" is a slang term for marijuana? Please tell me you didn't know this either. Never mind how I found out.

I wore a ponytail as a little girl. When a bully who was chasing me in our apartment complex used it to pull me up and out of the deep tree well in which I was hiding, I decided it was time to get a haircut so nobody could ever do that to me again. I cut it even after my big brother beat the crap out of the bully and made her cry. After over sixty years, Ms. Davie Lemer found me on Facebook; we are friends again, and all is forgiven.

Word-lover and word-game addict, here. Blame my family. My folks had a contest every Sunday morning to see who could finish *The New York Times* crossword puzzle first, in ink. When Larry and I were young teens, our folks took us on a road trip one summer in our Dodge DeSoto (the model with the huge tail fins, remember those?) up the Eastern Seaboard from Georgia to Montreal and back. They trotted out every word game they could think of to keep us from killing each other in the back seat. "My Father Owns a Grocery Store" was a favorite until one smart-ass would invariably think of, say, an "A" word no one would ever find in a grocery store—like "aardvarks"—which led to outrage from the other one. This ultimately required parental de-escalation.

During that trip, my brother and I watched *The Tonight Show* with Johnny Carson on a motel TV the night Jerry Lewis recited his famous Announcer's Test: "One hen, two ducks . . ." We memorized all ten verses—each verse longer and more convoluted than the previous one. For the rest of the trip, we performed endless recitations. Thus, it became the spoken, ear-worm version of "Ninety-Nine Bottles of Beer on the Wall." We rattled our dad so much with our constant blather he got utterly confused and frustrated in heavy Montreal traffic, driving past road signs he didn't realize were bi-lingual. The sign with an arrow said "Pont/Bridge," which was both the French and English version. He took the turn one street too early. The memory of him yelling, "Where in the goddamn hell is the Pont Bridge!" became one of our favorite family stories forevermore.

Our parents are gone now, but Larry and I recite "One hen, two ducks . . ." when he and his wife, Ellen visit us every Christmas. We also sing Tom Lehrer songs and Pogo's beloved Christmas carol, "Deck Us All with Boston Charlie, Walla Walla Wash and Kalamazoo!" We're not above playing "My Father Owns a Grocery Store" either—despite both of us being in our seventies. God help us.

I've always been a creative. Music. Drama. Art. Writing. God endowed me with vocal talent. My brother can't sing his way out of a bucket, and he is not especially artistic, but he is the ultimate arts supporter, and he is very smart. I'm smart too. But not like Larry. Yale graduate versus art school. Maybe I have a few self-esteem issues.

My mom was a newspaper columnist and a poet. When she died, I found all her old columns for *The Arizona Republic and Phoenix Gazette* and bound volumes of her poetry. Damn, she was good.

As little kids, my brother and I loved to invite our neighbors over and put on plays in the backyard. Our stage was the porch of the log

4

cabin my dad built us with his own two hands. The logs were courtesy of the Phoenix newspaper where he worked—huge cardboard tubes left over after the newsprint paper rolled through the presses. My dad stained and shellacked every one of them and built us a mighty fine cabin.

My first showbiz trauma came when I was five on the porch of that log cabin. During a pivotal scene in which I was the pioneer mother rocking her baby and singing a sweet lullaby, my baby doll's head fell off, hitting the porch with a horrible thud. I've struggled with stage fright ever since.

When I was twelve, my mom drove me every Saturday into midtown Atlanta, dropping me off for art lessons in a big Victorian house on 15th Street. The odor of the paint, the supplies, and all the tools I wasn't sure how to use, the art I produced—none of it could compare with expressing myself through music. I was simply compelled to sing, so my art took a back seat. Who knew that as a mature adult I would attend The Atlanta College of Art across the street, then Savannah College of Art and Design at the Atlanta campus, and graduate with a BFA in art, *summa cum laude*, a mere forty-something years later? Weird.

I have sung my way through a lovely, music-filled life. For my fiftieth birthday, I did a one-woman cabaret show at the Rialto Theater in Atlanta. It was a raging success, and I did great, considering I spent the entire weekend prior curled up in a fetal position on my bed, praying my doll's head wouldn't fall off.

I have lived in Newnan, Georgia with my husband, Rick, and our two boys for over four decades. I have driven the forty-five miles to Atlanta and the forty-five miles back for many of those years. I am weary from that drive and the traffic. Thank God I'm retired.

I'm not singing now. I am quiet. Strange.

June 10, 2021 marks our fiftieth year of marriage. We've paid off our mortgage and prepaid our burial expenses. We're not moving to a "home." Ever. Carry me out in a pine box, and please don't put me on display. Better yet, turn me into ashes. I'd rather be remembered through the lens of the living or, even better, by my retouched headshot.

Our two sons, Nick and Scotty, are my heart. Our precious grandsons, Harper and Sawyer, are my joy. My husband, Rick, is my love.

I flunked spelunking almost fifty years ago. Before we were married, Rick and I were invited by our mutual friend, Steve Hudson, to go caving on a "fun" weekend in the North Georgia mountains. Steve was already well-versed in the sport and promised to teach us what we needed to know. Steve's practice session had us rappelling off a forty-foot expressway bridge at midnight down to an unfinished section of I-285 before the highway was even open to traffic. Then, Steve had us climb back up to the bridge using rope foot-slings tied with prusik knots (Google it.) and pulling ourselves up with sheer arm strength. I was abysmal at both the descent and the ascent, which should've warned us all I was not built for spelunking. We should've just gone to a movie instead, but we did not heed that warning.

The most fun I had the entire weekend was barreling up the highway in our friend's Jeep singing along to Crosby, Stills, and Nash and camping cuddled next to Rick in a sleeping bag. And I'm no camper—that says something right there.

The caving episode was a cataclysmic disaster. I was terrible at—and didn't enjoy one bit—wearing a carbide lamp on my head while lowering myself into deep, dark holes in the earth. Ditto on bellycrawling along ink-black, pebbly passageways, squeezing myself like a sausage through dank, labyrinthine tunnels barely two-feet tall by two-feet wide. I enjoyed even less chimneying across bottomless, menacing crevasses—my back and butt pressed against cold vertical rock with my feet pushing on the opposite wall and total oblivion waiting below.

Inching along sideways ever so carefully, it became instantly clear to me this activity was sure as hell no Disney attraction. There was no net, and in one wrong move, a person could fall down into the perilous darkness and die. Yep, I began to freak out, finally having a meltdown half-way through a narrow, rocky tunnel leading toward the exit. I stopped mid-bellycrawl sobbing. Like a cork plugging a bottle, my body was blocking the last thirty feet of egress, halting all forward motion for everyone else behind me. A whole lot of frantic encouragement commenced from the voices in line bringing up the rear. Still, I was pitiful, frozen in place. I responded, wailing, "You guys shouldn't have made me first in line!" They reminded me no one wanted to be discovered years down the road as skeletal remains in that godforsaken shaft, least of all me. So I forced my ass into gear, and everyone eventually emerged to breathe fresh air and bask in the sun again. The whole thing was brutal. But I still say, at least I tried; therefore, I was the most game date ever. Also, spelunking is at the top of my list: "Things I Will Never, Ever Do Again."

I have a bum knee, and I hate that. Even after knee-replacement. Ain't that a kick in the spokes?

I love lamb. Medium rare. Else why bother?

I have a lovely studio workspace above our detached garage in which to paint. Although, these days I spend more time writing.

I would refinish my hardwood floors only a) it's too expensive, b) the thought of moving every stick of furniture out of the first floor makes me want to take a nap, and c) I'm old. Who cares?

I was a co-conspirator in a heinous crime as a kid on Christmas in 1962. My dad was ultra-desperate to find a last-minute gift for Mom the day before Christmas, so he took Larry and me shopping. Nothing passed muster until we entered the Lenox Square Mall pet store and stood before the live, capuchin monkey mugging for us in his cage. My brother and I swooned, gushed, and kind of forced my dad to pull the trigger on that purchase. Worst idea ever. Dad had lost all rational thought by then, bowing to the pressure of his procrastination and our adolescent pleas.

After Christmas Day was done and we were all in bed, the story goes my mom spent the evening alone with a bottle of scotch talking to the monkey, wondering what Dad was thinking, and where had she gone wrong. It only took a week before the monkey disappeared, along with the huge cage that had displaced the entire contents of the breakfast nook in our once-tidy kitchen. "Returned to the pet store," they said. Poor Dad. Poor Mom. Epic fail. Mea culpa.

I drive a 2011 Hyundai Santa Fe, which means that 2020 or 2021 might've been years for a new car. Instead, those years have been the latest downers in years of unsettling, stultifying societal discontent and global upheaval. A deadly, world-wide virus. Lockdown. Crazy politics. Riots. Insurrection. The earth's poles are melting, while the people of earth are more polarized than ever. Civil discourse is dead or at least sputtering. I dare not predict how the rest of 2021, 2022, and beyond will fare. So, for me, 2021 is the year of the big reminder that peace, health, things, and people are not guaranteed. I can only rely on love, hope, and gratitude—the intangibles that cannot be taken from me without my permission.

But I still wouldn't mind a new car.

Labors, Deliveries, Growth, and Grace

LABORS, DELIVERIES, GROWTH, AND GRACE

As of 2021, Rick has been a veterinarian for over forty-six years. It is impossible to overstate his dedication, integrity, skill, popularity, delight in good outcomes, and despair over bad ones. His devotion to his clients and to their sick, injured, and helpless animals is legend. His kindness and his selfless, punishing work ethic are unwavering. Rick's complete and utter lack of insight into the rewards and, more especially, the personal ramifications of all of it for himself and his family went unacknowledged for many years. How the broader effects of his choices fanned out into the world from one situation, decision, event, or career seemed to float beyond him.

Rick's very early professional years, beginning in 1977 when he started his own practice, were focused on proving himself as a large-animal vet to a then-rural community around Newnan, Georgia. He was a head-down, nose to the grindstone, no boundaries kind of vet. Farmers and large-animal owners clamored for him. They were in need, and they showed it.

Just after we moved to Newnan that year, Rick walked out of a grocery store one afternoon to find a note under the windshield wiper of his newly outfitted, baby-blue F-250 complete with a custom veterinary unit filling the back bed. The unit was shiny, new, and bright with chrome handles and white fiberglass drawers, compartments, and doors for storing equipment, supplies, and medicine. The cost of the truck was a pricey fifty-six hundred dollars. The custom veterinary unit was an added expense of four-thousand dollars, but it was its own best advertising. There was no mistaking who this guy was as he drove around town—the vet had arrived. One random person in town did pull up beside Rick at a traffic light to ask Rick if he was driving an ice cream truck. Seriously. Rick was amused and kindly set him straight.

The note on Rick's windshield in the Kroger parking lot read: *Heard you were here. Welcome! We are so glad! We need you!* It was signed by Dick Blackwell—an airline pilot. He, like a lot of pilots in the area, owned a couple of horses and some acreage. Dick and his wife, Shirley, would become wonderful clients and friends, among many.

For decades, Rick worked hard to make a living and show his love for his clients and family. He maintained a brutal work ethic, being on call 24/7 and available to minister to anyone's animal at a moment's notice—no matter what. They needed him, and Rick needed them. Our family needed him too, but we learned to enjoy him while we could. For in a moment's notice, on any day, the phone could ring, and Rick could vanish.

———

Rick's programming as a young boy—second eldest in a large family of six children—was to work hard to show love. His mother, Libby, was busy as a stay-at-home mom raising six children, cooking, and cleaning while listening to news-talk radio in the kitchen for adult companionship. His dad, Joe, Jr. was gone a lot, working as a salesman for a chemical company.

Rick's Italian grandfather, Joseph T. Berta, Sr., was bigger than life, rich, blustering, and incessant, asking even from the time Rick was a little boy-child in the 1950s what Rick wanted to be when he grew up. This great man was Rick's bête noir—his role model and inspiration. Although Joe, Sr. never knew it, his family gave him the affectionate nickname, "The Big Pizza."

Rick's grandfather rose in business as the son of an immigrant without two coins to rub together to become, through sheer will and grit, a wealthy executive on the board of the Pittston Clinchfield Coal Company.

Not only did The Big Pizza question Rick, but he also told him countless stories about growing up and what life was like for him. Joe, Sr. wanted Rick to grow up to be a success, despite the inevitable trials that would lie ahead, so he spoke of overcoming adversity and working hard. Joe, Sr. had also seen too many offspring of wealthy, successful men struggling to chart their way through life spoiled by their daddy's money, navigating without a rudder, and often lacking a moral compass. He would require his grandchildren to have both and to steer their own ways through tough waters but not endlessly. They had to choose a destination. To do that, they had to have a plan and know what they wanted.

"Why, my formal education ended at the eighth grade," The Big Pizza would say, hitching his pants up above his oversized belly— perhaps a Freudian variation of pulling oneself up by his belt rather than his bootstraps. "My folks were so poor I had to quit school because they couldn't afford the five-cent bus fare to high school and back." Joe, Sr. always added, "They passed out brains before they passed out diplomas anyway, ya know. BUT," he would catch himself, clearing his throat and warning, "you, young man, you must keep going. Get your education. Have a plan. What will your path be when you do?"

The Big Pizza regaled Rick with many stories over the years—sometimes annoying Rick but always captivating him. Joe, Sr. spoke of how he went to work after the eighth grade, circa 1910, starting in a menial job with the coal company. Regardless of his low-ranking employment, he did the best job he could do, no matter what anyone asked of him.

"Even if you're just a dogcatcher," Joe, Sr. would interrupt himself, leaning forward, shooting a keen eye at Rick, and over-enunciating, "be the very best dogcatcher you can be."

Then, leaning back in story mode again, Joe, Sr. explained the details of that menial first job in the coal mine: He sat all day between two conveyor belts sorting out coal from stones, tossing out the stones. His stories continued on and on, for years, all to show the effects of work and human will over circumstance.

"So, kid, what are you going to be?"

What little kid is equipped to respond to that question and make the answer stick, especially when peppered every day by his intimidating role model? As a defense mechanism, Rick thought of an answer early on—one he hoped his grandfather would accept. I suspect it was because Rick grew up in a house full of cherished dogs—Hercules, Heidi, and Blitz among them. The dogs ruled the roost, lounging on hairy, sheet-covered furniture in every room in Rick's house and looked forward to their daily runs in the woods with him almost as much as Rick did. His grandfather liked ponies and horses.

As a young man, Joe, Sr. had seen ponies pulling ore carts out of the mines "because horses were too tall to walk inside in the shafts." After earning his wealth, Joe, Sr. would purchase ponies and horses for all the adults and grandchildren in his family, building a riding ring on his expansive property in Pennsylvania. The Big Pizza, too, had a clear affinity for animals.

"I want to be a veterinarian," Rick would reply, hoping for some respite from the constant barrage. His grandfather accepted that answer from his young grandson, but he never stopped asking the same question. Rick thinks it was because the old man was okay with the veterinarian thing, but Joe, Sr. really wanted engineers—the people he considered the very smartest in the entire mining industry.

Rick's dad, Joseph T. Berta, Jr., became an engineer but not the kind relating to mining or coal. No doubt Joe, Jr. wanted his own identity, having been so long in the shadow of his old man's greatness and frank intimidation. No, Rick's dad had a master's degree in chemical engineering. Joe, Jr. launched himself into a different career independent of his father. Even still, he never quite escaped from the strong gravitational pull of the old man's orbit and expectations. A sense of competition always haunted Rick's dad. He needed to be as good as, or better than, The Big Pizza. His efforts in that vein would prove consequential to everyone around him.

So it was always the same question to young Rick and always the same answer. Until one day, it was time to decide for real, and the young boy was a young man—off to college at The University of Georgia in 1967. By this time, Rick had answered the question the same way enough times he believed it himself and began his journey.

———

I was a high school junior in the fall of 1966 when Rick and I met on a blind date. We dated off and on until the beginning of my senior year in the fall of 1967 when Rick bundled himself off to college. Packing his luggage, along with his familial baggage, he left for school to begin his travels down the pre-veterinary path. Rick spent his freshman year at UGA competing for a slot on the varsity wrestling team and winning a partial scholarship. I was deep into high school musical performances and drama productions. We couldn't have been more different in our interests. Differences notwithstanding, we still saw each other on occasional weekends when he made the hour-and-a-half drive home from Athens.

We dated more consistently during the whole summer of 1968 after my high school graduation. Then, I left for my freshman year at Stephens College in Columbia, Missouri, and Rick went back to UGA. We wrote each other letters, but the distance wasn't working in our favor. I didn't know he had sustained a herniated disc in his neck requiring surgery and could no longer compete in athletics. He didn't know I had traveled to Hollywood to sing in a televised talent competition and lost—confidence shaken and disillusioned with showbiz. Later, with athletics only a painful memory, Rick explored the fraternity route and became a brother at Phi Gamma Delta—one of the best on campus.

Rick had left home a shy, reserved guy. The fraternity transformed him into a gregarious, hail-fellow-well-met. He made lifelong friends with his frat brothers who gave him a chance to come out of his shell—sophomoric high jinks included. These were guys Rick could depend on and who had his back no matter what. Even today.

I came home in May of 1969 after my freshman year at Stephens, and our relationship reignited as I found Rick far more mature and vastly more interesting. Then, after I returned to school that fall, I made it through only one partial semester before dropping out and coming home for good in November of 1969.

I felt lost at school; I missed Rick terribly and was tired of living so far from home. Our differences had become less important than our common interests. Rick didn't consider himself a writer, and he certainly couldn't type worth a damn, but he was a deep thinker, well-read, and spoke intelligent, persuasive words. I was drawn more and more to him by our conversations, his thoughts, and his keen wit. Rick was even a fellow Episcopalian. He liked me more, too, for the same reasons. Very much so, in fact. By 1970, we were engaged.

———

We married in June 1971 and spent that summer happily renting a tiny duplex on Park Avenue in Athens, Georgia. We joked about our Park Avenue address and the house that sat on a weedy, gravel lot behind the Gulf gas station.

"Y'all come see us," we told our friends, "and we'll show you our fancy digs and then hit the town Park Avenue style!"

Rick needed one physics class in order to graduate and complete Tuskegee's veterinary school admission requirements. The University of Georgia's veterinary school had put him on the waiting list for admission, so his chances of getting in there were less than great.

While rules have since changed, in those days, vet schools had certain regional agreements about who could even apply. If you lived in Georgia, The University of Georgia and Tuskegee were your only choices. Auburn's vet school was off the table. So Rick decided one physics course would not be too high a hurdle for a chance at gaining admission to Tuskegee's veterinary school and an entire future. He was told they would wait for his transcript before making their decision on his application. Completion of the course didn't guarantee admission, even so. Rick would have to complete his class, send off his transcript, and hope they accepted him.

Rick busied himself with summer school as I tried my newlywed-best to feather our modest nest and find a job. The kitchen was minuscule; only one person was able to squeeze in at a time. I had already demonstrated a complete and utter lack of success at the nearby laundromat, using way too much soap in the washing machine which resulted in just what you might expect—overflowing bubbles approximating an *I Love Lucy* episode, which I found unamusing, as did the proprietor who asked that I not return.

I was due a successful domestic accomplishment, and as it so happened, I had the potential that same day to have it. A neighbor had dropped off a sack of fresh-picked vegetables at our door while I was at the laundromat, and I set about to making something special for dinner.

I peered at the long, green vegetables in the bag. They were ripe and still warm from the summer sun. Reaching in, I took them out and laid them on the counter—four nice, big, fat zucchinis! I marveled. I had already put two Cornish hens in the oven to roast, basting them with butter every fifteen minutes, and they were approaching done. Then, as they were just finishing roasting, showing off a gorgeous golden skin and smelling divine, I retrieved a skillet to begin the vegetables. I washed and sliced the zucchini. I grabbed an onion from the tiny pantry and butter from the refrigerator. I peeled and sliced the onion, cutting a generous cube of butter from the stick and placing both in a skillet to sizzle. After the onions were soft and smelling fabulous, I put the zucchini in the skillet to sauté. Just as it was finishing, Rick walked in the door.

"Time for dinner!" I chirped, as a new wife and domestic goddess would. He sniffed the air rich with butter, onions, and Cornish hens.

"Wow, smells great!" he declared, sitting down at the table, eager to partake.

I served Rick his plate at our little black, melamine table on the sun porch off the kitchen. As I sat, I saw him looking down at the gorgeous meal I had prepared. I had surprised myself with my new culinary talent, and I was so proud of my dinner. Rick took a bite of the zucchini.

"Well, there's a first time for everything," he whispered, forcing a smile as he chewed. My eyes wide, I gave him a quizzical look. "Sweetheart, I have to say," he began, choosing his words, "I have never, ever in my life had sautéed cucumbers."

Before I could say a word, he added, "But these are the best sautéed cucumbers I've ever had!"

The next day I set about finding a job to bring in a little income during the summer. I visited the career office at The University of Georgia where I had heard they could help me find a job. They would give me a typing test to determine my fitness for a secretarial position. I had been a good typist in high school typing class, and I typed my own papers while in college, but I was rusty. I had typed very little in the last several years. What I discovered was employers don't want to engage in on-the-job training by hiring rusty typists. They want accomplished secretaries who could whip off letters and memos without mistakes.

My typing test proved, without a doubt, that they would not be hiring me for a job. That summer, the only available jobs the career center knew of were clerical. I left, head hanging and discouraged. I had proven I couldn't do a simple load of laundry, I didn't know the difference between a cucumber and a zucchini, and now I couldn't type well enough to even get a clerical job. Given time, I could brush up and get my typing mojo back, but I didn't have the luxury of time. I needed a job, and I needed one pronto.

That led me to walking into the Athens Howard Johnson's to apply for the waitress job they advertised.

I had never been a waitress, and I didn't know how to be one, but by God, I just knew I could figure it out. How hard could it be? They didn't seem to care I was unqualified, either, because they hired me. My first shift would start the next day at six o'clock. In the morning.

I earned all-new respect for waitresses—whom we call servers today.

I lasted one week at Howard Johnson's. My departure wasn't only about my frank ineptitude, the long hours, my aching body, and the occasional snarky customers. It was also about the post-menopausal grand dames gracing this particular establishment with major attitude that came with decades of waitressing tenure and entitlement. Crusty, four-star generals in aprons fighting for hierarchy and territory, they were in constant conflict over the air-conditioner thermostat. That battleground was won and lost multiple times a day—the temperature inside the restaurant alternating between glacial and a heat approximating Death Valley. Every day was an incessant, un-winnable war, and I was in the crossfire. Overall, I feared if I stayed, I would either suffer and die from the toxic, emotional back-and-forth or from physical exhaustion and a cracking good case of pneumonia—perhaps all the above.

Forced to admit I couldn't hack it, I surrendered, hung up my apron, said "so long," and dragged myself home in defeat. I was now a complete, proven failure. The rest of the summer I vowed to work on my typing and domestic skills. Although I would need a job after Rick finished that quarter, I knew without a doubt waitressing would not be it.

———

In August 1971, with Rick's physics class completed and final transcript sent off to Tuskegee, we waited. We would need to hear if the vet school accepted him before we could make final plans for our entire future. Because our time in Athens would be so brief, we had used my parents' address in Atlanta as our permanent return address. One day, the phone rang in our tiny apartment, and my mother's breathless voice greeted me on the other end of the line.

"There's a notice here of a registered letter that only Rick can sign for at the post office," she said. "You all need to come home. This could be the letter you've been waiting for!"

I hung up, anticipating our entire lives wrapped up in one registered letter. If accepted, Rick and I would need to hurry to Alabama to begin school in September. If rejected, we had no clue what we were going to do. Well, I knew I wouldn't be a waitress.

Rick didn't have a Plan B if the news was bad. We had an inkling of what the letter might be, however, since rejection letters are not usually of the registered variety. Even so, we wouldn't know for sure until we made the hour-and-a-half trip to Atlanta to open the letter. My parents huddled with Rick and me in the post office as Rick opened the letter that would reveal whether their daughter had married a loser.

Unfolding the letter, Rick read aloud, "Dear Mr. Berta, Congratulations!"

We hooped and hollered, high-fiving and back-slapping right there in the middle of the sedate United States Post Office as people stared. My husband—my parents' son-in-law—had done it. Rick was going to be a doctor.

Awhile later, my mother shared with me a comment made by her snooty Buckhead neighbor about Rick's vet school acceptance.

"Well, it's a shame Susie couldn't marry a professional man, a real doctor," this neighbor had sniffed.

My mother said she just smiled and remained silent, though utterly peeved. She knew this snooty lady's son had already failed to launch, had no job prospects, and was still living at home, hanging out in the basement. Yes, sir, Rick Berta—the grandson of a poor immigrant miner, her daughter's husband—had found his compass, set his sails, and directed his rudder. He was off to vet school with his wife—her daughter—to do great things as a doctor. *Well, Rick will be a doctor, and you are a snob*, my mother thought to herself as their chat ended and she turned to go. Snooty Lady had a worthless son, and they both knew it. Mom didn't need to say a word.

With Rick's undergrad degree and vet school acceptance in hand, we set off for vet school in Alabama in 1971, finished it in 1975, and once again set sail on another adventure—horse country in Virginia.

———

In 1975, at the ripe age of twenty-six, Rick started his first job as a real, official veterinary medical *doctor* at Woodside Equine Clinic in Ashland, Virginia. Rick and I hadn't had time to find a place to live, so in the sweltering heat of a June afternoon, we moved ourselves into the "rustic" space upstairs above the clinic's barn.

"The barn will be temporary, baby," Rick promised me. "I'm sure it's a nice barn, and we can talk about this for the rest of our lives." Oh, how right he was.

The Virginia heat rivaled the Alabama heat, turning roads into wavy, liquid mirages and cars into ovens. Imagine my thrill at our new accommodations—no air conditioning save one rickety floor fan. There were no screens on windows, no bathroom, and a mattress on the plank floor. Flies from the stalls below zoomed around our heads, bumping into our faces. Pungent Eau de Manure perfumed the air, wafting through the windows and up the staircase.

The owners cordially invited us to use the bathroom in their house nearby until we could find a place of our own. It was then I swore to Rick we would find permanent digs very much sooner than later. Rick was too overwhelmed with the job that lay ahead for him to even consider looking. So I did. After a couple of false starts—the barn being the first and the second being a single, upstairs bedroom in a woman's house just to get us out of the barn—we found a rental house with air conditioning, a kitchen, and a washer and dryer too. It would do.

Rick put his education to use at Woodside and began learning more about the actual world. He now had a mentor and taskmaster who worked too hard and never rested. Milton Kingsbury, DVM was the very definition of boundless, kinetic energy. He was tall and lanky, wore a perpetual sunburn on his face and neck, and spoke in a clipped, authoritarian voice. He rose ultra-early, worked super late, and required the same of his newest hire—young Dr. Rick Berta. They wore green cotton, wrap-around smocks with the veterinary insignia and clinic logo stitched on the breast pocket. Even in the heat of summer they had on neat, button-down shirts and ties underneath—Milton's edict.

"We are professionals, and we must look professional."

Milton taught Rick invaluable, real-world, post-graduate veterinary medicine while showing him how to overwork oneself into exhaustion. This reinforced Rick's familial programming and helped solidify it as though carved in stone. Milton gave Rick a practice vehicle to drive—a dust-covered, wood-paneled Ford Esquire wagon. Loaded into the back compartment were large wooden boxes housing pullout drawers filled with equipment, supplies, and drugs.

Then, Milton sent Rick out to conquer the world.

Milton's veterinary partner was the esteemed Olive K. Britt, DVM. She was a UGA vet school grad in 1950-something. Olive was renowned and respected for her knowledge and a trailblazer for women in the veterinary profession. Her clients were top notch; among them was Penny Tweedy at The Meadow when Secretariat won the Triple Crown in 1973. Olive was older than Milton, calmer, and more sedate—a perfect balance to Milton's intensity. Rick was learning his real-world equine medicine at the feet of two masters, and he knew it.

Mary Ann, Milton's wife, offered me a position in the practice's office working alongside her. She was as intense as her husband, and frankly, I sensed danger in too much family entanglement. So I secured a job as a typist-transcriptionist where I was tucked away in the medical records department at Crippled Children's Hospital in Richmond. My typing proved exemplary—thanks to my four-year job as a secretary at the Alabama Exchange Bank during our vet school days in Tuskegee.

We carried on for two years in Ashland, Virginia. Rick worked day and night as I worked during the day and waited night after night for him to come home. I never knew when he would arrive or in what shape. Rick's day job often flowed right into his night job, and his goal for it all was to survive and help the animals without killing any. Surviving was my goal too. Thriving would come later.

One late night, Rick shuffled through the kitchen door, head-down like a teenager trying not to get caught breaking curfew. He raised his head and showed me his fat lip and a scraped, bulging nose as little flecks of dried blood scattered on his face and a row of black stitches poked from his upper lip.

"What the hell!" I gasped.

"Horse," Rick mumbled. "I trusted the owner to restrain her animal while I was at the ass-end of it trying to be a good vet. My mistake."

"What happened?"

"Oh, she was riding on a country road. School bus drove by. Side mirror hit the horse. Lucky it didn't kill 'em both. Turned out its tail was broken. Never believe 'em when they say they can restrain their own animal. Like I said, my mistake. I don't want to talk anymore. It hurts."

That was a hard, real-world lesson to learn. Rick was fortunate the horse's kick missed his teeth, but it split his upper lip clear up to his nostril and scraped, rather than broke, his nose. At the emergency room, the attendant pinched Rick's nose, rocking it back and forth, asking, "Does this hurt?" Rick showed great restraint by not punching the guy, demanding his lip be sewn so he could leave.

Later, when Rick got his sense of humor back, we staged a photo with his battered mug posing next to a folded newspaper bearing a taped-on strip of paper with the doctored headline, "Ali Loses in 3rd Round to Upstart Newcomer, Berta." At least we could laugh. I think I have a picture of that somewhere.

During our two years in Ashland, Rick made equine house calls to all kinds of places—from gentrified professional horse farms like The Meadow to well-kept residential farms to backyard hard-pan dirt patches surrounded by drooping wire fence in the godforsaken backwoods of Virginia. He delivered foals, cured colics, de-wormed horses, administered vaccinations, diagnosed lamenesses, and sewed up everything that could be sewn. Rick saw it all.

On the occasion someone hauled a horse into the clinic, Rick might get to participate in a surgery. I was present for one of those one weekend. The owner suspected colic, but the horse was still standing, so he trailered her in. Once the mare arrived at the clinic and was backed out of the trailer, she stood long enough for Milton to put his stethoscope to her belly.

"This lady is going to need surgery," Milton said, matter-of-factly.

On the spot, as if on cue, the mare went down, collapsing in pain. Milton and Rick anesthetized her, positioned her, and opened her belly. They found a long portion of intestine swollen as big as a 12" diameter sewer pipe, hard as stone. It took the strength of both vets to lift the heavy intestine outside her body.

"Sand colic," Milton proclaimed as soon as he made his lengthwise incision. Sand—lots and lots of it—flowed out like water gushing from an open faucet. Enough sand spilled on the ground to fill a child's sandbox. She was from an area that had pastures with sandy soil and had been ingesting small amounts of sand with each graze. Over time it built up into a fifty-pound blockage that wouldn't wait. Once the intestine was emptied, they flushed it clean with sterile saline, sewed her up, and gave her medication.

She would wake, stand, and live another day.

———

And so it went. In 1977, after two years in Virginia and six years of marriage, we were pregnant. The baby was due in mid-May. We joked about putting me in a clean stall with fresh hay and having Rick deliver it—pure cheesy, veterinary humor.

It was the hottest May on record, and I was nearing ten days past my due date. Fat, swollen, sweaty, cranky, and miserable, I emphatically declined an invitation to attend an outdoor barbecue for Senator John Warner and his wife, Elizabeth Taylor. Yes, that Liz Taylor. Not even a famous legend with violet eyes and the sixty-eight carat Taylor-Burton diamond could beckon me out into that heat in my condition.

But when my time came at noon on May 26th and I knew what was happening, Rick was not home. I reasoned my labor wasn't too far along—no water had broken, and the contractions were still far apart—so I got my keys and proceeded out the door to drive myself to the hospital. I had begun to master independence as a vet's wife, having no expectations around Rick's availability—ever. But as if by magic, Rick pulled into the drive.

"Wanted to come home and check on you," he said, smiling, hanging his farmer's-tanned arm out the window. "What are you doing?"

Blinking back happy tears, I couldn't believe he was there. "Having a baby," I said, straining to speak. "Let's go!"

It wasn't long before I realized what a miracle it had been Rick came home when he did. I closed my eyes, flooded with relief he was driving. My discomfort was becoming more intense by the minute. I would have been a danger to myself and others. But as we got off the freeway and headed for the hospital, what did my sweet, overworked husband do?

Rick hung a left and wheeled it into Jack in the Box.

"If you're OK for just a sec, I need to eat," he reasoned, "and I figure we'll be at the hospital for a while."

Stunned, trying to craft a measured response that would not catapult me into a stroke, all-out labor, or result in my injuring him, I replied as succinctly as I could. "I'm OK," I managed, wincing, "but for God's sake make it fast." We were fifth in line.

The wait was neither fast, nor was I at all measured by the time we pulled out of Jack in the Box. I was hurting. I was vocal. I was anxious-sweating and irritated. The food smelled good too, which didn't help my state of mind. I dared not eat since I didn't know what the future held for me, and I wanted to be ready for anything.

Turns out, not eating was a good move because I ended up having a C-section many hours later, giving birth to a nine-pound and eleven-ounce boy-child-giant we named Scott on Memorial Day weekend in a hospital filled to capacity.

In those days, husbands were not allowed in the operating room, so I went in alone—bolstered only by the kind encouragement of medical strangers around me. C-sections aren't very warm and fuzzy births. I was highly anxious and awake with only a cloth partition stretched across my chest preventing me from viewing the proceedings. Rick couldn't be there encouraging me to push, holding my hand, taking pictures, kissing me, or laying our newborn baby on my chest.

No, it was a certain, unwelcome detachment and anxiety that sat itself heavy upon my chest, instead, keeping me from the camaraderie and magical experience of the natural birth I'd imagined and so hoped for. I felt no surgical pain at least—thanks to the magic of an epidural—except for when the baby was pulled from my body.

I honestly think it should be called a C-Suction. Nobody tells you about that part. My heart felt as though it were being sucked out along with my lungs and every internal organ I possessed. When the tugging was over, though, the baby delivered to the world and my innards returned to homeostasis, I heard that baby cry. It was the most beautiful, soul-filling music in the world. The nurse held him next to me, face to face, and I burst into tears, sobbing with relief, joy, and exhaustion. He was finally here, and we were at last united. I longed to hold him, but that would have to come later.

Post-delivery, I would even have to spend a few hours in the public hallway until a room was ready. Without introduction or a howdy-do, a nurse leaned over my bed rail and grabbed my flabby belly, digging deep to knead my also flabby uterus like bread dough. I gasped as she squeezed hard where the fresh staples held together my hours-old incision. This was Medieval torture. Rick was with me by that time and tried his joke on the nurse—the one about how he had been prepared to deliver the baby in a stall with fresh hay. My hazy recollection is that she was not amused. By this time, neither was I.

I spent a week in the hospital—standard operating procedure in 1977 for C-sectioned mothers. It gave me time to rest and get to know my little one. We tried to breastfeed, but it was not meant to be. Another big disappointment. But in the overall scheme of things, we had a baby—a beautiful, healthy baby.

Rick missed the new parents' dinner the hospital offered to couples after delivering their babies in favor of a sick or dying animal. I can't remember which, if I ever knew, but that one stung. And I had to deal with it, whether I liked or understood it. Rick's absence would be a harbinger of our future.

At least I didn't have to drive myself to the hospital. Rick was there the day of the birth. We had a beautiful, if not giant, son we nicknamed "Sarge" because he had a full head of reddish-brown hair that stood straight up like an official military high-and-tight cut. Rick visited when he could and was there to take me home. That's all that mattered; that's what I told myself anyway. That was my story, and I was sticking to it.

We brought that beautiful, beloved baby home, thus launching ourselves right into the confidence-obliterating terror of the care and feeding of a first child. All the nest-fluffing and parenting books in the world could not have adequately prepared Rick and me for the exquisite awesomeness and the stark reality of bringing home a living, breathing, tiny human whose very survival depended on us not screwing up.

My folks flew up to help. My mom was, of course, wise about a lot of things, but feeding newborns after almost thirty years wasn't one of them. Both of my parents were preoccupied with doing it perfectly. So was I. Genetics, I presume. I had already failed at breastfeeding, so we all obsessed over filling baby bottles with powdered formula and sterile water to the exact level required. I mean exact. Like, if we missed the measurement mark on the bottle by a fraction of a millimeter, the child could suffer certain death or disfiguring rickets at a minimum.

Fortunately, we were visited early on by the Kingsburys' farm manager, Jimmy, and his family who stopped by to pay their respects and congratulate us. Jimmy's wife, Theresa, had their fat, happy ten-month-old baby, Jobe, slung on one hip. Jobe was dressed in only a diaper, sucking on a pacifier, blissful in his countenance, looking like he had just played in a sandbox full of dirt. Theresa walked through the kitchen door just as we were fixated on filling Scott's next bottle, and she served up a word of advice with a side of southern drawl.

"Aww, y'all don't need t' fuss s'much," she said. "If I kin raise up this young 'un, y'all shorely kin raise that 'un!"

We had to agree and thanked Theresa kindly for her wisdom.

After that, we breathed easier; she was absolutely right.

———

We left Virginia in June 1977 almost immediately after Scott's arrival, coming back to Georgia to start Rick's practice in Newnan. It was time for him to fly solo. We chose Newnan for its lovely environs, farms with large animals aplenty, and proximity to Atlanta—only forty miles up the road—for me, the city girl.

When Rick was in vet school, he studied large- and small-animal medicine, the whole gamut. Early on in his education, I was envisioning coming back home to Atlanta where Rick would don a white coat and work at a veterinary clinic and come home every night at 6:00 p.m. How wrong was I? I suppose my first clue was when he accepted the job in Virginia horse country. I still held out hope we would return to the white coat and city life, but by the time we left Virginia for Newnan, I knew what I was in for. Ever the game and supportive wife, I said, "OK, if that's what you want then let's do this."

Still, it took me awhile to get used to the whole large-animal practice thing. And the not white coat. And the not vet office. And the not getting home at 6:00 p.m.

First National Bank officer, Ron Duffey, took a chance on us and granted us a loan for that brand spanking new truck and fiberglass veterinary insert. We converted a bedroom in our house into an office. I fielded phone calls from clients, some of whom could talk a blue streak, therefore holding the phone line busy and keeping Rick from calling in. No cell phones. No computers. And no expensive base station and radio. Still only phone booths.

I sent Rick from pillar to post on his veterinary rounds, acquired a microwave to heat his dinners, and perfected the art of doing a large-animal veterinarian's laundry. Basically, that meant hiking our water bill sky-high because I washed everything he brought home—twice with Tide, separate from the other laundry, one time in cold water, the next time in hot. Sometimes I could add Clorox, but on the things that weren't colorfast, vinegar also came in handy.

Every day, Rick brought home all kinds of biological grahdoo on his clothes despite his efforts to avoid it, especially during foaling or calving. Rick learned to put the O.B. chains on the baby and hand the owner the short end of the chain. This way, the owner was an active, willing participant in the birth, excited to be standing so close to the action between the business end of the animal and the vet. Aww, how sweet.

In truth, the owner was a human shield.

When the baby was pulled through the birth canal, liquid stool in the colon came squirting out like a fire hose, baptizing the owner, and sparing the vet from the bulk of it. Invariably, though, Rick still got his fair share of collateral splatter to bring home on his coveralls.

If a foal or calf were stressed from the birth and not breathing well, Rick would pick the baby up by its hind legs and swing it from side to side to create negative pressure in its little lungs. Afterbirth and slimy grahdoo got slung hither and yon in that process, adding to the stuff already on Rick. It was hard on a man's back and arms, too, when that baby was seventy or eighty pounds.

Then, if its breathing was still not up to par, Rick would clear the baby's nostrils with his fingers, hold its mouth closed, put his lips directly on the baby's slimy nose, and blow. Again, he was collecting even more birth fluid and biological matter.

These are but a fraction of a vet's exposure to, and tolerance for, wearable biology, and the exotic laundering opportunities afforded to the wife of the large-animal vet. And also why Rick showered and brushed his teeth—twice—as soon as he arrived home.

The years flew, and Scotty became a toddler, and then a little boy who loved riding with his dad on calls. I now had two jobs—or three when you count parenting. Duh. I helped Rick part-time with the office and got another part-time job as a secretary at a tiny Episcopal church down the road. Rick no longer restricted his practice to just horses and saw all kinds of large, four-legged creatures. They qualified as large animals as long as they weren't dogs or cats. Although, once (or so) he did neuter a barn cat in a farmer's bathtub.

Kids who grow up on farms see a lot of nature and know much more about animals than your average apartment-dwelling city kid. Scotty was like a farm kid without the farm, riding around with his dad, visiting farms and animals, seeing how things were, learning the ropes, witnessing birth, life, sickness, death, and injury. Those calls coming in for help with animals in labor were always dramatic and played out either for the good or the not so good.

Timing was everything. Cows are usually in labor for four to six hours. Horses take only thirty minutes to an hour, tops. There was no real knowing how long an animal might have been in distress if someone had not watched them carefully. As a result, by the time Rick arrived on the scene, unhappy, non-viable births were all too common. Scotty had seen enough of those, too, and was getting discouraged.

One day, Rick and Scotty went on a call for a fellow whose first-calf heifer was in labor and having trouble. When they arrived, Rick went into action and was able to deliver the live calf. After he cleared the slimy newborn's airway and laid it on the grass, he knew exactly what to do.

Knowing the calf would stand on its own anyway, Rick told Scotty it was his job to get this baby up. The owner found a towel. With great expectations, Scotty gently rubbed that calf so he could do his critically important job and help it stand. When it stood, that child was rapt—full of wonder, pride, and reverence for the new life and his part in it.

Later, when Scotty was playing at his friend John's house, John said they had a new baby. Would Scotty like to see him? Scotty was happy to oblige, being a professional in the birthing business now. As they peered into the bassinet at the new little sleeping bundle, Scotty smiled and whispered to John's mom with the assurance of one who knows all about these things.

"I know how you got this baby, Miss Jane. It was borned right out your fanny."

It wasn't long before we got a phone call from Miss Jane. She was clearly not amused.

Bless her heart.

——·——

Our second son's delivery five and a half years later, in 1982, was a planned C-section.

27

Rick and I consulted our calendars. When the doctor suggested November 30 as a possible surgery date, we had to tell him that just would not do. Rick would be testing a beef cattle herd for brucellosis and tuberculosis on November 27. He would be drawing blood from each cow for the brucellosis test and injecting tuberculin into the underside of each cow's tail for the tuberculosis test. Three days later, he would be examining the undersides of cows' tails on November 30.

So we planned my C-section around a herd of bovines.

In deference to Rick, he was, after all, a duly accredited veterinarian conducting important work securing the health and wellbeing of the United States food source—work which would also bring in a paycheck. I could live with that. But the next day, December 1, 1982, would be sacrosanct—the day reserved only for our baby's birth and nothing else. Nothing would get in the way, or our children would grow up without their father because I would kill him with my bare hands.

The first day of December dawned a dark, cold, and rainy day. We had to leave for Atlanta at Zero Dark Thirty to avoid traffic and get to the hospital by the prescribed time. Rick got behind the wheel of our Volkswagen Super Beetle, and I eased myself into the passenger seat. This arrangement felt familiar from five and a half years earlier in Virginia, but at least this time I wasn't in labor.

He inserted the key and . . . nothing.

I hadn't been driving for a good while, and neither one of us had thought to check the car before it was time to go. We got out of the car. Rick attached a rope to the bumper, and with his practice vehicle, he pulled the little red, crippled car up our steep driveway and onto the street. The car was pointing in the right direction at least, downhill, since the street was at about a thirty-degree angle. All we needed now was the long straightaway to get the car's momentum going and someone to pop the clutch with it in gear in order to start the vehicle.

The consensus was for me to do the clutch popping while Rick pushed off the car. We realized the problem right away; I was too big with child to fit behind the wheel of our tiny VW. Rick would have to sit in the driver's seat and pop the clutch.

I would push the car.

So with nary a single witness at 5:30 a.m., Rick put it in first gear, depressing the clutch as I pushed the VW, grateful to my very toes that the downhill was in my favor, and I wasn't in labor. The engine roared to life, and we were golden. I didn't even have to run to get in.

Rick stopped the car, and as it idled, I once again eased myself into the passenger seat and shouted, "I am Woman!"

We were on our way.

Rick was there for the birth of our son, Nick. In the years since Scotty was born, modernity had come to obstetrics and hospital rules, so Rick was allowed in the surgical room during delivery. Not knowing his profession, a nurse helped him don a surgical gown, cap, and mask, asking him if he was squeamish. She patted Rick's hand, advising him if he felt like fainting to just let her know. He decided it was time to try the same tired joke about me, the stall, and the hay on a whole new audience.

"I do all my C-sections out in the field at midnight by car headlights. This is nothing."

The nurse's eyes opened wide, and then our obstetrician said, "He's a vet, people!" They all laughed, relieved, and a tad shocked at this corny, comedic veterinarian in their operating room.

We brought our beautiful, second son home to meet his big brother, and Rick was there all day. I did not have to kill him for being absent, which made me very happy.

At least for a day.

———

It wasn't long after Nick's birth in December 1982, in the freezing-cold dead of winter, Rick got a call from a client in Moreland, Georgia. He had found a very young calf down, stranded on the man's side of the property fence in his pasture. It didn't belong to him, but his neighbor wasn't home, and the man feared the calf was dying.

Rick arrived to find the little calf hypothermic indeed, lying prone on the ground and in imminent danger of freezing to death. He gathered the baby up in his arms, placed it in the cab of his truck, covered it with a blanket, and brought it home.

Rick laid the calf in our bathtub to warm it up slowly so, hopefully, the calf's brain wouldn't swell. But despite Rick's valiant efforts, the calf became vocal and "commenced to hollering," as we say in the South. The little guy's brain was swelling.

Our phone rang right about then.

"Hello!" I screamed into the receiver.

"MMMAAAANNGGHHH!!" hollered the calf from the bathtub, the earsplitting sound bouncing off the tile walls and echoing throughout the house.

"Susie? What the hell was that!?" asked the voice on the other end of the phone.

It was our friend and lawyer, Pope Jones, greeted not only by my boisterous hello but the raucous, desperate bleating of a dying calf. I explained what was happening, and we ended the call so we could tend to the calf. We weren't sure if there was a city ordinance against having baby bovines in bathtubs but felt sure Pope would keep it under his hat, citing attorney-client privilege if it came to that.

Scotty paced like an expectant father, back and forth down the hall, popping into and out of the bathroom to check on the calf, stroking his body, and offering tender words of comfort. Then, the bleating stopped. The calf was silent and still. Scotty wondered aloud why, even though he was pretty sure he knew. We explained the calf had expired.

Scotty understood, as he had seen dead animals before. His tears rolled, but he held no malice toward his dad. Our son knew we had all given it our best shot. When Rick took the dead calf away, he called a farmer with a backhoe and had the calf buried. Scotty reasoned at least the little calf had people around him when he died and got a decent burial instead of freezing in the pasture all alone. This child had become quite an empath and philosopher, even at the tender age of six.

As Nick grew up into little-boy toddlerhood in the mid-1980s, old enough to ride with his dad, he also went on calls. Nick saw his fair share of animals. But around that time, Rick was getting very busy. So busy that a normal day became a lengthy exercise in mere survival. The nature of Rick's daily work became a constant, hectic road rally, motoring around several counties from call to call and never stopping. Those were exhausting trips, even for Rick, and they were no place for a little kid. So Nick's brief role as Dad's sidekick came to an earlier end than Scotty's.

I was juggling as fast as I could by then, too, and for years after. I counted on girlfriends for adult company and socializing. I also relied on part-time daycare, then preschool, then elementary school, and then high school to keep and educate the boys while I worked various part-time secretarial jobs. We all came home in the afternoons and managed for the most part without Dad. Doctor visits, parent-teacher conferences, sports, tutors, homework, meals, discipline, church—basically raising two boys as a single parent—were all under my purview. When I started singing more, the boys had babysitters. It was tough on everyone—that daily life.

The boys missed their dad when he was out ministering to the sick and injured in the animal world, but when Rick was home, he took them in his lap and read them stories, played ball, and took them swimming. Rick was still a good dad doing dad things. They were proud of him. Likewise.

That's not to say we didn't have our occasional awesome vacations together and fun times. The national parks were the best. By the 1990s, Rick managed to hold the world at bay on occasion, and we drove the boys out West several times. Nick was an adolescent and Scott a teen. We visited Montana, Wyoming, Yellowstone, Yosemite, and Muir Woods. We took them another time to the Great Smokey Mountains and up the Blue Ridge Parkway all the way to Washington, D.C. to tour the White House. *Yes, Virginia, there once was a lovely White House tour before pandemics and insurrections. Just a simple hi-ho to your congressman, a wait in line, and a sign in. Then, a nice, quiet walk around once and done.*

Georgia has some perfectly lovely beaches, too, which were only about a six-hour drive from our town. Rick and I made some of those vacations happen with the boys too. Some of those trips were tied in with veterinary conventions, so we could write off some of the expense. Thank you, IRS.

Traditionally, Rick's one-week vacation became a three-day vacation. As long as we've been married while Rick was working full-time, whenever we took a rare week of vacation time, it took him at least two days to slow down after our arrival at our destination and not look over his shoulder for the next farm call to race to with his hair on fire, the next difficult surgery to perform, or another problem to solve. Two days before our vacation ended, Rick started mentally gearing back up for the onslaught upon his return home. So, a one-week vacation, left him about three good, quality days to enjoy. Sometimes you gotta take what you can get and let it be enough. It is a choice. We have excelled in that, believe me.

You know, as warped as this may sound, I wouldn't change a thing. Every day of our lives has brought us to where we are today.

If I hadn't had the life I've had as a veterinarian's wife, I might have been married to a rich guy and be dripping in diamonds, married to a performer, or not married at all. I might not have learned how to wash a vet's clothes or tried to save a dying cow in our bathtub. I may not have grown in understanding about what it takes to be a veterinarian and a vet's wife or really appreciate all those single moms out there.

If I could give my younger, married self some advice now, I would tell her this: "You have found the right man. You love him. He loves you. There will be good times as well as trouble ahead. You are strong, and you are smart. Whatever happens, you can do this. Cherish this life. Never give up."

There's a saying, "We will not regret the past nor wish to shut the door on it." That's from an anonymous group of folks that want to stay anonymous. Surely you know who I mean. Anyway, I like that saying a lot. They have another good one about regret and gratitude: "An honest regret for harms done, a genuine gratitude for blessings received, and a willingness to try for better things tomorrow will be the permanent assets we shall seek."

Amen, y'all. Amen.

VET SCHOOL, LOUIE, AND SUZANNE

In October of 2016, Rick and I took a short, fun weekend road trip to Nashville to see Adele in all her concert-y delightfulness. She did not disappoint. Before leaving for our trip, we had discussed maybe trying to look up some long-ago friends who lived there—Louie and Suzanne—with whom we had lost touch from all the way back in veterinary school about a million years ago. Clearly, Adele is still in my head. "A million years ago?" Adele fans will get it.

Veterinary school was forty-plus years ago, from 1971-1975, when landlines, twirly phone cords, and the Southern Bell Company were the only communications options down South with pay phones on every corner. No one "computed." We typed on IBM Selectrics with little state-of-the-art rotating metal balls striking the ribbon and page. We still wrote in cursive and read paper books. I-85 stopped at the Newnan exit and took back up somewhere in Alabama. Now, it's an eight-lane autobahn to eternity.

When Rick and I met Louie and Suzanne at vet school, we were all young and callow, brimming with energy, drive, promise, hope, and willingness to sacrifice. We shared a heavy load and a common goal.

Newlyweds and mere babes—I was twenty-one, and Rick was twenty-two—in 1971, Rick and I happily and bravely emigrated to a strange and foreign land called Tuskegee, Alabama. It had a town square, bank, courthouse, a few shops, offices, and G's Diner—the local greasy spoon and gathering place for students and townsfolk to eat and yak. A ways out from the square were the undergrad and veterinary school campuses.

Tuskegee Institute—now Tuskegee University—was, and still is one in a group of historically Black colleges and universities in the country known as HBCUs. When the UGA vet school wait-listed Rick and Tuskegee accepted him, we went for the sure thing. Rick and I packed our bags and set off for Alabama.

We eagerly settled into our new home about a mile off Tuskegee's square. It was a modest twelve-by-forty-feet corrugated sardine can perched upon cement blocks on a corner patchy, grass lot just down the street from the tiny, brick rental house Louie and Suzanne occupied. We had cheap linoleum floors and shag carpet of the '70s brown and gold variety, no dishwasher, three dogs, and a tiny bedroom crammed with one sole furnishing: a king-sized bed fitting like a custom-cut jigsaw puzzle piece snugly up against all four of our fake-paneled walls. We installed two window air-conditioning units. Those rattling, white-noise machines bothered and constantly blessed us with lifegiving cold air, for which I was grateful to my toes every second of those horridly hot, humid Alabama days and nights. If there had been a speed above high, say "wind tunnel," I would have gladly opted for that one.

We found if we turned off the A/C during the day when we were gone, there would be no recovering in the evenings from the heat buildup in that tin can. I proved it when I first tried that off and on thing, and it did not go well.

Arriving home after my first day of work at the local bank, I opened the door and fell backward from the intense blast of hot air. It was as if I had opened a veritable oven door, perhaps even a portal into the sweltering seventh circle of hell. Stumbling forward and stepping inside, breathing instantly labored, eyes burning, sweat already streaming, I discovered my new tapered candles bent over double on the table. Had there been a pan of rock-solid, frozen lasagna set out on that table in the morning, I felt sure it would've been thoroughly baked and bubbling. After that incident, we agreed the obnoxious rattling A/C units would also be our constant lifeline by always remaining on and the resulting electric bill would just have to be a major budgetary expense—worth every damn dime. Cheaper, I joked, than new candles every day. And we could reserve any baking for our actual oven. Priorities.

Rick and I were also situated smack in the middle of a larger geographical area, a long, diagonal swath of land affectionately known in the South as Tornado Alley. When the sky turned black, the winds picked up, and it started raining sideways in sheets against our windows, the rain turned into icy marbles ping-ping-pinging on the windows and metal roof. Then, when our little perchy sardine can groaned, vibrated, and rocked, it was our cue to evacuate.

All three dogs and two adults clambered outside and into our little red VW Beetle clown-car as we shoehorned ourselves in and spilled back out down the street at the front door of Louie and Suzanne's tiny brick house. Sopping wet and smelling of wet fur, we all took shelter, huddled close together in their hallway. The tornado missed us, as they say, by a mile. I mean that literally—one mile.

Later, Rick and Louie were out walking in the area where the tornado had touched down and saw a piece of broken farm equipment at the base of a tree. They looked up and scanned the tree's scraped bark on one side of its limbless trunk—from the top where the tornado had blown the tractor into it from God-knows where all the way down the barkless trunk and gouged earth where it lay in a twisted ruin. That was what had missed us by a mile. One blessed mile. Whoever said, "Close only counts in horseshoes," has never lived in Tornado Alley.

Every day, Rick and Louie went to their respective classes, labs, and clinical rounds. After each long, hard day, they studied late into the night. Through our bedroom door, I had a perfect view down the long, straight hall of our sardine can into the kitchen. Rick sat at the kitchen table by the front window every night, surrounded by books and papers, a reading light glowing harsh and bright over his shoulder. Through the window, I could see the kitchen light shining at Louie and Suzanne's, too, just down the street.

On the weekends, the four of us socialized in the evenings, taking turns hosting at our home or theirs. There wasn't much to do in town, and we were all broke anyway. We were compatible though and laughed a lot. Suzanne and I kept each other company when our husbands weren't home. Even just a grilled cheese sandwich and tomato soup lunch for an hour on a Saturday afternoon together gave us joy. When they weren't in class, Rick and Louie went deer hunting together in the Alabama woods on the weekends. We ate a lot of venison. It was cheap, plentiful, and helped poor vet students survive on a budget. There was venison for breakfast, lunch, and dinner: steaks, roasts, ground burgers, sausage, chops, casseroles, and stews. Every covered-dish party featured some version of venison. All these years later, I must think long and hard before venison passes my lips.

There was, however, always one annual departure from venison at the traditional cookout held by juniors and seniors from the vet school. This affair was the all-out Rocky Mountain Oyster Fest. (Those who don't get out much and don't know what a Rocky Mountain oyster is should Google it.) Over the entire academic year, vet students saved every castrated bovine and porcine testicle, hermetically sealing them in O.B. sleeves in large-animal clinic freezers. At the proper time, these delicacies were thawed, sliced, breaded, and fried in a large kettle filled with oil over an open fire. The large ones, that is. Smaller ones were fried whole and popped in one bite. I declined to partake, but Rick relished the moment.

"You can eat anything breaded and fried as long as you have a beer with it," Rick declared.

Oh my God, my mom's snooty friend may have been on to something.

I worked full-time at the local bank on the town square all four years, showing up six days a week to perform my duties as executive secretary to the president and vice president.

Alabama Exchange Bank president, Allen Parker, was an older white man in a predominantly Black town—a well-respected, civic-minded, big-hearted soul, often hiring wives of vet students when there were openings. Mr. Parker was kind enough to employ me when no one else had or would. I was still a rusty typist when I showed up in 1971, and I knew nothing about banking. I learned all of that on the job, thanks to him. (Lookin' at you, UGA career office).

Mr. Parker lived with his sweet wife and two little yip-yip Pomeranians in a modest brick ranch just down Main Street, halfway between the bank and the corner lot on which our tuna-can trailer was situated. A staunch proponent for the Black community, Mr. Parker granted an unsecured loan to a local, prominent Black lawyer and civil rights activist, Fred Gray, by providing bank funding to finally litigate the infamous "Tuskegee Syphilis Study." Parker required no repayment until the case was settled.

I was fortunate enough to walk right into a position being vacated by a senior student's wife. Richie and Sue Savino were from Long Island and would be moving back there after graduation. Sue was brilliant and friendly. She trained me and showed me the ropes. Richie was innately funny. His Long Island accent and sunny personality made everyone around him happy. A burly guy who looks at every dog and says in a laughing falsetto, "Hoo Hoo da pwuppy dwahwg!" was immediately our kind of guy.

After four years, I had learned how to type like the wind and be a phone-answering, task-juggling, problem-solving, customer-service rendering, multitasking secretarial whiz and general Girl Friday. I took Lionel Richie's phone payments in person when he was still a Commodore. I filled baskets on the lobby tables with matchbooks bearing the bank's logo and watched daily in amusement as customers opened wide their purses or paper bags, dumping them all in. I typed loan papers, insurance forms, and letters. I essentially did whatever needed to be done, including roasting the bank president's fresh peanuts each week.

The bank's vice president, J.T. Daniel, Jr., was probably in his forties at the time. He was a sweet, sunny man whose large, wooden desk was positioned next to mine behind the polished wood, courtroom-style banisters that encircled the bank lobby. J.T. was a paradox. He wore his fastidiousness—always neatly dressed in pressed slacks and polished shoes. I noticed his hyper-clean, manicured hands right away when he opened an envelope, taking a small mother-of-pearl pocketknife from his pants pocket and slowly slit the envelope with careful, surgical precision, pinky up.

J.T.'s desk, however, was a rat's nest. It was piled at least two-feet high with papers, books, folders, and things unseen. For years, J.T. and his desk were the butt of good-natured jokes, but he could produce anything he needed as effortlessly as Elvis could sing. Mr. Daniel also had a regular hobby. I bolstered him with compliments on the days he came into the bank proudly brandishing yet another handmade, shiny, green-glazed celery dish from his weekly ceramics class.

After four years, that was a lot of peanuts and celery dishes.

My co-workers were all southern to the core—most of them well over forty—and had names like Dovie and Miss Louise. Many grew up in Tuskegee, lived in Macon County, had never left, and were fine with that. Others commuted from "out of town," which included Auburn or tiny Notasulga whose population was in the hundreds.

That full-time, six-day a week job of mine at the Alabama Exchange Bank brought home the princely sum of three-hundred dollars *per month* with no benefits.

It was a unique, four-year adventure during which I earned my secretarial stripes and bragging rights and gained a ton of valuable insight. I witnessed true perseverance, generosity, kindness, and engagement daily in friendly, inclusive conversations and community awareness—at my job, in the town, and at Rick's vet school. It was an eye-opening, sociological experience as Rick and I learned what it was like to be a white minority in a predominantly Black community.

We also knew that even though we were in the minority there for a short while, nothing in our experience could ever match the civil rights inequities suffered by Black citizens and students who struggle every day of their lives to be heard and given equal standing under the law.

At graduation, May of 1975, the veterinary school issued DVM degrees to the graduates, mostly males at the time, and each female spouse received a PHT degree: Pushing Hubby Through. I swear; I am not kidding.

When Rick and Louie had their DVM diplomas in hand, we all left to go our separate ways with a great flourish of hugs, tears, best wishes, and mutual promises to keep in touch.

Rick and I immediately pulled up anchor in Alabama after graduation and sailed north up the interstate all the way to Ashland, Virginia, for Rick's first job at Woodside Equine Clinic. Then with a new baby, we came back to Georgia in 1977 where he would open his own practice in Newnan. We were forging a new life a million miles from Tuskegee and our friends in the tiny brick rental.

Louie and Suzanne immediately settled in Nashville after graduation where Louie opened a small-animal practice in a little, red outbuilding behind their house.

Once back in Georgia with his one-man, large-animal practice revving up, Rick was out running the roads until all hours. I spun plates raising our first-born, fielding client calls, managing the office in a converted bedroom in our home, and holding his dinner in the oven night after night.

We visited Louie and Suzanne only one time in Nashville, circa 1981, with matching toddlers in tow—theirs a girl and ours a boy. The visit was pleasant but brief. We recounted memories of our old bond—the husbands as struggling veterinary students and the wives working hard to pay the rent. Louie and Rick welcomed the chance to compare notes as professional, honest-to-God veterinarians. Then, we left to live our separate lives, and we all four let the connection fade away.

So in 2016, as we planned our quick weekend trip to Nashville to worship at the altar of Adele, we contemplated Louie and Suzanne after so many years and the distance between us. Due to our time constraints, Rick and I decided not to look them up. We let it slide. "Next trip, when we have more time," we said.

Then, just a few days after we got home from Nashville, Rick came into the den wide eyed and tight lipped. He was holding a recent veterinary journal at arm's length, stabbing his finger at one spot on the page. Once Rick moved close enough for me to focus on the spot in question, I saw it. We could have easily missed it altogether. Rick could have skipped reading this edition. He was behind by a couple of months on his journals anyway and catching up would mean he might have to skip one or two to keep current. But he didn't skip one. He chose one. This one. And now he was pointing to the only thing that mattered in that moment.

It was only one line of text nestled in the middle of a short list of several other names hiding in plain sight on a busy page filled with distracting, eye-catching headlines, article callouts, pull-quotes, and requisite gross-out photos of surgeries, growths, and gory wounds. Photos like that are a veritable siren call to any professional seeking answers to interesting medical dilemmas and provide the ultimate visual distraction. So what were the chances Rick would notice, amid all that noise, one quiet, brief line of text? Slim. But he did. He saw it, and then so did I.

Rick was pointing to the name of the old friend we had just decided not to look up on our trip. Listed was Louie's name, followed by his date of birth and date of death.

Both of us were stunned.

In times like this, a predictable emotional pattern follows in response to events of the universe over which we have had no previous knowledge and absolutely no control.

The shock turns to denial and anger: *This can't be true. How the hell . . . what the hell . . . this isn't fair! He's too young—in his sixties! This isn't some faceless stranger; this is Louie, OUR Louie from vet school!*

Then to guilt: *Of course it can be true. Why haven't we visited before now?*

We experience irrational thought: *An old friend dies in August, it's October, and we never heard him go? We could've and should've heard about it. We should've been more connected.*

Then the reality: *We would've been too late this time, even if we had decided to visit this past weekend. It's October. He has been gone since August.*

Then the regret and the sadness: *We could've kept up with them, but we let them go. And they, us. Now he's gone. We feel awful. Sad. Helpless.*

Then we were hit with another stunner; I went online and found his obituary, which listed the name of his surviving wife. Her name was not Suzanne. This wife was not the wife we knew so long ago. Where was Suzanne? What happened? Was she alive? Did they divorce? Did we have the right to ask or know, having detached so completely for so long? I tried Googling Suzanne's name, but she was nowhere. The many photos of Louie online—either through his practice's website or on the funeral home tribute page—showed no sign of her.

It was as if Suzanne didn't exist. How did I have the right to be concerned for her, after all our silent, disconnected years? I suddenly remembered her maiden name. Why did it visit me so effortlessly after forty-plus years, when some days I strained to recall a famous name in a Jeopardy clue?

How do you let someone fade away when you were once close enough to know her maiden name and huddle together in a stifling hot hallway with a bunch of wet, smelly dogs while waiting for a tornado to pass?

When I am still, quiet, open to forgiveness, and letting go, acceptance comes—to everything there is a season. Sometimes folks drift apart. They do. People come and go, but certain ones that go also remain. They remain as ever-present memories. They are the folks who leave a mark on your soul with a shared history that doesn't disappear, even if they—or you—do.

We expressed our condolences to the family on the funeral home website and told Louie we still loved and remembered him from so long ago and that we had visited this time. And we lifted Suzanne's name up to the universe and sent our love.

It would have to do.

MAY DAY, MAY DAY

Each that we lose takes part of us;
A crescent still abides,
Which, like the moon, some turbid night,
Is summoned by the tides-
—Emily Dickinson

MAY 18, 1980

Mt. St. Helens volcano in Washington State exploded with the force of five hundred nuclear Hiroshima bombs, taking lives, destroying homes, spreading five hundred forty million tons of ash over twenty-two thousand square miles, and flattening trees for two hundred twenty square miles. It was the worst avalanche in U.S. history. Within two weeks, ash had drifted around the globe.

Rick and I were flattened that day, too, all the way across the country in little Newnan, Georgia by an intense, personal upheaval of our own. As sure as the volcano across the country had done its worst, a tragedy exploded our lives, raining down on us its own brand of suffocating emotional ash. It was the worst cataclysmic disruption of our young, thirty-year-old lives, leaving us devastated, bewildered, and empty.

Our firstborn son was nearing three years old. Our second son wouldn't even be conceived for almost another two years. They could not know, nor did they suffer, when disaster visited our little house on Dixon Street and time stood still in 1980. But the daughter who should have been their sister, due to be born in August, stopped moving in my womb that day in May.

On that perfectly ordinary sunny day in May, life slipped silently away at our house. I was twenty-six weeks pregnant, carrying our little girl inside of me. My friends were planning a baby shower. The nursery was ready. And in one moment, I felt her go motionless. There was nothing else to signal catastrophe—only sudden, haunting stillness. Just like that, a quiet, deadly landslide took a living, moving person inside of me. I knew in my heart what was happening. I desperately didn't want it to be true, but my mother's instinct was strong, and I knew an unmistakable, epic calamity was at hand. I was choking on the ash that rose in my throat. I knew in the time it takes to flick a light switch or drop a bomb that everything was instantly different and always would be. The damage was done. Why it happened, I didn't know. But in that moment, I knew I was suddenly carrying a corpse.

My doctor's answering service told us to come to the hospital ER right away. He would meet us there. Rick was actually home. It had been a rare, tranquil Sunday—until it wasn't. We sent our toddler over to a friend's house and made our way to Atlanta. We were quiet but hardly calm on the ride up. I was terrified, afraid to speak, and so was he. We held hands tight all the way.

Once we arrived, we checked in, took a seat, and waited—silent, sitting close, arm in arm, hand in hand. They called my name, and as I stood to enter the exam room, Rick let his hands gently follow down the full length of my arm as I slowly stepped away from him and toward the door. The nurse ushered me through the opening, and I entered a portal that would deliver me into Reality, Questions, and Painful Answers.

Could she see the ash rising in a plume above my head, from my throat, my heart, my child? The nurse turned the ultrasound screen away from me. I squeezed my eyes shut as I lay flat on the table that felt in that moment like a steel slab in a morgue. It did not take her long, which was a bad sign. She wiped the ultrasound goo from my skin and clicked off the machine without speaking. Trying not to relay the results with her expression, my nurse did not possess a good poker face—not even close. I was so hoping she would tell me I was not feeling what I was feeling. Or more accurately, not feeling in this case. I desperately wanted to feel the return of the kicks and turns, to watch my belly undulate with movement. It did not. The nurse's expression told me I shouldn't and wouldn't be expecting that now. Or ever.

The nurse escorted Rick and me across the hall into the doctor's office. I searched her face yet again. She avoided my gaze entirely this time—her head down, brows furrowed, and lips tense. Whatever denial is it is certainly powerful. I already knew the answer in my heart, but until somebody told me out loud what had happened, I would reside in an awful limbo of shock and disbelief. As long as it remained unspoken, maybe it wouldn't be real—like the doctors on television who say out loud, "Time of death: 3:00 p.m." Until they do that, death is not official.

We got our official pronouncement right there in the office. There was no way around it. The bomb had fallen, indeed, and laid waste our twenty-six-week-old fetus two thirds of the way to forty weeks and full term. I was bracing for it, expecting it, and yet when it dropped, I could hardly process it. Rick and I held each other—my head bowed, tears brimming, then spilling over, rolling in rivulets down my face. I had no words. The doctor couldn't tell us why, other than to say something about how "This sometimes happens," "We don't know why," "This is not your fault," "I'm so sorry," and "We're going to take good care of you." All I heard after that was a rush of white noise and a faraway voice that sounded like nonsense as the hum of grief pulsed in my ears.

What I wasn't expecting was what would come next. Incredibly, "taking care of me" meant the doctor wanted me to go home and see if I would go into spontaneous labor in a few days, if not weeks.

"Excuse me?" I shot back, eyes wide, my blouse and slacks now sopped, ropy snot running from my nose. I remember thinking, what is this lunacy? Surely, he doesn't mean that! Astonishment and anger compounded my sadness. The doctor repeated himself gently, patiently assuring me he would follow me closely and this would be over "soon." *Define soon*, I thought. *Today, right now, is soon enough.* He would go back to his job and busy himself with pelvic exams and Pap smears and chit chat with pregnant women carrying living babies inside of them, and I would be the one waiting impatiently for "soon."

All I knew for certain was I was exhausted from the day, the worry, the questions, the answers, the grief, and the enormity of it all. So I threw my wadded, wet Kleenex into the trash can, pulled a fresh white tissue from the box on the desk, and with a high flourish, waved it in surrender. Rick and I left. Just like that. We just . . . came home.

Thus began our odyssey—an impossible journey requiring me to continue to carry on and . . . wait. It was horrifyingly open ended. There was the matter of our toddler's third birthday party coming up only eight days hence. How could I function? I remembered the upcoming baby shower and how I would have to break the news. Having to do so in addition seemed a bridge too far. What would we do with the nursery?

Our people rallied around us. My dear friend, Carol Harrison, generously offered to throw the birthday party at her house with cake and balloons for our newly minted three-year-old and a few of his toddler friends. All I had to do was show up and pretend to be sane, smiling in the maternity jumper that belied my actual condition. I was a mobile mausoleum.

We canceled the shower, food arrived, and sympathy cards replaced congratulatory cards. I felt fragile and oddly embarrassed. I was now an imposter who looked pregnant but who was grieving the lifeless body inside of me. Naturally, I didn't go out much.

One time I made a quick trip to the little store up the street just to grab some apple juice. The friendly owner behind the counter asked me as I was paying for the juice, "So when are you due?" Abruptly disoriented, my brain went full-stop, full-on mute, catatonic. Straining to produce a cohesive thought, my left frontal lobe rebooted in agonizing slow motion.

Focusing my eyes on the counter, I forced a weak smile and stammered, "In . . . in . . . Awwww-gust. Well," I added, expelling a sharp sigh and clearing my throat, "I-I-I-I gotta run." I picked up my purchase and made my getaway. He must have thought I was weird. And I guess I was. There was no way I could share with a stranger the news of my dead baby who was, incredibly, still in my womb. It was hard enough to share it with friends and relatives. This guy was not on the list.

Rick went back to work, and while he was sad and shaken, he still had to earn a paycheck. He did the man-thing and went head down, balls to the wall. I knew he was hurting, and during his long, arduous workdays, he got his solace where he could. On his large-animal rounds, farmers and their sturdy wives often invited Rick to join them for hearty, home-cooked southern meals. In their welcoming farmhouse kitchens, Rick spent a bit more time lingering at their tables, savoring their kindnesses along with his second or maybe even third full breakfast or dinner of the day. Often, they sent him on his way with bounties of farm eggs or fresh-picked garden produce for the "missus." When he got home, whenever that would be on any given evening, Rick brandished the humble farm gifts proudly. On the rare occasion our toddler was still up, he took over parent duties until bedtime. Later, we took time to care for each other, held one another other and talked. Rick was exhausted and usually fell asleep long before I was ready for him to. We did our best.

By late June, I was still not going into any kind of spontaneous labor. Blessedly, I was brought back to the hospital to make the delivery happen. "Soon" had been long enough.

May 18, 2020

Forty years later, things are growing again around the mountain in Washington state. Yellow wildflowers and blue lupines. Animals and insects. Butterflies and bees. The mountain is different now, changed forever. Shorter by over thirteen-hundred feet and burdened with the history of that explosive day four decades earlier, it survives as a sentinel and a witness to death, destruction, and resurrection. It flourishes now with new life. The people who died are still gone, but I like to think some of their children and their children's children live on to tell the tale of their forebears, to name them and keep them alive in that way.

Forty years later, our firstborn son, Scott, turns forty-three on May 26, 2020; our younger son, Nick, turns thirty-eight on December 1, 2020. They, too, continue to grow and flourish. They are my heart.

She neither grows nor flourishes on this earthly plane. She lives in the soft places of our hearts, minds, memories, and imaginations now transformed by that awful day four decades earlier—the day that changed us and her, forever.

Life goes on. She, too, survives somewhere, as an unseen sentinel and a witness to death, destruction, and resurrection of spirit. She would be forty now.

Her name is Sarah Kate.

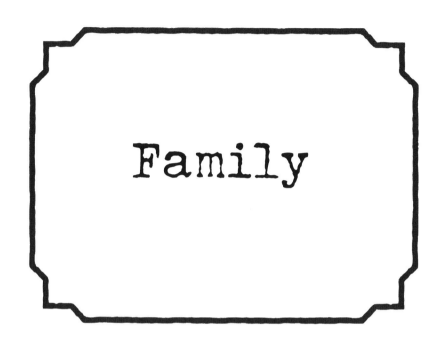

Family

ONCE THERE WAS A MAN...

There is absolutely nothing a person can do about their parentage. We're born, and we get who we get, whether we like it or them. When we marry someone, it's like being born to another set of parents. There is absolutely nothing we can do about that, either. By marrying a person, you inherit their parents—even if those parents are no longer living. It is what it is. Everything we are as an individual and as a couple harks back to our upbringing in one way or another, small or large, for better or worse. We can't choose our parents, but we can choose what kind of role model we want to be, going forward.

———

...NAMED JOE

Once there was a young man named Joe Berta, Jr. who went to war—WWII. When he left, his young bride, Libby, went to live with the man's generous father, Joe, Sr., on his working farm outside Paoli, PA.

The young man enlisted because he wanted to go overseas and fight. He received military flight training, and he was so good at flying he was made an instructor. Then, Joe, Jr. got his chance to fight, and he flew missions through danger and over strange lands. He was on a bombing mission when his plane was struck by anti-aircraft fire, crashlanding on a beach in New Guinea.

With exceptional piloting skill, Joe, Jr. navigated his crippled plane past the water and landed safely on the beach. He and his crew spent two months wandering through the jungles of New Guinea, avoiding enemy Japanese patrols and head hunters. Finally, they encountered a British military post and were saved.

After the war, young Joe came home to Libby on the third floor in his father's house in Paoli. The old man's home was a busy place, not unlike many multifamily houses of the time. It was there Joe, Jr. and Libby had their first child, Joe III. Also home from the war and living in the house on the third floor were Joe's brother, Bob, and his wife, Roxanne—both couples making and having babies at a rapid pace.

The old man was kindly in his generosity. He was also a temperamental, bombastic Italian American who brooked no fools and held stubborn ideals, wholly dedicated to family. The story is legend in the Berta family about Joe, Sr.'s encounter with a health inspector in Peoria, Illinois way back when he was a young father himself and Joe, Jr. was a baby. The health inspector dared tell Joe, Sr. he would no longer be able to purchase the unpasteurized milk the pediatrician had prescribed for his hungry baby. They argued for a time before exasperated Joe, Sr. looked the health inspector in the eye and said low and slow, "Where are we?"

"In Peoria, sir," replied the inspector.

"What floor are we on in this apartment complex in Peoria?" Joe, Sr. asked.

The health inspector dutifully replied, "The second, sir."

The story goes that Joe, Sr. then pulled on the man's collar, bringing him nose to nose, and said, "This is a three-story building. I will take you up to the roof and throw you off if you come back. Get out!"

Young Joe, Jr. and Libby moved from the Paoli house and had more kids. He began a career selling chemicals for Hercules Powder Company, which moved the man and his family to Lancaster, PA. There Rick was born, and Joe, Jr. became Rick's doting dad. Then, the company moved them to Michigan—where Lisa was born; Delaware, where Patty was born; and back to Paoli, where Peter and David were born. Finally, now as a family of eight, they settled in Atlanta in 1963. The family had a lovely house in a beautiful neighborhood. All seemed perfect. For a time.

The years went by, and there came that middle-aged period when working people are moving up in their careers and on to other positions, advancing higher up the ladder. For whatever reason, Joe, Jr.'s career stalled. He had reached a level where he would go no higher, even with a college degree from UVA and a master's from Penn State. Desperate to find the magic formula for success, Joe, Jr. started a business he didn't know how to run, made some poor decisions, and eventually lost the business. Then, it was just wash, rinse, repeat. Joe, Jr.'s life began to unravel—thread by thread. He made some personal decisions that weren't very good, either. Matter of fact, they were abysmal.

Up until then, Rick, a teen, and his siblings were kids who didn't know of their parents' hardships and struggles, and probably didn't care to know, either. His dad had been the ideal dad. He had told his children to tell the truth. They were told to be honest and fair in all their dealings. Joe, Jr. told them there was a code for men to live up to, which he showed through example more than anything. Rick remembers when he was in high school, and his buddies wanted to travel to somewhere and leave school early. Rick tried to talk his dad into giving him an excuse, but Joe, Jr. said, "No, that's not the way we do things." Rick remembers him being an adviser for his Boy Scout Explorer Post, taking the Explorer Scout troop scuba diving in the Keys.

When Joe, Jr. had experienced yet another business failure, he started building a boat in their garage. The boat was just to keep him busy— "my therapy," Joe said. Rick's mother was not at all happy he spent money they didn't have on this boat when there were six children to feed. And what of her therapy? Joe tried to stay busy while his world crumbled around him. Libby kept the home and the kids together while hers crumbled as well.

His advice to his kids had always been, "If you get into trouble, you come straight to me." Over time, that fatherly figure with all the wisdom disappeared, evaporated. Rick watched him become a hollow shell. Joe, Jr. broke every rule he ever taught his son.

In February of 1967, just before Valentine's Day when Rick was a senior in high school, his mom and young teenage sister, Patty, were driving on I-285 and hit a bridge abutment. Patty was killed instantly. Libby was severely injured, in critical condition, with broken bones everywhere in her body. She spent long, excruciating months at Piedmont Hospital recovering.

When Libby finally emerged from the hospital, she was disabled, using a wheelchair, then walker, and finally a cane. She and the three children who were still living at home went to Joe, Sr.'s summer home in Florida. Rick and Joe III were at college, so Joe, Sr.'s was a place where she could rest and recuperate before returning to Atlanta to resume their lives.

Rick's dad slowly disengaged, finding work in Montgomery, Alabama in a shop that converted locomotives to electronically controlled switch engines in a railyard. He started coming back to Atlanta only on the weekends. Joe, Jr. was becoming more and more distant. Every weekend home became every other weekend home, then once a month, and then it was just random. Joe, Jr. was still the sole support for the family, though, and sent them money.

The family never knew when they would see him next.

Joe, Jr. managed to make it to our wedding in 1971, at least. Rick's folks were pretty good at covering up the dysfunction. In our wedding pictures, Joe, Jr. grinned in his white dinner jacket as he stood next to Libby who was smiling in a lovely silk, jacketed gown with her cane wrapped in fresh flowers.

Two years later, Rick and I were living in Tuskegee when the proverbial shit hit the fan.

Rick's older brother, Joe III, got a call from someone in Montgomery. They told Joe they hated to have to say it, but they'd seen an announcement in the newspaper.

"Your mom should know something, Joe," said the voice over the phone to Rick's brother. "I will call her right after I've finished talking to you, but I wanted to tell you first, and then you should call Rick. Your dad has married a woman here. Her name is Elizabeth. He calls her Libby for short. They have a German Shorthaired puppy named Heidi."

Rick's mom's name was Libby.

Heidi was also the name of their dog in Atlanta.

My God. Rick's dad was not only a bigamist, but he was also a crazy bigamist.

Joe III called Rick right away and laid it out just as he was told. As the eldest, Rick's brother was the first to know, but in the long term, Rick was the kid who got to handle it. The rest of his siblings lived far away, save one. Brother Joe had a wife and child and was working for their dad in Montgomery. Joe couldn't afford to confront his dad for fear of losing his job. Therefore, Rick was next in line and took up his grandfather's mantle of "Communicator and Defender of the Family Honor." Like his grandfather, Rick would brook no fools, either. He was not putting up with this shit.

Rick called his mother. Rick told Libby he was willing to call his father, go see him, and get this fixed. He also offered to give up his veterinary education and career in order to get a job right away to support her and the family. Luckily, Rick's grandfather had already stepped up and offered to support Libby and the last two of Rick's siblings still at home. Libby was exceedingly grateful for Rick's grand gesture. I was exceedingly grateful for the big-hearted, beneficent, old Italian who not only saved Rick's mother but our future as well.

Although Libby didn't need Rick's offer of financial support, she did accept his proposal to visit Bigamist Joe and talk to him. Time for Rick to call his dad, set up a face-to-face, sit his ass down, and tell him to fix this.

Rick and I went to see his father privately and put the cards on the table. Seemingly cowed and chagrined, Joe, Jr. promised to file for divorce right away and end the marriage to Rick's mother.

After that, however, Montgomery Libby was still clueless. Rick's dad had clearly been stalling. Out of nowhere, she fired off a letter to Rick and his siblings chastising them for *how poorly you children have been treating your father*—her husband. *There have been no cards, no gifts, no calls*, she criticized. They *should be ashamed*, Montgomery Libby scolded as she closed her letter.

Since Joe had obviously yet to fess up to her, Rick replied with his own letter signed by himself and all his siblings. Rick's letter explained what Joe hadn't: She was married to a bigamist; that Rick had already talked to him about it; and that Joe had made Rick a promise, but obviously he hadn't followed through.

Ending the letter Rick wrote, "Maybe you can move this whole debacle forward and make him get a divorce from our mother."

We're pretty sure when she got that letter it was the night the lights went out in Montgomery.

Divorce proceedings between Rick's parents were begun post haste.

The family saw very little of their dad after that. Joe, Jr. continued to try assuaging his conscience with impersonal gifts ordered from Omaha Steaks every Christmas, until even those stopped.

Rick's mom kept their two-story family home in Atlanta, but eventually sold it to purchase a more physically accommodating one-level ranch with a pool for her own therapy. Both houses were, each in turn, the family's central gathering place on holidays and special events for many years. No matter how tired Libby became over time, she loved having family gather and was the ultimate, stalwart hostess. I've never met a stronger woman.

In 1988, Libby's body could no longer sustain her, and she died peacefully in her sleep. Her children, family, and friends attended her service and internment next to her daughter, Patty, and the munificent Italian patriarch, Joe, Sr., in the Berta family plot in Pennsylvania.

When Rick's dad died of prostate cancer years later, we were on our way to Washington, D.C. for my brother's wedding.

Rick was not the least bit sorry we weren't attending his father's funeral. Rick had already said his goodbyes long before that.

Hobart Franks met Halberta Hiner before WWII. She was a smart, trig young woman with great legs who had a way with words. He was a bright, handsome young man who also had a way with language and a terrific work ethic. Hobie had been a dirt-poor Colorado boy—the baby in a family of five kids with a father, Robert, who would just as soon gamble the rent away than buy shoes for his children. Hobie's mother, Leona, was a round and kindly woman who put up with Robert.

Halberta's mother, Nellie, was a seemingly sweet but emotionally detached woman who swore she would never have another child for all the pain Halberta caused, and she told Halberta so. Halberta's dad, Halbert, was a tender soul who became an alcoholic and died at the age of sixty-nine. He worked sixty-hour weeks in the auto detailing business he owned in Phoenix until the day he picked up a hitchhiker who rewarded his kindness with a blow to the head, robbing him, breaking his glasses, and blinding him. I still remember sitting on his lap as his young granddaughter—his whiskers scratching my cheek, his breath smelling odd, and the glass eye he could remove and put back in, which I found horrifying and wholly unnecessary.

Halberta was a sickly young girl, having had every condition of the times, including rheumatic fever, ear infections followed by mastoid surgeries, tuberculosis—later, polio and chicken pox. She spent much of her youth in bed, reading everything she could get her hands on. Halberta missed a lot of school but educated herself through her unquenchable curiosity for knowledge and words. By the time she attended Phoenix Public High School, she had fashioned for herself the nickname, "Tee." Her parents had bestowed on her the most god-awful name, Halberta, well-meaning, of course, after her father. Therefore, her whole name scanned as Halberta Hoover Hiner, and she would no longer tolerate it. Tee it was, and Tee it remained.

Hobie's family moved from Ridgway, Colorado to Phoenix where he and Tee met, falling madly in love. Hobie always said he fell in love with her because she was smart and had a typewriter. Tee said she fell in love with him because he was kind, handsome, and could write too. Tee finished two years of junior college; Hobie never went. At the age of twenty-two, they married in 1937 at the courthouse, both wearing suits. She held a gardenia corsage, and he sported a single gardenia pinned to his lapel.

When the war came, Hobie enlisted in the Navy, becoming a radio communications expert who never saw action on a ship based in California. His job was tapping out Morse Code and pressing his fingers on the keyboard of his manual Underwood at a hundred words per minute. Tee worked at a radio station, charting out tunes for the day's program. As word people do, they wrote each other beautiful letters during the war.

Afterward, Hobie returned to start their lives and a family together. He got an entry-level job at *The Arizona Republic and The Phoenix Gazette* and worked his way right on up the ladder. Tee got a job at the newspaper too, ghostwriting wry newspaper columns for a car dealer, which created quite a fan base for him. She said it was always a challenge to think and write like a man.

My brother, Larry, was born, and I came two years later. When I was seven, our father took us cross-country to Atlanta for a huge job promotion with the Atlanta newspapers. After that, as the family became more upwardly mobile with every year, our parents gifted us with cultural enrichment, theater, ballet, music, and art.

In 1963, we moved into a newly built, ultra-modern, split-level home with a bright orange door on the corner of Howell Mill Road and Peachtree Battle Avenue. It was the only one of its kind in our neighborhood in a part of town known as Buckhead—a lovely, forested neighborhood in Atlanta. My parents were busy people. Dad worked hard at the newspaper and involved himself in community pursuits as president of the symphony. Mom was a housewife, superb cook, arts volunteer, and mother simultaneously supportive—and ultra-critical—of a talented, hormonal teenage daughter, and mostly supportive—as I recall—of an academically gifted teenage son.

Dad never bowed to the stuffy rules many southerners had about what was proper or not proper in one's neighborhood. Hobie was the only guy in Buckhead with a field of Silver Queen corn in his side yard.

Now, when I drive through the streets of Atlanta where we lived, past the beautiful homes on Peachtree Battle Avenue, West Wesley Road, Habersham Road, and all the way to the Capital City Country Club in Brookhaven, I'm always shocked at how I took it all for granted. As a young girl, I was ignorant of my privilege and the obstacles others had to overcome; obstacles that were not and would never be in my way. No one ever stopped me from going anywhere or doing anything I had a mind to do. My dad never had to have "the talk" with his son—one that is required for young Black sons before they leave home. I was so naïve.

———·——

Rick lived about five miles from me on Conway Valley Road in an equally lovely neighborhood near Chastain Park. We went to different schools, together—as the old joke goes. He and I were introduced during high school by our mutual friend, Pat Fitzhugh, who was my classmate and knew Rick from their church youth group. None of us had any awareness of the rare, shining, sheltered life we had been gifted.

Later, the life my parents enjoyed would change drastically, and none of us would be prepared for it.

A few years before Rick and I married in 1971, my dad quit his executive job as vice president at the Atlanta newspapers out of pure conviction for integrity and good-guy-ness. Hobie had been passed over for a promotion. A coworker was tapped for the position, which would make him my dad's boss. This took my dad straight to the big boss, editor, publisher, president, and Grand Poohbah, Jack Tarver. Hobie laid out his thoughts about Tarver's promotion decision and what a terrible choice it was. My father explained that the man promoted was not a good guy, and in all good conscience, he could not work under this mean-spirited individual.

After an impassioned speech appealing to Tarver's own morality and humanity, Hobie waited for a response. After all, it had been Tarver who supported the integrity of the newspaper's Pulitzer prize-winning Ralph McGill, who preached racial justice at a difficult time in Atlanta's civil rights struggles. My dad was depending on that part of Tarver to rise up and support him, too, in the name of personal integrity. However, Tarver was unmoved, and that was that.

My dad quietly said, "I quit," and cleaned out his desk.

I can only imagine my mother greeting him at the door that day with his hat and cardboard box in hand, not so much as a phone call to prepare her. No more executive-level job. No more executive-level paycheck.

Surprise, honey. Sorry I didn't call! I'm home! Because I'm a good guy and I just quit my job on principle!

It would be a very long time, years, before my mother would gather the wherewithal to forgive him.

My father reassured Tee he could get another job. But like most people over fifty who leave their jobs, Hobie was overconfident and surprised to find he was, at every turn, either overqualified or too old. My dad would discover being a good guy didn't carry the gravitas he ascribed to it. He kept searching but also began drinking to ease the pain.

So while I was off having a personal meltdown at Stephens College, my parents were having their own crisis. No doubt it was a mixed bag for them when I called them to say I was dropping out of school and coming home—worried for me and my future, and yet I always guessed they secretly celebrated. *No more private college tuition! Yay!*

I came home in November 1969, looking to return to my old summer job at Parkwood Hospital in the arts and crafts room of the occupational therapy department and find an apartment. Licking my wounds from my short college stint, I found two parents swirling down the drain and trying to look like they weren't.

Tee and Hobie clung to their dysfunctional coping mechanism of drinking too much. During the day—not so much—but when the sun started over the yardarm, they began with their six o'clock cocktails, which soon became five "o'clocktails," and happy hour stretched to happy hours.

From my bedroom late at night, I'd listen to them in the den down the hall. They had a pattern, and every night I had a repeatable reaction. They bid me goodnight as I disappeared to my room. Hobie and Tee would settle into their comfy chairs in the den, consume more drinks, and predictably get overly mellow—okay, sloshed—as they sat in the dark and listened to classical music on the stereo at full volume.

Music lovers, they had an extensive record collection—vinyl LPs in those days—and even a smattering of brittle 78s. My parents stacked multiple records on the stereo spindle—each one dropping automatically in turn, giving my folks a good long session of uninterrupted anesthesia.

In one evening, they could listen to quite an array: powerful orchestral symphonies and melancholy Chopin piano nocturnes; a sensual, full-throttled Rachmaninoff Piano Concerto followed by a palate cleanser of operatic arias: Anna Moffo singing the "Bell Song" and the sublime "Flower Duet," both from Delibes's opera, *Lakmé*. Sutherland or Sills as Queen of the Night singing the bold aria from Mozart's *Magic Flute* in which "the vengeance of hell" boiled in her heart. Thrilling, heartbreaking tenor arias sung by Pavarotti ranged from Puccini's tender "Che Gelida Manina" ("Your Little Hand Is Cold") in *La Bohème* to a luscious "Nessun Dorma" "("No-One Shall

Sleep") from *Turandot* to the high stakes, frenetic, "Pour mon âmes/ Ah! mes amis" "(For My Soul/Ah! My Friends")" from Donizetti's *Daughter of the Regiment*, requiring the poor chap, Tonio, to squeeze out nine, flawless high Cs in a fortissimo chest voice within two minutes. Talk about tension and release!

Every night, I lay in bed trying to fall sleep, wishing for no ears— or better yet, wishing they didn't have any. I fumed silently. Why weren't they worried I might be disturbed by the decibel level which matched a jet plane taking off? Their cigarette smoke wafted down the hall to my room. I took to closing my door, but even so, I could still hear them talking during the brief gaps in the music as the stylus in the cartridge on the tone arm skated silently away from one set of grooves across the smooth vinyl to the next.

As the night got longer, their speech smeared—ice dropping into tub glasses again and again. Their voices were slow and unregulated as they slid into that silky smooth place only liquor and music could take them. Eventually, I would fall asleep, and the next morning, I'd rise to a new day programmed to repeat itself.

I was conflicted and angry they debased themselves every damn night in order to escape into oblivion. But they had been good parents, providing me with love, one hell of a fine music appreciation education, and sage parental guidance my whole life. They were hurting, deeply. *And they're alone in there, not out in public. The only person they're debasing themselves in front of is each other. And although they don't even know it . . . me.*

Me.

I could not bear to see them this way.

I loved them, but I no longer recognized them.

The day Dad took their private pain out into the world was the day I knew it was time for me to grow up and get busy finding my own apartment.

The phone call came in around 7:00 p.m. for my dad from a potentially prime employer with a newspaper in Tennessee. On central time, the newspaper was an hour earlier than Atlanta, calling at the end of their workday to interview him. Happy hours at our house was already in full swing.

My mom answered.

"Oh yes," Tee said, "he's right here."

To my utter shock and horror she handed the phone to Hobie. I did not then, and I do not now—nor will I ever—understand why she did that. He was, as they say, "beyond the pale." My dad could barely speak, and the words he did manage to slur made no sense. No surprise, then, this was a very short, colossally painful interview.

It was clear to me at that moment this was their house, and I was now a visitor. There was nothing I could say to them to make them change. My parents' pain was theirs to handle, and I needed to let them have it. It was my job to accept them, give them their space, take care of myself, and be an independent adult.

I got hired back at my old job at Parkwood. Dad helped me buy my first car. I secured a two-bedroom apartment at Nob Hill—a nice singles complex on Roswell Road inside the perimeter—and I conscripted two female workmates, who were nurses at the hospital, as roomies. I was twenty-years-old and on my way.

My folks managed for a couple of years. They quit drinking and held on to the country club membership just long enough to have our wedding reception there in 1971.

They held on as their society-minded, high falutin' business acquaintances drifted away. My parents held on through the sale of the Peachtree Battle house, moved closer to us to a little burg about twenty miles from Newnan.

Their new house was in Peachtree City, where folks toodle around in golf carts on special paths and enjoy a big, beautiful lake as its centerpiece. There, my parents could relax, free from big-city-Atlanta taxes, old habits, and dead friendships. The lake was right outside and across the cart path from their back door. Dad could fish. Mom could watch. They were happy. Hobie and Tee babysat our toddler from time to time. They visited us and helped us do projects at our little house in Newnan, which they had generously helped us purchase in the first place.

Our relationship was healed.

Their relationship was healed.

We all held on to each other like a cherished prize we had earned—which we absolutely had.

All of us later held on when my dad was diagnosed with esophageal cancer in early 1982 and had a remission in December of that same year, just as I was having another baby, followed two weeks later by my mom's emergency surgery to repair an aortic aneurysm. As soon as she got home, Dad's remission took a hike, which opened his cancer floodgates.

I spent my days, barely recovered from my C-section, driving Hobie back and forth every morning to Atlanta for radiation therapy. Mom looked after the new baby in the playpen I set up in their house.

As we made our road trips, I watched my dad squirm in pain, getting worse by the day. When the pain became intractable and indignities were eschewed for practicalities, I kept my eyes firmly on the road while he contorted himself in the passenger seat of my car to self-administer extra-strength, opiate suppositories—both of us praying for his relief.

We held on.

One year after his cancer diagnosis, at the age of sixty-seven, my dad was no longer holding on; he let go on May 24, 1983. A few days later, under cover of darkness, we quietly, reverently, and quite illegally emptied Hobie's ashes into his beloved lake behind my parents' house.

Mom held on for sixteen more years and let go in her sleep on May 23, 1999, when chronic obstructive pulmonary disease was done destroying her lungs at the age of eighty-three.

Shortly before Tee's departure, she showed me a slim book of poetry by her favorite poet, Rupert Brooke. She had wrapped it in a butter-soft, gold filigreed leather book cover. On the front page she had long ago inscribed her maiden name and the date, "July 22, 1935," in black ink. Also on that page appeared a faded penciled note, "See p. 123." On that page was the poem, Retrospect, and another of her penciled notes: "Mozart A major sonata. Words could be adapted to the music's flow and beat."

She asked me if I would work on it with her. I wrote out the tune and piano accompaniment by hand on staff paper, and after multiple iterations, we had our finished piece: "Retrospect," Lyrics by Rupert Brooke, Music by Mozart, Adapted and Arranged by Tee Franks.

In your arms was still delight,
Quiet as a tree at night
Dark clouds in a moonless sky.
Love, in you, went passing by . . .
...Oh infinite deep I never knew,
I would come back, come back to you.

I saw it as a plaintive love song to my dad, and it spoke of her hope to join him. God knows how I did it, but I sang it at her memorial service in her retirement home. It was the perfect tribute to both of them. Damn, that was hard. Perhaps I was able to sing it so freely because I knew my performance would also be free of her critique. Although, ironically, this time I thought she would've approved.

The next evening, under "dark clouds in a moonless sky," and "quiet as a tree at night," we deposited Tee's ashes in the lake to join my dad.

A few weeks later, the city drained the lake—something about dredging it to make it deeper.

Eventually, the lake was refilled and sparkling again behind my parents' old house, where strangers lived, fished, and drove their golf carts along the path. We have no idea exactly where mom and dad went when they flowed out and down the drain as love went passing by, but wherever it was, we know they went there together.

———

...NAMED RICK

Rick swore he would never, ever be like his dad. I begged him never, ever to do to himself or me what my dad did to himself and my mother by quitting his job on principle without even consulting her first. I did tell Rick to feel free to adopt the sweet, loving parts of both our dads if he liked.

And yet...

To be fair, Rick is not like his father—at least not in his dad's later unstable, decompensating years. Rick took the good from his father and left the rest, except for some dysfunctional problem-solving skills upon which Rick would improve later in our marriage. He is still the kindest, most caring, and most responsible man I know. As a father, Rick has been a role model for our two sons.

However, there was a time when Rick tried so hard not to be like his dad that he almost did just that. And that thing my dad, Hobie, did about quitting a job on principle without telling his wife? Rick almost very nearly did that too.

———

When Rick and I met on a blind date his senior year and my junior year of high school, he was painfully shy, and I worked way too hard at being scintillating. On that first date, we went to the 1966 sci-fi movie, *Fantastic Voyage*, starring a miniaturized Raquel Welch riding around inside a miniaturized submarine in somebody's circulatory system. It was the forerunner of 1989's *Honey, I Shrunk the Kids* but with Russian scientists and surgical assassins. After the movie, Rick and I had a burger and a coke. Running out of conversation, he took me home.

We were babies. We didn't know how to talk to one another—as evidenced by our first date and quickly followed by our second date. Rick and I went on a hayride and spent most of it smiling at each other and saying awkward things like, "This is fun! Isn't this fun? Are you cold? I'm freezing! Where's that blanket?"

Shoot me. Now.

It took us time to grow up and get to know each other—the real people we were. But we did. We both matured. Rick was a quiet man with a gentle way, and I lost my heart to him, even when he hid his so well. I loved his sweetness, warmth, and determination to achieve success—both in college and in what he hoped would be a subsequent veterinary career. Also, there was the way Rick danced, his smile, his sense of humor, his intelligence, and his handsome, angular jawline—all extremely appealing. And he was well read. I loved him deeply.

Rick says he fell hopelessly in love with my words, my heart, and my mind. He found everything about me beautiful—inside and out. I'd call that one dandy mutual endorsement.

If we had to choose again, Rick and I would still choose each other.

We married June 10, 1971, at St. Anne's Episcopal Church in Atlanta with The Reverend Blount Grant officiating. Our honeymoon was brief, but we didn't mind. We were headed to The University of Georgia for Rick to finish summer quarter and hopefully go to vet school. We stayed a single weekend at his bombastic Italian grandfather's vacation home in Tryon, North Carolina, and then we were on our way—full of promise with our cup running over.

———

Thirty-six years flew by.

Between 2007 and 2010, things were suddenly very dark for Rick and me.

With two other partners, Rick had built up a fine small-animal practice, which was popular and well established by this time.

He and I were plugging along until we both hit a kind of wall. In 2007, I was recovering from an exhausting four-year return to college to finally earn my degree, while Rick found himself in the middle of a disquieting professional conundrum. Things had started changing with his partners and the veterinary practice. The situation was perplexing, and it was overpowering him. Like the metaphysical mystery of Schrödinger's cat, Rick's problem was a puzzlement; the solution not straightforward. He had no answers and no insight into any.

Rick was, and still is, honest to a fault. He won't tear the tags off mattresses. He would give up his life for his dog. He is a kind, brilliant vet. But none of that served to help him, then.

Large-animal partners since 1985, Rick and his veterinary partner built the small-animal hospital in 1990. The UGA extension service had warned them the demographics of the county were changing ever-so steadily from rural to suburban. True to prediction, as the years went on, land was becoming more expensive and not as conducive to farming for a profit. Highways widened, and pastures became shopping malls. Families sold their holdings because they could no longer afford the tax on their property. Dairies were closing, and the average age of cattlemen was between sixty-five- to seventy-years-old. Many younger family members couldn't afford to continue farming, and cows and horses were not as plentiful as they once had been.

Many of the farmers still raising cattle were electing to do their own routine maintenance, buying wormer and drugs from the feed store, and calling Rick mainly for emergency work. As a vet, Rick depended on a balance of steady, regular work as well as emergencies to pay the bills. Emergency work only would not cut it. The economics of curing a sick cow changed. Too often, it would be more economically advantageous for the owner to send it to slaughter than to spend past a certain amount of money for Rick to cure it.

Rick and his partner saw it all happening, and the small-animal hospital was born as a result.

The two large-animal vets were also exhausted, tired of looking out over the hood of a truck twelve to twenty hours a day. One of Rick's great joys of large-animal practice, however, had always been visiting clients on their farms and ranches, making friends, and sharing stories and meals with families in their kitchens. He would forever regret having to give that part up. The sore muscles and long hours, not so much.

It took a time or two before they found the right fit in a third doctor for the small-animal hospital. They made some costly mistakes along the way, but finally hired a young female vet who had great diagnostic skills and a winning way. She became a partner. Now they were three. All was well for a time. Years.

Then, by 2007, like those two roads in Mr. Frost's famous yellow wood, the practice philosophies of the partners—once in sync— began to diverge, making all the difference. The other two partners were forging a new and different philosophical route, which was one Rick did not wish to travel.

There were disparities of opinion over changing policies, fees, protocols, and pace. The friction was becoming untenable for Rick.

When his singular effort to persuade his partners not to go there fell on deaf ears, Rick's resistance to the change was taken as belligerence. All he knew was this was not the practice he wanted to run. While all three partners practiced excellent medicine, the trajectory of the business model was changing with or without him. As a minority of one, Rick's hands were tied.

Rick came to me and sat down one night after work.

"I don't want to be there anymore," he sighed, head down.

"Wait, what? This is the practice you started," I said, terror rising from my gut and tightening my throat.

"Not anymore. I don't recognize it. It's not what I built, and it's not where I want to be. I'm miserable, and I need to go. But I don't want to pull your dad's 'Honey, I'm home because I just quit my job' trick and not talk to you first." He held my hand.

"I'm grateful for that," I assured him in the sincerest, calmest voice I could manage while I was screaming primally inside my head.

The old, familial baggage of my dad quitting his job and the chaos that ensued for my parents had just dropped itself at my feet with a thud. Similarly, the work failures of Rick's dad and his own parents' mess dropped at his feet too. We were both terrified.

Rick and I talked for a long time. I told him I loved him, and I would support him no matter what decision he made. I reminded him he was a fine person with a good heart who had built an amazing practice and was exceedingly well respected with his numerous client-fans.

I also told him I was so mad at him for letting this happen I could hardly see straight. I have never been known for holding back.

The next day after Rick left for work, I tried to sit with my feelings. Impossible. I went, alone, to the movies to see Sandra Bullock and Ryan Reynolds in *The Proposal*. It was midday. There was no one in the theater but me and a couple of old people eating popcorn in the dark. They were laughing in all the right comedic places. I was in tears the entire time.

It took a long, ugly while to settle the business divorce between Rick and his two partners. On September 11, 2009, at a meeting in a lawyer's office, the painful division was finalized. The date, September 11, was not lost on us.

Then it was over, and Rick was free.

He had consulted me, at least, before pulling the plug, and we weren't drinking heavily, either, like my parents so long ago. I'll give him that. But Rick had done the second half of the Hobie Franks thing and assumed he could find another job immediately once his practice divorce was over.

Time was of the essence. We had COBRA insurance for a short time, but it ran out. I wasn't working for a company that provided insurance, either. As the situation began to look dire, I worked on creating a cookie baking business so we could stay afloat. Rick had a non-compete clause to honor. He called around to his vet friends to ask if they had any job openings or part-time opportunities. He was able to pick up a few hours of work here and there but nothing permanent. Every day, Rick came through the kitchen door bent and bowed—a defeated Willie Loman.

About a month after he left his business, Rick walked into Family Friend Animal Hospital. He was calm but direct in his request for a job. Fortunately, the practice was a toenail past the non-compete area in his business divorce agreement. The practice was a fledgling business trying to make ends meet. At first, they didn't know if they could afford to hire a second vet, much less keep the current employees afloat. Rick offered to work on a percent commission only with no benefits. He'd had enough of practice ownership and the headaches that came with it. He just wanted to work, practice good veterinary medicine, and earn a paycheck. The owner sent Rick away, telling him they would talk it over amongst themselves. The owner's wife told her husband he would be crazy not to hire Rick, who could bring in new clients, grow the practice, and give her husband some time off! Bingo—the call came in that same afternoon.

"We're taking you to lunch," the owner's brother and practice manager said. "We can start you part-time and then go full-time if it works out. We think you will be a perfect fit here."

And, indeed, he was.

IT'S SIX O'CLOCK, THE LIGHTS ARE OUT, AND THE POOL IS ON FIRE

Rick and I have had some incredible times over the years; unforgettable times, for all sorts of reasons. Some years ago, in May of 2002, our elder son, Scott, was getting married. Rick and I were hosting the rehearsal dinner in the backyard of a house we had rented for a few weeks at the beach. It was the perfect location—just a mile down the road from the church where the wedding would be the next day. Our shindig was totally outdoors. There was no Plan B. When I think back on how much was on the line that weekend, I can't believe we pulled it off.

Rick and I planned the party to be an outside affair because, frankly, the interior of the one-story brick vacation rental was dated. But the backyard was what sealed the deal. It was potentially dreamy. There was some yardwork to be done and landscaping to be improved, but I saw it all in my mind's eye and knew straightaway it was the right place. Encircled by tall, thick greenery, the grassy backyard was private and lush. A large, sparkling swimming pool anchored the space. Surrounding the pool, a spacious flagstone patio flowed out to meet a generous stretch of lawn large enough to accommodate a dining tent with ample room left over for our crowd to mingle "en plein air," converse, enjoy cocktails, and glom catered appetizers. They could then have a lovely dinner followed by speeches and toasts under the tent.

For months, I worked hard on the details for the party as Rick worked just as hard at the clinic. This was the story of our lives. Rick was devoted to his veterinary career. Next in line was his family who got Rick's fully committed attention when he could either hold the world at bay, or just get out of town. Leaving town was the best way Rick could detach from work demands. God bless him. I finally just accepted the trade-off. If Rick put forth his best effort when he did get away, his no-boundaries devotion to work when he was home just had to suffice. Rick promised me he would get two weeks completely off for the wedding. Until then, I was on a mission—totally on my own as the sole party planner.

I was slowly but surely getting details checked off my to-do list. Caterer—check. Tent, tables, chairs—check. Centerpieces—check. Floating pool candles—check. Outdoor lighting...

Well, that was a problem.

The yard was large, and the harsh spotlights at either corner of the roof weren't sufficient to light the far reaches of the lawn. I wanted twinkle lights around the tent, patio, and bar, which was doable. Still, there wasn't a way to illuminate the expanse of grass farthest away. There needed to be something in the way of soft, romantic light for that area so guests could use all the available space without tripping over each other in the dark. I was wracking my brain to come up with something and was down to my last neuron when I saw them. Right there they sat in the tchotchke aisle at Kroger along with the summer picnic supplies, pool floats, and mosquito repellents.

Lanterns. Beautiful lanterns.

They were a nice size, metal—copper not plastic—and classy with frosted glass on all four sides. They would last for years, which was a big plus. They were attractive enough to house a thick candle or two and sturdy enough to safely hang from the shepherds hooks I would bring from my own garden—an even bigger plus. We needed maybe fifteen lanterns to do the job. They were only ten bucks each—the biggest plus of all! And I could bring them home after the party and use them in my own yard. Sold.

Rick and I rented the house for several weeks to have plenty of time to spiff it up before the rehearsal dinner, engage in the wedding festivities, and have a week to recover afterward. When it was time, I drove down to the beach alone, and Rick planned to follow a few days later. I trusted he would be there when he said he would be, but I had learned the hard way over the years that Rick's timeline always had the potential to be a tad fluid; I always suffered a low-level hum of anxiety until I saw the whites of his eyes in front of me.

As soon as I got to the beach house and saw the interior of the house again, I knew a phone call was in order.

"Rick," I stammered, "The interior is, um . . ." I strained for words as I surveyed the dated, unbeach-y dark furnishings and faded upholstery. "Not okay. Guess I didn't pay as much attention as I should've when we did the rental walk through. It was the backyard that sold me. So, now something's gotta happen inside. Even though we're not entertaining indoors, if someone needs the bathroom . . . I'm gonna need some more things from home."

"No problem, babygirl, I will bring whatever you need." Rick was emphatic and determined to keep his word. He was, indeed, exerting his best effort with flying colors.

I itemized a long list that included everything from lamps to vases to rugs to yardwork tools and more to brighten the place. Bless him—Rick got everything I asked him to bring. When he drove in the driveway at the beach rental the week before the wedding, I breathed a sigh of hope and relief. Rick's car was so tightly crammed with stuff it was comical, Beverly-Hillbillies-full to the brim. No one was happier to see him than I was.

Our younger son, Nick, showed up on leave from college to help. He and Rick set upon the landscaping chores with an exuberance I wished Nick had displayed when he lived at home. Bushes needed trimming, flower beds needed cleaning out, lawns needed mowing, and mosquitoes needed spraying. We probably did thousands of dollars in environmental damage with Rick's industrial, backpack fogger. My friend, Leanne, arrived, and we made a run to the local nursery to find hydrangeas, geraniums, gardenias, more green shrubbery, and hanging baskets to decorate and beautify the yard for the party. We barely got it all to fit in the car, but I was prepared to make two trips if necessary. This was some serious party atmosphere I was determined to create.

All the blooming perennial plants were placed—some nestled together in their pots, strategically camouflaged behind a short brick wall in a semi-circular bed next to the house. Some were grouped around the yard, snuggled into pine straw islands. Hanging baskets of ferns and flowers shared the shepherd hooks with the lanterns on the opposite arms.

It was then Rick posed a critical question he had not thought to ask until that moment.

"Um, babygirl, what are we doing with all these plants when the wedding's over? Are we taking them back to the nursery?" Rick asked this like a typical husband—unaware of what every wife would already have known; there was no way those plants were going back.

"What?" I laughed. "Are you kidding me? No, of course not. We are taking them home to our house to plant in our yard!"

Rick looked stunned for a moment, "Really? So do we really need all of them? There's no more room in our cars." A light clicked on in his eyes. He brightened.

"Oh dear, what a pity," he whined in mock distress. "I guess I'll just have to buy a trailer and hitch it to the jeep for the trip home," Rick laughed—delighted with his sudden awareness of a golden opportunity. This was a man-dream come true: a covered trailer to haul man-things, like wood for campouts and whatever else men dream about carting around.

It was as easy as that.

The day of the party arrived. The tent was up, open bar and tent furnishings in place, lights all strung and twinkling, shepherd's hooks planted, and flower baskets and lanterns hung. I was thanking the beach-weather gods for the clear skies and the glorious full moon above as I filled each lantern with candles. Just the weekend prior, the skies had let loose with a two-day, frog-strangling rain that would have canceled all our plans had it happened on our night. Again, we had no Plan B. What the hell was I thinking? We were at the mercy of nature's whimsy. And yet, we forged ahead—determined to have the perfect evening. Call it denial. Or hubris. Or dumb luck. I'm pretty sure it was all three.

Rick and I left with the wedding party for a quick five-o'clock rehearsal at the church just a few blocks down the beach. Our dearest friends, who were there to help, assured us they would oversee the final details during our brief absence. We left, knowing everything was in good hands. Just how beyond good, we would have no way of predicting.

As the food arrived and caterers were setting up, the guitarist positioned himself on the patio and started preparing for his gig. It was now approaching 6:00 p.m., and guests would be arriving soon to the magical fairyland we had worked so hard to create. We would be getting back, too, just moments before them. The lanterns flickered with warm candlelight, casting a beautiful soft glow on the foliage and out onto the grass. The floating candles in the pool were lit. The string lights twinkled.

The guitar player was Scott's pal and fraternity pledge brother from college, Jonathan Burke. Jonathan plugged in his amp, and every electric light in the yard went out.

Then, one of the lit floating pool candles quietly bobbed its way toward the pool wall and was gently sucked right into the opening of the intake valve. It stopped there, still lit, and began to burn the access cover—a rubbery, plastic-y lid recessed in the concrete pool deck directly above.

Driving back from the church rehearsal, Rick and I were but moments away, unaware of the chaos that had befallen our party before it had even begun. When disaster struck, our dear friends who were left in charge stood wide-eyed and slack-jawed in momentary disbelief before shooting into hyperdrive.

Leanne miraculously remembered where the extra fuses for the string lights had been stored after Rick finished daisy-chaining the strings together around the tent, bar, and patio earlier in the day.

She retrieved the fuses while Gary grabbed a ladder to work furiously with the light strings. Humphrey raced to help, and Kathi focused her attention on the caterers, servers, and bartenders whose food and beverages were still in need of last-minute order. Dan grabbed the first thing he could find to pry open the pool's intake access cover. As smoke seeped through the seams, Dan found himself firefighting with the business end of a long-handled butane lighter.

In the span of minutes, these angel-friends had replaced the fuses and restrung all the lights properly so as not to overload the fuses again. The butane lighter served as the perfect pry bar—providentially not exploding—and the offending candle was removed from the intake filter, the soot wiped from the lid, which was then replaced over the opening, not too much worse for wear. Much fanning dispersed the acrid smoke as the food was placed and ready and the bar was open.

When Jonathan plugged in his amp again, all was well as big sighs of relief blew across the yard. The party was back on!

Enter now our wedding party who marveled again at the beauty of the sparkling scene, which appeared to be just as we had left it earlier.

Moments later, dinner guests began arriving. They oohed and aahed, mesmerized by the twinkling lights, the lanterns, the full moon, the pool aglow, the soft guitar. Neither they, nor we, had a clue about what we had all missed by mere minutes. Except, I did notice that our dear friends were glistening with flop sweat, had facial expressions like deer in headlights, and had already been amply served at the bar. It wasn't long before they brought me an adult beverage and took me aside to fill me in.

I went a little weak in the knees, aghast. I hugged my friends, hard. They had saved us, and I was immensely grateful.

The evening turned out to be perfectly divine and memorable for each guest for decidedly different reasons. For the unsuspecting partygoer, it was just a lovely, romantic rehearsal dinner under a full moon in a beautiful setting.

For those of us in the know, it was a goddamn miracle.

Four years later, our son was divorced from the bride he toasted that night and married the following day in the little church down the street from our beach rental. And in a final, metaphorical irony, the beach house was demolished a few years later—much like their marriage—and the land split up into three lots of new, high-priced condos.

I saved my lanterns; they now sit in rows along the edges of our sidewalk leading to the front door of our home. I filled them with strings of small outdoor globe lights that (properly) plug into the outside receptacle. The glow always reminds me of that one beautiful night.

Rick's covered trailer has served us well all these years too. He's hauled everything in that thing, as predicted long ago, from yard equipment to camping gear, to furniture, and a complete collection of artwork I took to an exhibition. I also find it very handy on occasion for plant runs to my favorite nursery. A gardener never has enough plants.

We still have our dear friends—our family of choice—who share years and years of stories, laughter, love, sadness, deaths, births, and memories. And will as long as we live.

Lessons were learned that night so many years ago. I learned not to overload string lights. I learned that I'm a damn good wedding and party planner—a lucky one at that. I learned to be thankful for calamities beyond my control that turn out okay because of dear, dear friends and, in the case of the weather, because of serendipity and sheer, dumb luck. I learned to turn off pool intake pumps before floating burning candles on the surface. I learned, that despite their best efforts, people can screw up, they get divorced, they hurt, and so do those around them, and life goes on. I learned that devoted friends are there when you need them and will do anything for you. I learned that nothing is forever—not beach houses, string lights, and sometimes marriages. And I was re-assured my husband could separate from his job, show up for us, and really give us his all. Ours was one marriage we vowed would not be demolished. Ever.

My lanterns require a little rehab now and then, but don't we all? I love having them, along with my memories of what was, for a short while, the loveliest and most miraculous of times.

MAKE YOUR GARDEN GROW: THOUGHTS ON A MARRIAGE

The summer of 2016 was the hottest in living memory. How did my husband and I celebrate our forty-fifth wedding anniversary that June? Clinking ice-cold champagne glasses at the Ritz? Nope. We took a trip to visit the Atlanta Botanical Garden. Outdoors. In the heat. We wanted to take in the bountiful flora and fauna and marvel at the latest art installations by Seattle glass artist, Dale Chihuly.

We had considered lots of (economical) options. By this time, Rick was semi-retired, which had its pros and cons. In our case, Rick and I had more time to do stuff but less money to throw around doing it. Go to the movies, a play, a show, an art gallery or two? Eat out locally? Grill a juicy steak and stay in? Certainly not a European vacation or a trip to anywhere very far. Semi-retirement meant my husband had to work the following day.

Inveterate gardeners, Rick and I love to make our garden grow, and we know it's only through hard work and commitment that we can accomplish that. So we worked in our garden on that blazing hot Georgia day in June. We started gardening in the morning, as every gardener knows to do, but the time slipped by as we pushed into early afternoon in the ever-escalating heat. It was like the Hadron Collider when they smash gold particles together, and for a split second, the temperature reaches 7.2 trillion degrees—only way more sultry with one hundred percent humidity. We surrendered by 1:30 p.m., showering, dressing, and driving northward to Atlanta to spend the rest of the day and evening outside appreciating someone else's garden.

Our trip to the city was typical. One minute we were sailing along on I-85. The next minute we were in the middle of crawling vehicles with no apparent cause. Historically, Atlanta traffic is predictably unpredictable, especially at or near the University Avenue exit. From there, it's a toss-up which part(s) of the downtown connector will follow suit and bungle up traffic even more.

This day, sure enough, we crawled from University Avenue as multiple police cars screamed past us on the shoulder headed north. Finally arriving at the I-20 ramp, we saw the jumble of blue lights as we rolled by, but there were no mangled vehicles, no wreckers, no debris, no nothing save a small triangle of bright yellow crime tape flapping with the breeze. We made it to the Botanical Garden around

3:45 p.m., which was only about forty-five minutes past our target arrival time.

Little did we know, arriving closer to 4:00 p.m. would help us. It turned out there was a day admission until 5:00 p.m., after which there was a different admission for Chihuly Nights. To avoid paying double entry, they advised us to "chill" until 4:00 p.m., after which time we could buy access at the day rate, which would also include the entire evening. Since we were hot already, just the thought of "chilling" gave me all the incentive I needed to go with Plan B.

Enter the ubiquitous gift shop, conveniently located immediately to our left—it was the perfect way to kill fifteen minutes and cool off. There, Rick and I could most definitely chill.

We both bought hats we'd wear for the rest of the afternoon until sundown. Rick grabbed a new ball cap, and I spied a large-brimmed, black sun hat with white stitching and an elegant bow on the right crown. With hats in hand, we searched for our anniversary gift to each other.

For our anniversary seven years earlier, we bought ourselves a large terracotta pig for the garden path when we were building a detached garage. Our toddler grandson, Harper, loved it and dubbed it "Pig Pig." To this day, good ol' Pig Pig gets a pat on the nose every time we walk down the path.

Rick and I wanted to purchase something as lasting as Pig Pig. We didn't know what it would be but knew we would know it when we saw it. We thumbed through coffee table books and handled a variety of trinkets, baubles, and high-priced tchotchkes. Nothing suited us. Plus, there was the budget to consider.

And then, there it was. It was love at first sight: a smart-looking, kinetic whirligig. It bore two different hammered-copper flowers that spun independently yet welded together on the same metal pole. We could relate. It was perfect for our garden and for us. The metaphor was inescapable. It was us.

We emerged from the gift shop just after 4:00 p.m. happily wearing our new headgear and toting our unique anniversary gift to each other. Rick gallantly ran to the car to deposit the whirligig as I fanned and blotted myself, complaining in a good-natured way—I hoped—about the heat to the woman standing next to me. I waited in the shade, checking my phone. Beads of sweat dripped from my forehead, off the tip of my nose, and dropped onto the pavement. The local news app popped up on my screen with breaking headlines, and the mystery of our earlier adventure with traffic was solved. My heart sank.

Somebody shot a person and dumped the body from a car on the interstate. "Ughhh," I groaned quietly. Now knowing we had come so close to that scene made it feel more personal. I felt a quick stab of alarm, followed by sadness, and then an adrenalin rush of pure anger. I cursed and fumed in my head. *The shootings and the violence these days are outrageous, and there's no solution in sight.* Rick returned, smiling, and I closed my phone with a sigh—grateful for the interruption, my life, my day, and him. The heat instantly became more bearable. With a sudden new perspective, how could I complain?

I had no way of knowing that only two days later, the worst mass shooting in history at Pulse, a gay bar in Orlando, Florida, would sucker punch the entire world. Death and mayhem laid itself at the world's feet, like a grotesque offering at the altar of terrorism and hate, and we would be helpless to prevent it or dispose of it. Not since 9/11 had so many been murdered and maimed in the U.S. As a world community, we would at once be divided and united, taking sides, arguing about religion and guns and gays, and plunging ourselves into shock, sadness, anger, and grief.

I could not know that on that sad day, I would reach back desperately to retrieve the memory of our evening in the garden only two days earlier and hold onto it for solace—a healing balm for my soul.

So Rick and I stepped up to the booth, bought our admission, and strolled into another world.

And it was good.

We would continue with our splendid day, and we would have no more thoughts of bad things. We wandered up and down flowered paths, meandering slowly and without purpose, taking everything in as the afternoon sun bore down and the day slowly turned into a hot, sticky night. There was the rich, loamy scent of garden soil; sweet blooms and botanicals full of color and chlorophyll; bird calls and flapping wings; sparkling water spilling over things and down into brooks and fountain bowls. A rare, barely-there summer breeze floated through, carrying soft conversations and laughter all about like soft music. Branches slightly swayed, and green leaves rippled. Blissful cool caressed our sweaty necks. Glass sculptures were lit and glistened like fire and ice. The angular architecture of the city in the distance jutted over the top of a round, verdant hill. There were marvelous metal garden gates forged from garden implements and giant botanical topiaries of animals and beautiful goddesses. Majestic, crimson crepe myrtles lined either side of a long walk, bending benevolently toward each other to form a high, arched allée.

Rick and I continued to amble along happily, chatting now and then as we smiled, admired, discussed, enjoyed, people watched. We posed for a selfie, and I wondered how we might look by our fiftieth or sixtieth anniversary and how we might feel looking back at this photo. I took plenty of pictures of our surroundings, doing my best but finding it impossible to capture the immensity of a complete experience in a photo. Holding hands, still sweating, blotting, and fanning, we stared in awe and silence now and then. Rick and I were happy to take it all in, all of it: the garden, the people, the glass sculptures, the fountains, each other, even the heat.

What a gift it is to just "be"—alive, content, and in no particular hurry, especially in the company of a lifelong partner and love of forty-five years. There were no deadlines or rushing as we walked through so much sensual stimulation. Our phones only served as cameras. We were present. In the moment. The gardens alone were breathtaking, and combined with so many artful, Chihuly glass installations, it was a feast to savor. We happily gorged ourselves on it all.

As with any fine meal, there's a time to stop. Satiety becomes anesthetizing when one is full to the brim and cannot ingest one more morsel—be it food or art. We had fed our senses in every way but one: dinner. We found our oasis and took refuge in the garden's glassed-in restaurant. It was blessed relief from the heat, and we rested our eyes and aching feet, still seeking sustenance for body and soul in dinner. The provisions were delicious and welcome—our conversation lively, enjoyable.

As is his custom, Rick engaged our server in a friendly chat. We discovered her to be a student working on an art degree. Rick and I both related to those times in our lives when we were tackling something difficult.

It was the same way we had approached our marriage and still do—working hard; having integrity, passion, and communication; overcoming obstacles; and supporting each other. The only way out is "through." Build bridges, hold hands, and walk across together. Enjoy it all if and when you can. Love and appreciate it all—nonetheless.

Come to think of it, that's the way we garden too. It ain't all fun and games. Things die; bugs descend; body parts ache; the work can be backbreaking; there are no guarantees; sometimes, you must go back to basics and begin again. But commitment, faith, encouragement, and perseverance bolster a weak body. Through it all, we honor our promise to tend our garden. And the results are, more often than not, thoroughly rewarding.

All of that flew through my consciousness as we chatted with our young, tattooed millennial server. I hoped she would follow her path and succeed. I said a silent prayer for her success. I ran through my favorite Bernstein piece in my head, "Make Our Garden Grow" from *Candide*, and thought about how people make their gardens grow or how they fail.

Our server took our photo, and we paid our bill. Thoroughly sated in every way, we went back out to wend our way back through the garden, happily holding hands, back to our car, and back home.

The roads were clear by the time we headed south. I craned my neck as we drove by the crime scene we had passed earlier. There was no trace of the flapping, yellow tape or flashing lights; no sign that a soul once-living had been taken away at that spot. I don't know what I thought I would see. Silly of me to even look. But I did. Because, somehow, it mattered. Some ill-fated stranger mattered to me. I wondered if they were married. Did they have kids? Were they loved? Did they love someone? Did they live nearby? Did they have a garden? I hoped my thoughts made some cosmic difference. I thought of it as a personal benediction of sorts—my silent sendoff in case they had no one to whom they mattered, just as the strangers two days later in Orlando would matter to me.

Driving home, I was deep in thought as I marveled at our longevity as a couple. Bernstein played again in my head. Being married forty-five years hadn't happened by accident any more than having a beautiful garden was accidental. I had been twenty-one, him twenty-two and we could not yet understand what chaos life would lay at our feet. But we were intentional, stubbornly committed, and we hadn't just survived forty-five years but had chosen forty-five years. Some years were happy, and some found us besieged and barely hanging on. There had been forty-five years of lessons, times to celebrate and grieve, opportunities to learn when to listen and when to talk, children and grandchildren, sickness and health.

After forty-five years, our marriage felt secure, comfortable, reliable, loving, respectful, and still—always—intentional. We did the work, accepted the things we could not change, changed the things we could, and after so many years, we earned the wisdom to know the difference.

Our forty-fifth anniversary enriched us in many ways, most certainly with a cosmic reminder and reality check: nobody knows what the next year, month, day, or even the next moment holds. Rick and I vowed to make the best of this one. To be present. To be kind. To hang on. To work hard at loving someone and being loved. To take a hand and smell the roses, care for others, be intentional, and have a garden.

And wherever or whatever our garden is, we will continue to make it grow.

CHECKING A BOX BEFORE IT'S TOO LATE

In 2003, I wanted my college degree.

I had devoted many years to supporting Rick's career and raising our family. Rick's veterinary career was firmly established and now slowing down. Our grown children were out of the house. I wanted my turn at bat. It was my chance to stand over the plate and swing for the fences before it was too late—before I was either dead, or worse, senile.

By the time I got around to it in 2003, I was "an ancient" at age fifty-three. None of my old (and few) college credits transferred. I would have to start from scratch.

This news should have deterred me. It did not.

I figured the journey would be difficult. Just how difficult it would be came as something of a surprise. It's true what they say that ignorance is bliss. It's what allows people to get themselves into some very deep kimchi. I was no exception.

My lifelong career was always in music, and the lack of a music degree had not stood in my way. I had sung with the ASO Chorus, taught music at a private school where they didn't need the paperwork and held music summer camps at local churches. I performed all over the place in shows and concerts, cowrote and performed a two-woman musical show, *Old Friends*, and sang in cabarets and more weddings and funerals than I care to remember. I was a paid soloist in a large, midtown Atlanta church—St. Mark United Methodist. I celebrated my fiftieth birthday writing and performing an ambitious one-woman cabaret show, *All Grown Up*, at the Rialto Theater in downtown Atlanta. I even got a week's stint with the touring company of *Music Man* at the Fox Theater. With all that, a music degree was unnecessary. I didn't need or want it.

What I wanted was to learn something different, and always having been artsy, I chose a four-year art degree in graphic design. The Atlanta College of Art accepted me based on a portfolio that, looking back, was lacking but showed potential. As non-traditional students of a certain age are wont to do, I took it all very seriously. I was stubbornly committed to succeeding in school, much like I was in my marriage.

Unlike the first time I went to college as a kid, dropping out after a year and a half, I pushed myself this go-round to be the best student I was capable of being. It was jarring when the old neurons that had been out of academia for many decades had to be rudely jostled awake, dressed for school, and readied for serious, scholastic battle.

I held my own amid a bunch of fresh-faced, cocky eighteen-year-olds. I had something they didn't have, something for which there was no substitute and would sustain me in the hardest times: the wisdom that comes with age and life experience. I swore I would not quit the veritable four-year marathon that taxed me, tested me—physically and mentally—to the absolute max. I would prove to myself I could do something I didn't know whether I could do. Getting up at 5:30 a.m. and navigating Atlanta's rush hour traffic daily were just the beginning.

Starting over meant core freshman classes like English Composition, English Literature, Psychology 101, Math, and World Cultures—plus all the art and art history classes and subsequent assignments I would be required to accomplish after coming home from my part-time job as staff soloist at the church. On any given day, my commute one-way meant a forty-five- to ninety-minute drive, depending on the famously unpredictable Atlanta traffic. Optimistically, on the days I worked, I would arrive home at 10:00 or 11:00 p.m. followed by homework—lots and lots of homework.

On Sundays, I commuted to St. Mark both ways and sang two services, requiring me to leave home at 7:00 a.m. and arrive back home around 2:00 p.m. The balance of the day? Schoolwork. It was an unsustainable agenda, and I realized it would be necessary to leave my St. Mark job after a year of that grueling schedule. While the pay wasn't much, I had loved singing there for nine years and made many lifelong friends. But something had to change. So, yes, I quit. It was a matter of priorities and reality. I simply could not do both. I was resolute I would finish one or the other.

Still, with laser focus on my goal and no job to distract me, I struggled. My age became a double-edged sword. I may have had the advantage of valuable life experience and mature discernment, but my classmates had more energy. There were lots of all-nighters. Tests to study for. Papers to write. Projects to complete. The hard, wooden seats of the drawing horses hurt my over-fifty butt and lower back after hours-long studio classes. My feet swelled after sitting in a chair for half a day in my foundation classes. Spending long semesters standing in photo darkrooms, bending double over silkscreen tables, and standing at painting easels all took a toll. I wrote virtuoso essays and studied long hours for exams. I was crushing it with a 4.0 average.

My fellow students called me Mary Poppins. Each day, I came over-prepared to class, cramming art supplies into every available space in my portable art storage bins and zippered pencil pouches. I wish I had a nickel for every time I heard, "Anybody have an extra eraser, Conté crayon, 2B pencil, pencil sharpener, stapler, Exacto knife, scissors, tape . . .?"

I bought an entire box of acrylic transparency sheets for a screen-printing class and charged a dollar per sheet. My classmates were all too happy to pay, and I made a few bucks for my trouble. I had an extra shawl tucked away for young, bare shoulders in cold classrooms. I took photos in art history class and posted them online as study guides. I was their art school mother. In turn, they gave me encouragement and offered up generous assistance and moral support when I was flailing.

It was art school symbiosis in action.

My drawing teacher and I had a good laugh over my first drawing session with a nude model. Of course, a man's anatomy would be no surprise to me as an old married lady. But I had to admit I was as self-conscious and nervous as a schoolgirl. My teacher assured me I would be just fine.

The day came. Heart racing, I straddled the wooden drawing horse, propped up my large drawing pad, and waited for the grand reveal. The model entered, fully clothed, and stepped behind a screen. Soon, he emerged naked, walked to the center of our circle, stepped up onto the raised platform, and took a pose. He was poetry in motion. The room was silent. I was awed, awash with relief. My teacher was right; I was just fine.

As I picked up my sketch pencil, my relief was instantly supplanted by the awful awareness I had been worrying about *the wrong thing* all this time. Instead of clutching my pearls over a naked model, I should have been thinking about whether I could draw him, which was the entire purpose of the class. This was never supposed to be a therapy session for me to address my fears of a naked male body in my midst. This was a figure drawing class—nothing more. I would have to prove myself now as an art student, someone who draws. Duh! It took me a good while to learn, and after drawing many nude models, I finally got (excuse me for saying this) the hang of it.

As exciting as the whole art school experience was, it was equally arduous and demanding for Rick. He had been entirely supportive, but even he was weary from what it took to deal with my exhausting timetable and what it took for me to check the boxes. He was a captive audience forced to listen to dramatic primal screams emanating from my basement workspace. Rick ate a lot of dinners solo while I spent late nights working in the screen-printing studio or the computer lab. I dragged in at all hours—freshly traumatized by the latest rush-hour traffic and covered in paint, printmaking ink, screen-printing goo, or smelling like the chemicals in the photo lab tanks.

Occasionally, Rick had my dinner waiting. More than once, I had only enough energy to bend over my plate, prop up my head with an arm, and open my mouth just enough to allow a narrow rivulet of drool to escape. Despite my pitiful attempts at eating Rick's late-night dinners, my body's stress hormone, cortisol, was skyrocketing daily. I was subsisting on snack food during the long days, and I was getting fat, which wasn't helping either.

This whole scenario wasn't altogether unfamiliar. We had done it for many years when Rick worked, and I was his support system and laundress, working and raising two children. I had been a domestic Ginger Rogers, dancing for many years—in heels and backwards—with a veterinary Fred Astaire. Now, we had simply switched roles. Rick and I promised each other we could get through it, and the bonus, we told ourselves, was that it had a finite end. It would only take four years—four long years of baptism by fire.

I was baptized early on by white-hot computer fire. There is no substitute for hands-on art: a shard of vine charcoal in one's hand, the sound of it as it is drawn across a sheaf of hot-press art paper leaving black dust on both, the smell of paint and deep satisfaction of pushing it around on a canvas and learning how to deal with art materials and equipment. But everything else—*every single thing*—required computers at some point.

The same was true for photography class. We did use actual film in non-digital cameras and learned how to take the film out of the canister in the dark, readying it for development in another dark room. We taught our hands to feel and see in the blackness. It was an acquired skill and discipline—a photographic braille. We handled enlargers, tongs, and trays filled with chemical developers into which photo paper was floated. We did this all in the dark, save one red bulb glowing dimly on the wall. But after all that hands-on experience, we then learned how to scan negatives and images, manipulating them on the computer.

Notebook paper? What's that?

Students, take notes on your laptops or record lectures on your devices and transcribe them on your computers later; download your homework from the online blackboard program; upload your homework when you're done; write your papers with Microsoft Word; make your presentations with PowerPoint; create and edit video in Adobe Premier; lay out your graphic designs with Quark. Oh, by the way, next month Quark will be obsolete, so learn a whole new program called Adobe InDesign and do it pronto; use Adobe Photoshop and Illustrator for images and graphics creation and manipulation and Dreamweaver for web design; utilize Acrobat for your PDFs and Genuine Fractals for higher image resolution; make your spreadsheets with Excel and query your data in Microsoft Access.

So many software programs—so little time. I never fully mastered any of them, but slowly I managed to grasp enough to be semi-proficient in what I needed to accomplish. I learned so much, but after a time, I grew weary of the swift, unyielding pace of graphic design. During one memorable all-nighter in the graphic design computer lab alongside tireless youngsters, I was in tears and at my fifty-four-year-old wits end.

Amin, the whiz kid sitting near me said sweetly, "Wow, your eyes are red."

To which I replied, sniffling, "No duh."

"Hard, isn't it?" he intoned. "How bad do you want it?"

The next day, I switched majors to painting. It wasn't because I didn't like the computer or the program; I did. It wasn't because I wasn't good; I was good. And it wasn't because painting was "easy;" it was not. My graphic design professor tried his best to talk me out of changing. He said I shouldn't go because I was good.

I switched majors because the relentless pace of commercial graphic design was sapping not only my energy but my soul. I found myself in a world in which speed was not only regarded as a virtue but a requirement. In a digital age where kids are already proficient, I was a rank beginner, and I was too slow. My life experience would not give me an advantage in the computer lab as I tackled the technicalities of a whole new digital language, except having the discernment to know when it was time to change course.

I had spent inordinate amounts of time persevering in that lonely computer lab, long after all the young kids left for their triple mocha lattes at Starbucks on their walks back to their dorms to order Domino's pizza. At my age there were other, better places for me to be at three in the morning—like home in my bed sleeping next to my beloved husband. The rapid-fire world was not for me then, and it is not for me now. It is for the young whose hair has yet to gray; who don't need time to play with their grandchildren; who speed through their tasks and jobs and still possess the energy to exercise at the gym after work, take a shower, and go speed-dating at the local pub. Even their dating is fast. In my day, "fast" when related to "dating" meant something else entirely. God, I'm really *that* old.

Still, I persisted. I used computer programs to my advantage as a support for all my schoolwork—not as a be-all-end-all path to a commercial, graphic design career. The programs I learned in graphic design classes all had their place in my other pursuits, and I was glad to have the knowledge. Matter of fact, I designed this book's cover.

By graduation day, I had acquired a painful knee in need of surgery, frayed nerves, and a weight problem. I was more than ready to finish and get off the whirling carousel. In four years, I felt like I had aged twenty. But I crossed that stage in 2007 to receive my diploma—victorious as a college graduate, *summa cum laude*.

I was—as were my family and friends—elated, proud, so very grateful, and relieved it was over. I had done it. It took a village with support and encouragement from so many. We had done it.

Then, I went straight to bed for a month.

SHE MADE ME LAUGH

FEBRUARY 20, 2020

Despite my bumps with technology during college, I continue to strive to stay on top of ever-changing technology. While so many folks my age are lacking computer savvy, art school gave me a tremendous head start. Today, computers are an essential part of living, and I feel bad for those who struggle. And I have my moments, too. Trust me.

I'm not an expert tech aficionado, far from it. But I've learned a bit about hardware, peripherals, and portable gadgets. The digital world is always changing and never ending. It is imposing, demanding, and fascinating. Technology and I have come to an agreement—a truce of sorts. I "do" technology at my pace; it doesn't rush or judge me, and it serves me well, eventually. At times, there are spats when it misbehaves, but I've acquired patience for the most part and discovered the magic fix when things go wrong in technology and often, in life, which is this: When things go wrong, relax and reboot.

Rick has little need for technology but for an occasional time or two. Professionally, he has certain technological equipment in veterinary medicine that he has mastered: the ultrasound and digital Xray machines, fancy diagnostic monitors, testing equipment, and endoscopes. But digital gadgets outside of the office? Not so much. Rick does have an iPhone, and he has sort of learned how to email and text, although he is not yet sure which of those is which. I'm hoping one day soon he will get "Reply" and "Reply All" straight—those can be game changers. He also has a personal iPad for limited use, reserved mainly for the weekly newspaper and the Daily Jumble. Rick likes to use emojis. He has learned how to say, "Alexa, put milk and ibuprofen on the shopping list." Sometimes he even remembers to check the app on his phone at the grocery store. I'm proud of him. This is huge progress for a self-proclaimed Luddite (a person who rejects modern technology) who relies on a bulging pocketful of ratty, folded papers he affectionately calls his Palm Pilot.

"These will never crash, and they are un-hackable!" he jokes, pinching them tightly between his thumb and forefinger, waving them for effect. "And I can EAT this Palm Pilot and destroy all evidence."

Rick is teasing me with a playful grin, but I know the man is dead serious—still funny as hell.

Word: *I do not mess with his Palm Pilot.* Those inelegant scraps of paper—worn, torn, and cherished like a well-loved, velveteen rabbit—are his reality and touchstone. They contain phone numbers of clients, veterinary labs, and friends who long ago abandoned their landlines in favor of their cellular numbers, which he has not yet updated. There are formulas for prescribing medication dosages; a scribbled list of chores awaiting his attention, with marks heavily applied over the ones he has accomplished; wish lists of things to acquire someday and where to find them, like the name of the shop that sells a certain bamboo fly rod and its item number copied from a paper catalogue dated 1998. And so much more.

I suffer a bit of anxiety every time Rick declares his preference for his Palm Pilot over all things digital and virtual. What if, one dark day, this precious paper Palm Pilot should accidentally go through the wash? Oh, rue the day! He could not conceive of it. Nor can I bear the thought. But nothing is forever—not computers, not people, not even paper Palm Pilots. All things serve us in their time. I just hope Rick's Palm Pilot's days outnumber his.

Rick considers me the techno-whiz of our house. I can be good, but I can also be slow. I cannot always be both. He has no idea when I present him with an impressive Excel spreadsheet that it might have taken me hours to figure out one formula I had never learned before. Everything's relative, of course. Granted, the bar he sets by comparison is low, but Rick is proud of me and values my skills. I'm good with that. He has been known to volunteer for things, knowing full well he has my support, but more importantly, my computer skills to help him do the job.

We joke, like Glenn Close in the movie, *The Wife*, that I am a kingmaker.

As my skills and affinities continue to grow, I'm happy to explore other technological innovations. Historically, I am not that person who purchases something as soon as it comes off the conveyor belt. For the longest time, I did not see the benefit of having a microwave . . . until I got one. It was the same with VCRs, DVRs, and smart TVs. All game changers. All mindblowers. While fax machines are things of the past, they were useful for a time. So were buggy whips and manual typewriters. People who use fax machines now are derided as old fuddy-duddies. I got rid of mine years ago.

I'm still mulling over hybrid vehicles, though. For now, I've settled for backup cameras and GPS. But the microwave? Game-changer supreme. All those late nights when Rick would arrive home covered in goo, hungry, exhausted from his long days in large-animal practice and long after the boys and I had eaten dinner, I had only to pull the dinner plate from the fridge and zap it. Hot meal versus cold leftovers won out every time. Yep, microwaves are at the very top of my technological godsends list.

I've also installed smart speakers in several locations in our house. What wonders they are! They come in very handy—performing tasks, playing music and games, reading the news, making grocery lists, speaking and responding to commands, and telling you the square root of forty-two (which is 6.4807).

How I wish these things had been around when I was a kid! Math was not my strong suit. Emanating from sleek desktop cylinders, the smart speakers' speech is wrapped in silky, honeyed vocal artifice sounding like real, female humans—nice, girl-next-door types. But they are high-tech, disembodied wizards spinning wheels and knobs behind a digital curtain. They have names, too, although the choices are limited for now. "Alexa"—the largest unit and the mama-bear speaker at our house—is located most centrally in our kitchen (Isn't that just like a mother?). The other rooms have baby-bear speakers named "Echo." They are smaller, short discs that sit on side tables amongst the lamps, flower vases, and coasters so as not to be obtrusive. I look forward to the day Amazon will offer more names. It would be fun to name one Hal and another Dave. Or Big Brother. Or Hey, Dickhead!

I'm aware of all the warnings: These devices could be too smart (intrusive) for my own good; they are always listening, nosing into my business. I know that. I draw the line at listening, by the way, and so should everyone. None of my Alexa and Echo speakers have video screens, and I'm keeping it that way. Maybe I'll choose one with a screen one day and appreciate it like I did my microwave, but I doubt it.

Meanwhile, I'm not worried about surveillance. Listening in on me is a nothing-burger. I'm boring. I'm no spy and possess no state secrets, unless my superior score on Alexa's Puzzle of the Day is somehow relevant to anything that matters. The only thing I guard with my life is the recipe for my Christmas ricotta cookies (which really are of inestimable value to humanity, holiday or otherwise). As I am not in the habit of intoning recipe ingredients aloud like a seventh grader reciting "Thanatopsis," I can assume that secret is safe.

Otherwise, there is nothing in my daily life and conversations that should merit an iota of interest from the snoopy Gladys Kravitzes listening in at Amazon. I know they are there because *The New York Times* says so, as does the nightly news. Therefore, on the occasions when I speak about sensitive, personal things, or utter a brand name (There's data mining and consumer research going on. You know that, right? That, my friends, is the ultimate target—the motherload of all consumer data—our shopping habits.), or tell a little secret, or pull an all-out bitch session about my neighbor or a family member or the bloviated, talking yam in the White House, I simply open the app on my phone and erase the speakers' histories. And if there's a sensational hot topic or activity on the burner, I know how to pull a plug altogether. I practice "safe speaker."

It is possible to activate different "skills" with these speakers (Why are they called skills? Is it really a skill to play twenty questions with a robot? Whose skill is it, by the way? Is it the robot's or mine?). It's also satisfying to integrate the speakers with other smart features in our home like our thermostat and indoor lights. This brand of fun is, of course, relative. Better than a headache and not even close to the rush of a Krispy Kreme. I have also programmed Alexa and Echo with reminders. The speaker begins a reminder with a polite salutation, "Miss Susie," because I programmed her to say that. Is that too precious? Should I have her drop the cute, southern title? Wait. My house, my rules— "Miss Susie" it is.

"Miss Susie," Echo purrs from my bedside table every Sunday at ten-thirty a.m., "Here's your reminder: Wash your sheets."

When Echo chimes in softly with that one, it's right after Rick and I have gone to church. We have just worshipped together at the exalted TV altar of *CBS Sunday Morning*, relaxing in our pajamas while having brunch and coffee. It will have been an hour and a half of blissful enlightenment, sacred affirmation, and spiritual communion—a virtual eucharist that comforts, feeds, teaches, and at turns, alarms us like a cracking-good sermon. Its closing benediction is always masterful with trademark style. It's a spiritually restorative audiovisual montage of sensual blessings: bees buzzing around a pastoral, sunny national park as bison silently graze and kindly breezes blow; a clear brook rushing and burbling over logs and stones as sunlight sparkles on the water; eerie, other-worldly Northern Lights swirling aloft, green and iridescent from horizon out to infinity; a vaulted expanse of black sky studded with endless numbers of twinkling stars, punctuated by the sole sound of chirping crickets. These perfect little lagniappes for our souls are the last gifts of peace and hope before the political TV talking heads take over the airways and threaten to extinguish every good vibe in the world.

That's when we turn off the TV and Echo makes her entrance. She has us captive at that moment (because I programmed her that way). We are right there. Church is just over. We are finishing the last of the Sunday brunch my sweet, wonderful Luddite husband has prepared and served me in bed, on real trays with real love and his own two hands.

Rick and I have already read the Sunday paper. I access my Sunday news online—real news in virtual form. Rick's Sunday paper is tangible, tactile, made from actual wood pulp and ink that smudges on his hands, and crinkles with every page turn. Odd isn't it, that I'm the daughter of an old-fashioned, printing-press era newspaper man, and it's my husband who chooses real newsprint. He excels at reality. I confess I love him so much for that.

All morning, we have been churched, fed by the body of CBS, and washed in the blood of important, thought-provoking stories and art and music and theater and books and humor and nature and humanity and the creator of all things in heaven and on earth. Once all of that has happened, and not a minute before (because I programmed her that way), Echo ever so swiftly rips off the ecumenical Band-Aid and kindly harks us back to reality.

Dutiful, and then immediately penitent, we reflexively resent her visiting us with nirvana interruptus in favor of forced menial labor. Grudgingly, we accept the disembodied directive to wash our sheets for the week. And so, we do. Rick and I work together to strip the sheets off the bed. Real sheets. Real washing machine. Real work. This is our Sunday, after-church ritual: We wash away the figurative sins of the world with the soap of bless-ed, pain-in-the-ass reality and receive our absolution in clean sheets.

At 6:30 p.m. on Wednesday evenings, Alexa generically announces, to no one special (because I programmed her that way), "This is your reminder: Take the garbage and recycle bin out to the street." Rick and I both know the message is meant for him, although it's a mere formality. Invariably, he has already done it. Tongue firmly in cheek, Rick tells Alexa to stuff it. I am grateful for his reliability and preemptively willing spirit. And I have absolutely no doubt how he accomplishes that chore so well along with many others—it's the paper Palm Pilot.

I dislike entering dark rooms, so in each room where I have a smart speaker, I have plugged a lamp into a smart plug. As I approach, say, the den doorway I have only to utter, "Echo, turn on the den light," and—blink—it's on. I no longer must enter a dark room. Some might find this amenity unnecessary. Like I used to find microwaves.

What, my inner critic hisses, *you don't have a light switch on the wall at the doorway to simply flip on the overheads as you enter? Why you gotta make things complicated?*

To which I respond, *Nope, I don't. Now get off my lawn.*

My darling, wonderfully real husband always says, "I have my reasons, which are measured and insightful, and anyone who disagrees is itchin' for a fight."

I have my reasons, too, not the least of which is this: Harsh, overhead light is seldom kind. I prefer the softer lamp light—thanks. Aging, ex-stage performers like me know the value of lighting. Long ago, I adopted the old showbiz truism, "Never, EVER piss off your light or sound man." It's true. Really. Don't try it—you'll be sorry. You're welcome.

A curious thing occurred recently. I entered a room in my house with a smart plug paired with a lamp which was paired with Echo. I started to say the required command, "Echo, turn on . . ." and I faltered for just the briefest breath of a moment. Utterly astonished at myself I thought, *Where the hell am I?*

Echo is a machine, not imbued with human qualities like patience (because her creators programmed her that way). Hesitate even slightly during a command or give her the tiniest opening, and she will Shut. You. Down. My millisecond-long brain fart seemed so brief but was, in fact, plenty long enough for Echo to summarily turn herself off.

Now, in my dotage at a semi-spry seventy-one, I am not yet anywhere close to daft, and there is no bed reserved for me just yet in the memory wing of the retirement home I refuse to inhabit someday anyway. I am not losing it. I could dress up this tacky little piglet of a situation and just classify myself as "chill" which isn't untrue. But the deeper truth is that nowadays, this mature brain of mine is still mentally sharp, just slow...er, even slower than when I returned to college in my fifties and struggled to master all those new computer skills.

Therefore, I still haven't mastered—and may never completely master—the skill of mentally preparing to simply enter a room and swiftly announce myself to a robot. But this is one battle over which

I have no control. Control is a myth anyway. If I want results, I will have to play by Alexa's and Echo's rules and be a good Girl Scout. I must be prepared.

So when I paused that day to determine which room I was entering and my "chill" was turning to burning rage, I exhaled the sharp, quick breath of self-loathing to which all women relate on some level and silently admonished myself,

Oh, good grief, it's the bedroom. Just say "Echo, turn on the bedroom light!" Not necessarily fast. Just fluid. Decisive. Go.

With a clear, commanding voice and without hesitation, I spoke the words aloud.

"Echo, turn on the bedroom light."

Obediently, Echo snapped to attention, the lamp flicked on, and she emitted a little digital singsong affirmative. Thankfully, finally, the deed was done. And there was light. And it was good.

I was relieved, and yet my old-geezer inner critic paid me yet another visit on my metaphorical inner lawn: *Jesus. What is the point, really? You could've jolly well come into this dark room, fumbled around for the lamp, and turned it on with your own two hands in the time it took to negotiate with a heartless robot. How is this exercise even the remotest definition of "convenient" or "smart?"*

In response to myself, I thought, *I can turn off my lights from a horizontal position in my bed. Can you do that?*

And then I laughed. She made me laugh. Out loud. In that instant my negative, self-talking, inner critic melted away and I reminded myself, all by myself, to let her go; let it all go; to take both a deep breath and a different perspective—a kinder, positive, philosophical approach.

Try appreciation. This fit perfectly into the vacancy my inner critic had just left behind, like a cosmic puzzle piece of welcome grace.

My arms had been very full, after all—laden high up to my eyeballs with an unruly, puffy mountain of clean sheets still hot from the dryer. These were the sheets that were destined for the bed Echo had dutifully reminded me to change earlier in the morning. Like I said before, I hate coming into dark rooms. There was no need to fumble around wide-eyed and anxious in the dark, tripping over trailing sheets, catching my toe on the bed skirt, or stubbing my foot on the leg of the side chair while feeling around for the damn lamp on the bedside table. Plus, I don't even have an overhead light fixture in my bedroom (Consult old stage truism above.). No, I had been saved from all that. There really was a method to my smart-speaker madness:

self-preservation. And, okay, maybe a touch of techno nerdiness. Echo and I had worked it out. Technology and I had proven ourselves worthy of one another. Echo was fulfilling her digital duties. Because I had programmed her that way. And I was more than grateful for a second pair of virtual helping hands to literally guide me and light my way.

Rick's Palm Pilot can't even do that.

Thus endeth the Sunday lessons. Thanks be to Echo. To Alexa. To smart plugs and speakers. To Sunday mornings. Church. Breakfast in bed. Technology. Reality. Virtuality. Love. Rick. Luddites. Paper Palm Pilots. Nerds. Chill. Gratitude. Forgiveness. Perspective. Things seen and unseen. All of these and more, especially illuminated rooms and enlightened people, technology, and clean sheets once a week.

And microwaves. *Always* microwaves.

And the people all say, "Amen."

THE THINGS WE SAVE —
THE THINGS WE DON'T

JANUARY 12, 2021

Kids think life goes on forever. They haven't gotten the metaphysical memo of the big picture: Life is precious, and everything's relative; savor it. Wide-eyed at the starting line, the race looks long and endless. They cannot wait to be further down the track where the race is exciting, and they are older and flying free. To them, life has repeating finish lines that when crossed, they've made it to the next race and the next. They are bulletproof and immortal.

Rick and I are on the side of it where we are nearing the finish line. We know there are not unlimited races, laps, or time; we wish we, too, could take a couple more laps and have more races so it's not over.

I want to stand on the young toes of children, pin their sneakers down, and yell, "Don't be in such an all-fired hurry! Tempus fugit, ya dumb yanguns!"

I am not especially afraid of dying. I fear Rick's death more than my own. I don't want to live alone without him. But it's not mine to decide. I do especially fear, too, that when I shuffle off this mortal coil, our children will not cherish what we've left behind for them. I more than fear it; I know it. They tease us even now about our basement. They joke about how they are going to back up a truck and summarily sweep it all wholesale into a dumpster. Or worse, hire some stranger to do it. And they are right—partially. Our basement is full, full of stuff. Some—okay a lot of it—is entirely impersonal and disposable. [Make list here. On second thought, nope. Even my eyes glaze over at the thought.]

But what will they do with "their sacred boxes"? The large plastic containers I've stacked in the cupboard into which—for their entire lives—I have reverently placed memories, baby books, first locks of hair, carefully incised newspaper articles of their accomplishments, photos and programs of school plays, letters, and report cards?

What will Scotty and Nick do with the wooden chest full of our precious sterling silverware, half of which is from our wedding and half was my mother's—their grandmother's? What of our Wedgwood bone china? Our wedding Rosenthal crystal and the Waterford goblets that came to me after my mother's death?

Scotty doesn't even have a dining room anymore since he renovated his home to accommodate two more bedrooms after his lovely partner and her two sons moved in with him and his two boys. Nick travels light. He has been bustling up the ladder in the culinary world, moving to places that provide him the next rung to climb. He finally got to the top rung as executive chef at The American Club in Hong Kong and lives on Hong Kong Island. He married his profession (although he is dating a beautifully exotic woman named Olga). He will not be holding on to much of ours at our passing.

Maybe my anxiety about keeping valuable things for them is rooted in a deep-seated fear of inadequacy. Rather than things I cherish, what have I given them to cherish that they can tuck away as valuable inner furnishings in their hearts, minds, and memories? Did I do enough for them as a mom? Was I wise? Was I enough? Will their memories of me be sustained without the need for tactile reminders, bits and pieces of stuff they don't need or want? I need to ask. I need to know. If they will tell me. I am almost afraid to ask, though. Or am I more afraid they won't know?

Recently, I got a text from Nick—our Hong Kong dweller. "Mom," he said, "what's that saying you always use about what folks said during the Depression?"

"Oh, you mean 'Use it up, wear it out, make it do?'" I replied. "Got that from your grandmother who lived it."

"Yes! And what's that silly, sassy song you used to sing about cactuses and pollen?"

"Oh, yes, my dad, your grandfather, wrote that song," I replied, and I wrote out the lyrics, which were kind of blue—mentioning cactuses blooming and deserts perfuming and the willing pollination of the cowgirl by any cow guy who should be passing by. "That one?"

"Yes! And what's that movie dad has talked about for as long as I can remember with the Mountie who dispatches three bad guys at one time?"

"I asked your dad, and he says he remembers the scene vividly but has no idea what movie it was. Sorry. No clue, bud," I responded.

"I've been wondering what that movie was as long as he's been describing it without ever knowing if it was black and white, Technicolor, or otherwise. I've just imagined possible versions for thirty years. I realized yesterday I never even asked. I'm wondering if knowing would only diminish its value. I think the answer is less important than the acknowledgment," Nick replied.

"Yes," I responded, "you never know what you leave with another person, do you?"

He ended our conversation with the most incredibly beautiful summation, and suddenly, all was made clear to me. Apparently, a popular local character and Elvis impersonator named "Melvis" died recently in Hong Kong.

"Everyone in the city knew who this guy was," Nick told me. "It's been interesting to see the news hit different people each day. Sometimes you see them on the subway, reading an article about his death, or sharing the article that circulated heavily about a week ago. I don't think there were many tears, but about eight-million shoulders sagged off the beat, which ain't nothing."

His words hit me. That's it. The most important thing: to have made a difference no matter how large or small; to have been a positive presence in someone's life; to leave them with good memories, not stuff; to be missed and for shoulders to sag—whether it be eight million or eight—on one's passing.

Off the beat works for me too. And that really ain't nothin.'

It's everything.

Our revels now are ended. These our actors,
As I foretold you, were all spirits, and
Are melted into air, into thin air:
And like the baseless fabric of this vision,
The cloud-capp'd tow'rs, the gorgeous palaces,
The solemn temples, the great globe itself,
Yea, all which it inherit, shall dissolve,
And, like this insubstantial pageant faded,
Leave not a rack behind. We are such stuff
As dreams are made on; and our little life
Is rounded with a sleep.
—The Tempest

LOVE AND HOLIDAYS
IN THE TIME OF COVID

2020

Things were really weird in 2020. The holidays arrived, and we were still in the throes of a worldwide pandemic. Rick and I had a very small but fine Thanksgiving in November with immediate family members only. I had fun setting the table as I always do with my customary, artsy fall centerpiece, place mats, cloth napkins, chargers, china, candles, and sterling flatware. I trotted out my collection of ceramic pilgrim salt and pepper shakers from Publix—the adults and the children—a sizable collection of which I am both sentimentally proud and loath to admit. Our elder adult son, Scotty, and his better half, Val, cooked the whole meal, and it was fabulous. It started with morning Mimosas, a charcuterie board worthy of a magazine spread, and our traditional cheese ring—an appetizer that has reached epic holiday status in our family.

Rick and I thought it was the perfect arrangement: Scott and Val offered to cook everything while we would provide a clean house (at least the parts you can see) and a lovely holiday atmosphere. Deal! Meanwhile, I had forgotten one thing: Cleaning house is a lot of work. I only do it once a year at holiday time, whether it needs it or not (totally kidding . . . sort of).

By the time they stepped foot in our house, Rick and I had already had the carpets and furniture cleaned, moved everything back into place, mopped, dusted, vacuumed, cleaned the bathrooms, polished silver, rummaged through the basement for stored holiday décor and schlepped it all upstairs, searched the storage closets for all the stuff needed to decorate and to serve, eat, and drink everything. Then, I executed all last-minute things in a final flurry, with precious little time to shower and exchange my sweaty work-pajamas for presentable holiday wear. Funny how the mind forgets all the exhausting details when idealizing the big, finished picture. I think our house gets bigger every year. And we get older every year too. Our energy has limits. But I am not complaining. I was reveling in it all.

For Rick and me, while our bodies were already flagging, Barkis was still willin'. And joyous. When, at 9:30 am on Thanksgiving Day, Scotty and Val lugged in bag after bag and box after box of supplies and food items, I was awed. Clearly, they had gone to the utmost effort, with great love, and it showed. A turkey went into the oven while a ham was baking at their house across town, which Scotty monitored constantly with a high-tech, remote oven thermometer. Gee, and we thought of giving him a little dinky, digital meat thermometer for Christmas like the one we have. Silly. This thing Scotty had looked like a NASA space shuttle control panel. He's a pro now, with pro toys.

I am no longer the mother of rookie cooks with much to learn. I take my place now behind my adult boys, both fine cooks. Nick continues cooking as his profession and shows no signs of slowing down, still loving his executive chef position in Hong Kong. I am immensely proud of them both. And Val is Scott's perfect culinary complement, an absolute ace in the kitchen.

I plopped down at our kitchen island and watched, amazed. Stuff kept coming through the door in a seemingly endless loop, like the best and most positive version of Mickey's mops and water buckets à la "The Sorcerer's Apprentice" in Disney's epic animated 1940 film, *Fantasia*. Once the parade finally ended, our kitchen now knee-deep and piled high with potential, they got to work.

Magic ensued.

I was handed a Mimosa while a charcuterie board appeared, and Scotty explained each item after dropping the coup de grace in the center of the board—a small comb of sweet honey. Classy! There were big, fat Greek olives in a luxurious, oily mix, razor thin velvety slices of Smoking Goose Culatello in white wine, shaved Manchego cheese, and horseradish cheese spread; perfect cubes of Boar's Head Truffle Goat Cheese and Kerrygold Reserve Cheddar, creamy slices of French brie; spicy rounds of pepper-coated salami and Volpi Pepperoni Nuggets, bagel chips, Firehook sea salt crackers, and that all-impressive honeycomb.

After a while, renewed from a brief rest, delighted by the camaraderie, and fortified by hors d'oeuvres and morning adult beverages, I knew my job was only partially done. I had already set a beautiful table while my sweet Rick assembled our annual tradition: turkey cookies made from store-bought cookies and chocolate balls arranged to look like punch-drunk turkeys at best but fun and popular with the younger set.

Now it was time to clear the decks and bring on the serving dishes, meat platters, serving spoons, forks, carving knives, water pitchers, bread basket, and gravy boat. Then, there were the pans, pots, and utensils piling up in the sink. Dishwasher wanted—that would be Rick and me.

All hands were on deck now, many hands trying to make light work. Val toiled away making from-scratch dressing and gravy. The preparation involved an entire hen and some straight-up alchemy because I swear, the final product was supernatural. I would follow Val's dressing and gravy anywhere. Scotty assembled the traditional orange crescent rolls, popping them in the oven while running back and forth to the grill outside where he tended to his sweet street corn on the cob. Then, he made a trip back to his house to fetch the ham and glaze it to a fine, sweet shine at our house.

Once we had it all together, laid out in bountiful buffet style on the kitchen table, our family filled our dishes and strode happily down the hall with plates heavy laden into the dining room. We held hands around the table, stretched out a little further to reach each other than in past years, bowed our heads in a moment of spoken thanks and praise, and had our fill. I will confess, I wondered how Rick and I managed to do this whole thing for so many years when sometimes there were as many as twenty-six people for dinner.

Then, I thought how Christmas would most likely be weird, too, just like all the rest of party-pooping, pandemic-plagued 2020. And it was. There were no huge crowds. The previous Christmas I had made a humongous dessert platter fit for all our guests, neighbors, Santa, all his elves, and their elf neighbors. That was a spectacular effort and so much fun: a 3D, homemade gingerbread-house cake sprinkled with sugar snow in the center of a silver platter surrounded by snow-globe cupcakes I made with little trees and gelatin globes on top, all accompanied by an excess of store-bought chocolate Santas and goodies.

Nope, that was not happening in 2020. Things were pared down, for sure. No visitors from out of town. No dear friends or extended family of choice to add to the table. Just immediate family. And that was okay. I still set a beautiful table and cooked my famous roast beef. Rick was our ricotta cookie-making master for our neighbor gifts, and we still made reindeer-in-a-jar for the kids (mason jars decorated with pipe cleaners for antlers, googly eyes, a red pompom nose stuck onto the side, and filled with malted milk chocolate balls). Whatever we did, and however we did it, we put our hearts into it.

Because...

Because in pandemic days, there is always joy in the holidays tempered by uncertainty, sadness, and grief for those who are sick, those who worry for them, and those who are not here to sit at our tables.

Because the places I set at my Christmas table will always be, just like my Thanksgiving table, as beautiful as I can make them, just with fewer places than in years past but no fewer memories and no less important.

Because my food and table preparations aren't just for show.

Because putting forth my best effort is an offering meant to honor the occasion and the dear ones who join us at our table along with those who are absent.

Because I am not a wise man nor a king, but I bring what offerings I can. My heart. It's there in Christina Rossetti's poem:

What can I give Him, poor as I am?
If I were a shepherd, I would bring a lamb.
If I were a wise man, I would do my part.
Yet what can I give Him?
Give Him my heart.

I do. I give my heart.

Because I am thankful down to my toes that I am not waiting in long food lines at the local food pantry.

Because I am not, nor is anyone in my family, in the hospital dying of COVID-19.

Because my house still stands unharmed by fire or flood or hurricanes or tornadoes or death.

Because I pray for all those that have suffered any of these.

Because even now, we can give of ourselves in kindness and in service to others.

Because we have love in this world despite darkness and oppression.

Because I observe every holiday in my own way, at a table, with utmost love and reverence, whether it be with many or few, tired or not, no matter what.

Because Love is the alpha, the omega, and the bottom line. Always, always love.

Love came down at Christmas . . .
Love all lovely, Love divine . . .
Love was born at Christmas . . .
Star and angels gave the sign . . .
Love shall be our token . . .
Love shall be yours and love be mine.
—Christina Rossetti

CHRISTMAS EVE IN PANDEMIC-LAND

2020

I wish they had shown the empty pews.

Rick and were holding hands on our sofa, watching St. Philip Cathedral's 2020 Christmas Eve service in Atlanta on TV, and because of COVID-19, it was pre-recorded in a vacant nave.

The stunningly beautiful choral music was a recording too.

The camera panned from altar to lit candles to magnificent, vaulted ceiling to hanging garlands to the arched stained-glass windows—all of it above the heads of communicants who weren't there. Only clergy were present at the lecterns—the Bishop, and also the Dean, Sam Candler whom I have known since he was a youngster and now somehow sports gray hair.

Rick and I are both lapsed Episcopalians, but Christmas Eve 2020 was very different. That night, we tuned in because we needed the peace that passeth understanding.

In his sermon, Sam told the Native American story of the two wolves inside all of us: one evil, angry, and negative; the other good, productive, and positive. Whichever one we feed is the one that thrives. If ever we needed proof of it, 2020 provided it in full.

I wanted to see those empty seats and imagine ourselves sitting with and beside goodness and love—each of us feeding the wolf inside us with the Eucharist of new life and the incense and myrrh of Christmas. We are not alone. God be with us.

I wanted to see us living in absentia, in a pandemic, lifting each other up, extending our hearts in solidarity to our fellow humans, and praying for all whose spirits and bodies suffer, sputter, and die.

I wanted to see those hard, wooden pews as a stark testament to the sick, the dead, and those who care for them.

We needed resilience then, and always, in times like these. We must feed the good wolf and sing of the sweet Christmas birth of spirit and love.

In Dulci Jubilo!

THIRTY YEARS

JANUARY 2021

On January 15, 2021, I attended a funeral for a close associate I had known for over three decades—my JennAir cooktop.

That cooktop was pristine and beautiful when it came to our new house thirty-one years earlier. Rick and I had just purchased our "forever" home in 1989. Because the house had been on the market for a while and I had aesthetic vision beyond the awful gold shag carpets, heavy gold drapes, and the teeny tiny linoleum-floored kitchen, we got it for a song. That made it possible for us to add on to the entire back half of the house, creating a new, roomy kitchen, laundry room, and main floor bedroom. My knack for seeing the value of the "good bones" of a house, the proceeds from the sale of our starter house on Dixon Street, and a sum of money from our share of the sale of Rick's mom's house in Atlanta the year before made it all possible. I think of Libby every time I step foot in my kitchen.

How many appliances last for over thirty years? Very few. But this one did. It was a stalwart. And like Rome, all roads in our house lead to the center—the kitchen and the cooktop that sits in the center of the kitchen island, the center of activity. That JennAir saw us through decades of family meals, parties, and holidays; thirty-one years of boiling tea kettles, baby bottles, and small pots of hard-boiled eggs; big pots of homemade soup and chili; large stockpots of boiling water with just a touch of sugar for our summers of Silver Queen corn; heart-shaped Sunday pancakes on the griddle for our children and then our children's children. Around that island where our cooktop sits remain decades of memories of friends and loved ones gathered around it, talking, laughing, crying, fighting, apologizing, confessing, celebrating, busily cooking, drinking, toasting, eating, even singing together, and holding hands to say grace encircling the island and that cooktop. If an inanimate object can capture the "place" of a home, this one did. But nothing lasts forever, and our cooktop didn't, either. It was dead, and it was time for it to go.

After its unceremonious removal by the expert technicians, I bowed my head and said farewell to a dear friend as it went out the door, into the back of their truck, and onto the pile of other discarded appliances from the day's work orders. And when they came back through the door, I welcomed the installation of a brand new one in its place.

It was a thing to behold. Stylish, new, and beautiful. Modern and once again, pristine. I wondered if this cooktop would last another thirty years, and what it—and the world—would look like if it did. I knew in that moment I would never know the answer to that question. Sobering thought: I turned seventy-one this year. Alas, I am too damn old to survive another thirty years.

But the old cooktop was beneficent in its retreat. When it gave up the ghost, it did not take with it all the spirits and the memories. It kindly left them all in the room, in the air, in the hearts, in the minds, and in the very fiber of all who were here in our kitchen and around our island.

So what will the next thirty years bring, and how much of it will I get to see? The past thirty-two have certainly been eventful. By the end of 1989, when I was thirty-nine and Rick was forty, the Berlin Wall came down, there was a massacre in Tiananmen Square in Beijing, the World Wide Web was invented, we bought our "forever" house, and our boys were little. In 2020, a wall at our southern border was partially up, people protested in the streets of the U.S. for Black lives to matter, the people of Hong Kong protested in their streets for their independence to matter, we started experiencing a worldwide pandemic, and millions of people have died.

For the first time in my life, we experienced lockdowns, quarantines, isolation, and a general disruption of normality; politically things got messy and polarized; wearing protective face masks became political; it seemed everybody was angry, and a wild presidential election in November was the most impactful in my memory. There was an all-out insurrection at the Capitol in Washington D.C. on January 6, 2021, and people died.

We still live in our "forever" house—with landscaping and a garden we have tended over the years, a few new furnishings, some new playground equipment, a playhouse for our grandchildren they are quickly outgrowing, and a new cooktop.

Our house is minus two children who grew up here, but who still visit—one often, the other only periodically. One of our boys is now approaching his mid-forties, and the other is in his late thirties. Rick and I celebrated our fiftieth wedding anniversary June 10, 2021. We are retired. We are happy. In our very early seventies (emphasis on very early for my sake) we worry for our world now and wonder about a future thirty years from now that we won't live to see.

What will the world look like in 2051? It is my fervent hope it will be good, for everyone's sake. Everyone's. But I wonder if that's even possible. Will we, can we, all find common ground after all our schisms, enough to heal the separation and wounds we all suffer today? Have we ever?

The human condition is comprised of every second of a man's life—from birth, to standing around a kitchen island, to leaving the building forever. For another, it's from birth to a homeless shelter or a premature visit to the morgue. Austrian neurologist, psychiatrist, and Holocaust survivor, Viktor Frankl, says, "The meaning of life differs from man to man, from day to day and from hour to hour."

Historically, humankind has never been on the same page, and I don't know that another thirty years will change it. But what is a goal except something to strive for? Even our goals are different. But I wish, I pray, I hope with all my heart that mankind can find a common decency that is kind, accepting, inclusive, and unselfish.

Is that too much to ask?

If you will, in thirty years, come to our house, knock on the door, and tell them we sent you. I'll leave a memo on the island when we go, telling them to expect you. Please gather 'round the cooktop on the island and hold hands, sing together, and say grace for the world. That would make me so very happy.

And we'll know because we'll be there, in the air, around that island, in the room where it happens.

BEAUTY AND THE BEAST

2021

On March 26, 2021, in the time it took people to cower and embrace each other in bathtubs, basements, and interior rooms, to breathe in and out in the dark and pray, the beast came to call just after midnight. It was breathing, too, roaring in fact as it blew out lethal 170 mph breaths and exhaled against everything in its way as it sped across miles of my town, Newnan, Georgia. It peeled back roofs, shingles, siding as it beat windows into shards, walls into splinters, and turned order into utter chaos. It sucked up rooted trees, spitting them out on power lines, homes, garages, and schools. For good measure, it blew the trees it didn't ingest into broken, twisted missiles and roadblocks.

When it was finally done, the beast lifted itself away and disappeared—indifferent to the turmoil it left in its wake. And when quiet came, the people emerged to behold their places in the world. There was a collective gasp, and then the letting out of heavy, communal breaths of horror and disbelief. Then, there were voices calling out in the black night.

"Hey Pat, are you and Pam OK?"

"Yeah, we're alive! How 'bout y'all?"

"We're OK!"

"Help! I smell gas!"

"Oh, Miss Connie, your gas line is broken! I'll get my channel locks and turn it off!"

"Thank you!"

"Are you OK in there, Miss Nancy?"

"I am. Thank you!"

And so it went, into the first morning light, when the full effects of the beast's rampage were becoming visible. On his rooftop, a young man—our son, Scott—who turned off the gas behind his neighbor's house and checked on his other neighbors—stood and spoke quietly into his phone while making a video, panning across the ugly damage. Broken trees poked their sharp, black silhouettes upward, puncturing the dawning sky. Others lay like splintered Lincoln Logs tossed about everywhere in a suddenly unfamiliar, unnatural landscape. The unwelcome view was painful and harsh—a hideous, open wound—allowing him to see farther than ever before. The once quiet beauty of the place had been swallowed up by the beast and regurgitated, leaving a wretched, hopeless disarray.

And yet, in the quiet, half-light of dawn, as Scott prepared to speak, there were the sounds of birds.

He spoke for his—and all of—the broken neighborhoods in town when he said, stunned from the ordeal and so eloquent in his quiet assessment, "Any tree that is left standing is going to have to come down, so there are literally no trees left in Hollis Heights. A tree smashed Val's car and fell all the way through the garage, which is leaning in, so that's gone. All in all, we are incredibly lucky in our specific location. Broken windows, roof damage, siding torn off. We can get stuff out of the garage. We can fix things. We can plant trees. But this is unbelievable."

In a moment of stark realization, the pain obvious on his face, he took a long, deep breath, blew it out, and said directly to the camera now, "Well, two hours of sleep and the dawn is here. We must start figuring things out now. Thank you to everyone who has checked in on us. Thank you for all the offers of help. We will call on you when we figure out what we need. But we're okay. Getting power back will be a big bonus. But for now, we're gonna start digging out and making sure everyone has what they need around here. Oh, there's my dogwood tree! Wondered where that went. Thank you again for checking on us."

The video was still rolling as he stood looking out in one more long, pensive moment. Then, Scott said, his voice catching, emotion on his face and flowing through his words, "But we are the City of Homes, and these homes are still standing."

Indeed. At least some of them. It is the collective spirit of the people that still stands, for sure. We are Newnan strong.

At midnight, only a mile away on the other side of town, my husband and I were ensconced in our basement, too, after hearing the tornado warning, waiting for the storm to pass, and praying it would miss us. We had heavy rain—maybe even hail as best we could determine—tap-tap-tapping on our basement windows. Our home lost power, internet, and cable, but there was no loud, approaching train blowing over us. Rick and I could hear something coming from the south that sounded like a huge white-noise machine. And then it stopped. I called my son.

"Mom, we took a direct hit. We're ok," Scott said, raw emotion in his voice. "I'm going to look outside now. Oh. My God . . . there are no trees..."

Rick was already putting on his raincoat and boots. Wild horses couldn't keep him away from rescuing our son's family and their dog. Shortly after midnight, Rick drove as far as he could toward their house until the trees and debris prevented him from going any further. He parked and started walking, probably a quarter mile, with a flashlight in hand. This way and that, right turn, left turn, detouring around debris, through dark gaps in yards and streets, Rick found himself standing in the dark at what should've been the intersection by Scott's home. It was a foreign land. Rick questioned if he had come to the right place. A fallen street sign illuminated by his flashlight told him, sadly, that he had indeed found it. There were voices of people calling to each other as shadows wandered through yards looking out for each other and assessing damage.

Four traumatized boys and a dog trekked out of the neighborhood in the pouring rain with Grampa Rick—the two parents at their side, reassuring the children as they found their way to the car. Then, Scott and Val returned to secure and evaluate the damage at their house and the homes of their neighbors. By the time the boys, dog, and Rick returned to our house, our power had been restored. Four soaking wet children and a stinky, wet dog entered our house traumatized and crying with backpacks soaked through. They needed reassurance and a safe, dry place with power to unwind and try to sleep.

In Von Trapp fashion, Rick and I lined them up at the laundry room. We tossed their wet clothes into the dryer and wrapped them in dry beach towels, blankets, and Rick's warm, just-dried shirts fresh from the dryer. Hot chocolate was some comfort. Hugs were better. They all chose where they wanted to be for the night and bedded down. This small bit of control was all they had left after mother nature had just sent the beast to crush that concept. Choosing one's bed was a small comfort, but it was comfort, nonetheless. It was easily three in the morning before they were all asleep.

The family joke, later, when jokes were even possible, was that Rick's priority was rescuing the dog, since he's a veterinarian. Laughter is good medicine—even when it takes a while to remember how.

In the days following the beast's ugly rampage, the beautiful people of Newnan showed up. They epitomized how goodness survives and thrives, even when things don't. Volunteers with chainsaws, equipment, manpower, food, water, and supplies swarmed unbidden, yet oh so welcome, into Newnan's war-torn neighborhoods. Soon, piles of debris—six-feet high and climbing—were forming along the curbs of dusty, dirt-covered streets. Friends drove in from all over to help. They parked in undamaged areas and walked into the battle zone. Folks driving four-wheelers arrived to deliver people who couldn't walk that far but could offer help. The four-wheeler folks also loaded up much needed food, water, and supplies into areas that were inaccessible. Tornado relief groups began to organize and offer their assistance. Food banks and donation centers mobilized, staffed by their own workers and extra volunteers—ordinary citizens answering the call. The county fairgrounds became a central donation location where people could go for items they needed, showers, laundry, and mental health services. A phone number was established for questions and volunteer opportunities.

Charitable disaster relief organizations like the Red Cross arrived. Insurance companies erected tents at various locations and stationed claims centers underneath. Shelters opened. Churches made sandwiches, held clothing drives, walked the neighborhoods handing out water, food, and Easter baskets. Individuals roamed the streets pulling coolers, handing out bottled water, sack lunches, and snacks. Monetary campaigns were mounted for donations. Newnan was on the news nationwide. Calls and inquiries and volunteers from all over the state and country poured in to help. Utility workers and linemen worked tirelessly. City and county offices geared up to make recovery as efficient as possible, waiving building permit fees, and discussing policies to help with rebuilding.

Helpers showed up at the most incredible moments. Rick and I were working to clean up our son's yard, and I noticed the banisters on his front porch were hanging off, nails poking out. I yelled over to Rick, "We need a sledgehammer!" Before he could answer, a woman parked at the curb beside the house opened her truck door and emerged.

"I've got one!" she yelled back, brandishing the long-handled tool like the Olympic torch. "What can I do to help?"

This angel proceeded to march right over and knock those banisters off in quick order, happy to help. Then, she disappeared to offer her gifts elsewhere. Just. Like. That.

When the official report was released by the National Weather Center, it was declared that Newnan had suffered an EF4 tornado. The beast was a mile wide, skipping and jumping and barreling its destruction over as many as thirty-nine miles for over an hour. The official, combined preliminary report from Georgia Emergency Management and Homeland Security Agency (GEMA/HS), City of

Newnan, and Coweta County assessed the damage at 1,744 homes—one-hundred and twenty of which sustained major damage and seventy were completely destroyed.

Officials placed red, yellow, and green stickers on structures to advertise their status: green for "all is well," yellow for "damaged property but habitable," and red for "unsafe and uninhabitable." It was weird seeing them plastered on every house, like a twisted Passover story—all three stickers sometimes appearing in the same block.

All in all, the caring hearts, generosity, support, and love people have displayed has been and continues to be nothing short of mind-boggling, heart-warming, and absolutely beautiful.

And it is by no means over. It will be a long road to recovery. The cleanup and rebuilding will be a part of Newnan for as long as it takes—months, years. People are still living in hotel rooms and shelters. Many have lost everything.

In our part of town, only a mile away from our son, we had not one twig out of place. Our azaleas and dogwoods are in full, glorious spring bloom. I feel so fortunate and guilty. I caught my son standing alone, quiet, and wistful on our back porch at the end of a perfectly beautiful Easter Sunday afternoon. Face lifted to the sun, Scott was studying all our trees, taking in the green, green, green and the outrageous beauty of the blooms; our neatly ordered, partly shaded backyard, clean, and landscaped. I could see the pain on his face, reflecting what had happened on his side of town and how things would not be same there for a long time, if ever.

That evening, Scott posted something on Facebook that gave me a chill, a jolt of pride, and hope. Being a forester and a charity-minded guy, he would think of it, of course. He hoped when it is time to replant that everyone in his neighborhood (and elsewhere) would consider planting cherry trees. Scott would see if he could get the trees procured and find assistance in the planting.

Think of it! A Newnan Cherry Blossom Festival rising from the dead landscape, resurrecting neighborhoods, binding neighbors and an entire city together in solidarity, love, and remembrance. I can think of nothing better to serve as an offering and a living testament to the resilience of a community who rose above the suffering and planted hope and beauty in the aftermath of a dark, destructive beast. A beast who will not have the last word. #newnanstrong

The Music

MUSIC

In September 1980, only months after losing our baby and trying to convince myself I was a strong and powerful gladiator, I took hold of myself and strode terrified and weak-kneed into an arena to fight for my life. I needed focus and a way to step out of my sadness and into myself again—my "self" at its fullest and best. I desperately needed and missed my talent—the gift I had willingly subsumed for years in favor of supporting my husband's career. And now I was willing to fight to get it back.

I needed my voice. And I needed to sing.

So I entered the Woodruff Arts Center in Atlanta, stepped behind a music stand in a large basement rehearsal room, and started the audition of my life for a coveted spot in one of the preeminent choral groups in the U.S., conducted by the preeminent choral conductor in the world.

What was I thinking? My answer would come soon enough. The emperor's thumb would turn up or turn down, and I would know for sure.

———

Music has been in me my whole life. As a little girl, I sat beside our old record player at home and sang along with all the songs on the children's albums my parents furnished me. A little older, I sang duets with my mom in the car, always "Wind Through the Olive Trees." She was terrible. When I tried to harmonize, she couldn't stay on the melody, but I loved her for trying. In adolescence and into my teens, my parents took my brother and me to concerts and the opera. I remember sitting in the audience at the Civic Center watching some old guy play, thinking he was good. The "old guy" was famous classical pianist and virtuoso, Vladimir Horowitz.

My parents continued to educate me constantly. We saw Broadway musicals in the summers at Theater Under the Stars at Chastain Park. They took me to the Municipal Auditorium in downtown Atlanta on Courtland Street to hear Eileen Farrell sing arias and art songs. She forgot her lyrics, and cool as a cucumber, she stopped, laughed, and said, "It happens, folks!" and went on. I loved her for that. Forgetting lyrics had always been and would always be my Achilles heel.

I sang in my bedroom listening to Broadway, jumping from one single bed to the other singing "I'm Flying," "I Gotta Crow," and

"Never Never Land" with Mary Martin in *Peter Pan*, and "I Could Have Danced All Night" with Julie Andrews in *My Fair Lady*. I even sang all of Rex Harrison's songs too. I sang the leads in my high school musicals *Camelot* and *South Pacific*, won awards, and sang all four years in the auditioned all-state chorus.

Looking back, I realize I was insanely talented, and yet, five foot nine inches in bare feet and big boned in high school, I constantly wished to be someone else. Instead of towering over everyone and looking like tree trunks in knee socks (my mother said), I wanted to be a cheerleader type—a petite one, wearing size five saddle oxfords and long, thick socks rolled down twice just below the knee, thank you. I ached to have smooth, shapely thighs extending under the hem of a cute, short-short tartan skirt. At every pep rally, I studied those rah-rah kilts with the sewed-down pleats that showed off board-flat stomachs and small hips; pleats that opened into Vs that swayed during carefree strides and flew up during jumps, always falling perfectly into place afterward.

Alas, I was too tall. I was not the right body shape. And I was decidedly un-athletic. Three strikes and I was out of the cheerleading business.

My ability to sing like a bird, however? I figured maybe not everybody could wear that mantle, and so singing became my pleated skirt; my voice would be the beautiful legs on which I would travel in the world.

I got a summer job as an "occupational therapy assistant" at Parkwood Hospital, a psychiatric hospital in Atlanta owned by friends of my parents. It was basically arts and crafts— an emphasis on crafts. The job bore no resemblance to real occupational therapy on a professional, physical, or rehab level. I had an artsy-crafty creative bent, though, and I was pleasant and easy to talk to, so without any training whatsoever, I became the innocuous crafts assistant to the OT director.

I always had my guitar nearby and sometimes serenaded the staff and patients, which was a nice, therapeutic change of pace, doing worlds for my self-esteem and the patients' serenity. The music far surpassed, for all of us, the artless craft of binding pieces of wallet together using flat, brown plastic laces.

In September 1968, I left home in Atlanta to attend Stephens College—an all-girls school in Columbia, Missouri that had a terrific music and theater department. I was so sure I wanted out of my parents' house, and I wanted to go far, far away. What I got was homesick. Right away. Nobody was more surprised than I was.

One evening, during a moment of solitude and sheer melancholy in the empty dorm lobby, I propped my guitar on my lap and sang "Leavin' on a Jet Plane." Gradually, a crowd formed. My voice pulled girls one by one, quiet and curious, from their rooms to see where the music was coming from. Before I was done, there were girls sitting, standing, and still gathering from the halls to listen. When I finished, they wiped tears, clapped, and said they thought it was a record playing.

Wow, I thought, *maybe it's okay to be me.*

A few weeks later, I was invited to go to Los Angeles for a quick stint in a glitzy, televised singing competition, *The All-American College Show*. I had been hand-picked by talent scouts who came to Stephens.

Once I arrived on set, I was apprehensive and intimidated. The host was Denis James, and the judges were Cesar Romero and Ruth Bussey. Denis James was short; I towered over him. This was a huge concern for the show. They made me take off my pretty heels, gave me some ugly, flat elastic slippers, and then told me I should just sit on a stool with my guitar in my lap anyway. God forbid a female should out-tall the aging, image-conscious male TV show host. Hooray for Hollywood.

I sang "Scarlet Ribbons," muffing the words. Although they did a retake, I lost. Despite my chagrin at losing—I did screw it up after all—I promised myself I'd hold my head high. Still, I wasn't at all convinced I could or would.

Proven to be too tall for showbiz and Hollywood and having forgotten my lyrics and lost a competition because of it, I was no Eileen Farrell, either. I tried being philosophical. But I could not get past my lyric memory lapse having gone unforgiven by the show, and more importantly, now, by me.

Back at school in the fall of 1969, I was a sophomore majoring in theater and music before my confidence and patience started slipping. I'd had major surgery on my ankle over the summer because I kept turning and spraining it, and the doctors failed to mention I would still be in a cast and on crutches for the start of my sophomore year—all seven-hundred miles from home in Columbia-fucking-Missouri. The school was my choice. My parents' money. My bad. Stephens and I were, ultimately, not a good fit. The new dorm I was assigned to had three floors and no elevator, at least not one I was allowed to use. My room was on the third floor. There were no allowances for handicapped students like me at the time, and no accommodations were made. Up and down three flights on crutches got old real fast.

I honestly don't know if any school would have been okay.

I started to feel uncomfortable in my own skin. Often, even after making the effort to go to class, clumsily navigating stairs and campus with great effort on my crutches, I found myself turning around at the classroom door before I could make myself go in. Other times, I stopped outside the building, sized up the cement stairs at the entrance, and detoured to the campus student union for rest and solace: a couple of blondie brownies and music on the sound system.

The Beatles' "Hey Jude" was a just-released, number-one single, and it played all the time in that place. I wanted to take my sad song and make it better. Best of all, the coda of the song was one long refrain whose words I could not possibly muff: "Naahh, nah nah na-na-na-naahh, na-na-na-naahh, hey Jude."

Eventually, I just quit going to class altogether, even after my English teacher wrote emphatic notes on my papers, encouraging me to write because I was "terrific." I was a ball of confusion and discomfort, pulling at a string from that ball ever so constantly, trying to become smaller and smaller until eventually I might just disappear.

And one day, I did.

In November of 1969, I just upped and quit before they could ask me to leave.

After some "R&R" and soul-searching while living with my parents who were having their own crisis after my dad quit his job, I found my sea legs and went back to my old position at Parkwood Hospital. After several months, I had secured not only my own apartment but also my independence. I was happier and philosophical. In those days, I fell back on the stupid rationale that men had the careers and women didn't necessarily need one. I would be just fine, I consoled myself—not truly appreciating what a rare opportunity I had just squandered by leaving school.

Now that I was home, things were heating up between Rick and me. By 1970, we were engaged, and in 1971, we were married.

And just like that, the singing took a back seat.

I never really stopped singing completely, but I became a pale, solitary version of my real potential. Oh, I had kept my voice in fair shape by singing and playing my guitar at night while Rick studied during his four years of vet school. I sang and accompanied myself as I sat cross-legged on our bed at the end of the long hall in our tuna-can trailer, door closed so as not to distract him. Four years of that, and if I hadn't mastered it earlier, I definitely mastered the fine art of sotto voce and pianississimo.

I sang to myself again for a two-year gig after that when Rick started his first job out of school and was working all day and into the night in Ashland, Virginia. In his absence, I emoted with soulful, elegiac ballads, sitting on our bed until he came home at night. Being truly alone, I could express myself with a full range of dynamics. I was good company, and my own music therapist.

In 1977, after we had our first baby, we moved to Newnan and started Rick's large-animal vet practice. For the next three years, I was busy and tired serving two masters: my husband and baby. Rick was gone day and night, having to cover a large geographical area to support us. I worked the phones in the office we created in the back bedroom of our house while diapering, feeding, playing, and caring for our baby.

Until Rick's practice took off, we got a paper route to pay the bills, reporting to a cold, dark building off the town square every midnight to assemble newspapers. With the backseat down flat, we stacked the newspapers high like fortress walls surrounding our carefully placed infant car seat—infant included—in the back of our VW bug. Then, we drove around in the black of night delivering the paper everyone takes for granted, knowing it will be in their driveway or mailbox when they wake up each morning. If you get the chance, thank your newspaper delivery person. The job is brutal. We lasted a couple of months. By that time, Rick was busy enough to ensure our financial security, and we could clean the newspaper ink from under our fingernails once and for all. The irony, too, of delivering the very same newspaper my dad had left so long ago was not lost on us.

Meanwhile, I sang lullabies to little Scotty and kept up my solo solitary serenades while Rick worked. We joined a tiny Episcopal church with no choir, and I sang some solos accompanied by an old-fashioned, foot-pump organ played by a spirited spinster who sang along lustily with the hymns. In the summers, I played piano and guitar at vacation Bible school where I led all-out, catchy, Bible-kid songs like "Ezekiel Saw the Wheel," "Father Abraham (Had Many Sons)," and "Don't Build Your House on the Sandy Land."

Yes, I was singing—sincerely, maybe, but not seriously. Something was missing. Something big. Something more compelling and fulfilling than my cloistered bedroom ballads, little church solos, and artlessly fun Bible songs. I may have been singing, sometimes in service to others, but what about honoring me, feeding myself in a deeper, more satisfying musical way?

In 1980, I got my answer. The loss of our second baby, Sarah Kate, gave it to me. Life is a gift to be cherished. If we're lucky enough to get a life, we need to make it count by using our gifts and expressing ourselves with them. Often, tragedy brings recovery, courage, and/or delusion. Maybe in my case, I got a bit of all three.

So I made the call. It was official. My audition was on the calendar.

———

There would be a music theory test and a vocal audition for a limited number of coveted spots in the Atlanta Symphony Orchestra Chorus, which meant I would have to do battle against other more experienced, fierce competitors in the presence of vaunted maestro, Robert Shaw.

Like I said, what in the ever-living holy hell was I thinking?

I might have been delusional at that point. After all, I had lost in a Hollywood TV show competition. Who said I could match up to this next challenge? Somehow, I hushed the nay-saying voices in my head, gathered up my courage, and went all in. I wanted desperately to succeed. I thought of the old saw, "You lose every game you don't play." I was willing to fail, but I would never know if I didn't take my shot. I knew full well auditions can be subjective and no matter how good one is, sometimes it's not in the cards. But I wanted to take the chance, so I ginned up the courage to go forward.

My time until the audition was limited to just a few weeks before I would have to ride my chariot on in there and slay my gladiator fears, pass a written theory test, vocally match some random pitches played on the piano, sing a piece of my choosing, and then sight-sing one of theirs. Dear God, I would need to brush up—and fast.

I began with a trip to our small town's local pawn shop on the court square where one could find a gold mine of fun stuff, including new musical instruments for sale as well as all kinds of music books and sheet music. If the sheet music wasn't in stock, Rochelle would order it. Local proprietors, Hershall and Rochelle Norred, along with their assistant Don Berry, were always there at the front, smiling, laughing, welcoming, and happy to chat. Hershall was a lovely soul who had his charms, as he always called me the prettiest gal in Newnan. I did not ask him if he said that to all the girls; I didn't want to know. If he was a bullshitter, he was a sweet one. The pawn shop offered me the material goods I needed to pursue my crash refresher course. I left with a series of music theory workbooks numbered one through twelve and went to work as soon as I got home.

I memorized scales and refreshed myself on musical terms, time signatures, note values, and key signatures. I polished my audition solo to a fine shine and practiced pitch-matching, sight-reading, and sight-singing until the world went flat.

Then, the day arrived.

When I was greeted by a volunteer at check-in, I was nervous. I said something stupid like I hoped I was in the right place. I might as well have asked, "Is this where the gladiators register to die?"

I finished with the written test and handed it in to the volunteer who told me they would call my name when it was time for the rest of my audition.

Hearing my name, I descended the stairs, knees weak, gripping the handrail and hoping not to fall as I entered the large rehearsal room to face my jury. Two people sat at a long table—the one and only Robert Shaw himself and his executive assistant, Nola Frink. In later years, Mr. Shaw would no longer preside personally at the general auditions, leaving that job to Nola and others, and they would add a screen, so singers were all anonymous. But lucky me, I got to stand face to face with God himself and then try to open my mouth and make a sound. It couldn't be just any sound, either. It had to be good. It had to be exceptional. I had to soar. I petitioned all my angels and the good Lord above to help me through it.

I sang scales. I sang pitch patterns in response to those played on piano. I sang my solo audition piece. Then I heard God himself say, "Step up to the music stand, turn to page eighty-nine, and sing the alto part, please." It was Bach's B-Minor Mass. I would be sight-singing the alto part—that I had never laid eyes on—in the fucking Bach B-Minor Mass, the choral masterpiece with all the baroque runs and counterpoint. I heard myself in my head: Oh, dear God, help me. How will I ever do this? I forced a fake smile and nodded at the pianist to begin. I cannot explain what came over me except sheer, miraculous grace.

I sang that mother for all she was worth.

A week later, the letter came. I was accepted. I had done it! I looked at the letter again to make sure it said what it said. "Congratulations," it began. I had won my spot and my life would be forever changed. I would sing again. I took a chance on myself, put myself out there, and I was scared, but I did it anyway. How could I soar if I didn't shoot for the stars?

I looked again, and there was another letter in the envelope. I had been invited to audition further for the smaller, select Chamber Chorus. Invited! Apparently, one didn't just make a phone call and say they wanted to audition for Chamber Chorus; it was invitation only.

The audition for Chamber Chorus was no less terrifying. As a matter of fact, it was worse. We were separated into voice sections, and all those auditioning for a voice part—in my case, Alto—were seated together, grouped in a semi-circle in the Robert Shaw Room on an upper floor of the arts center. We were facing God and Nola, who were seated at a long table not ten feet away. Everyone would hear everyone else's audition. It felt a little like a firing squad, in that Shaw heard us one by one, down the line in order, and this time we had names.

"Miss Berta," he intoned politely. He pronounced it "Bare-tah," anointing my name with a touch of European panache, instead of the usual anglicized "Burr-tah," while looking up with steel blue eyes to see which one of us would be the next to die. I stood, back straight, arms forward, and balanced the thick music score in my shaking hands, ready for battle. "Please sing the first sixteen bars of the Alto part beginning on page thirty-two."

At least we had been given the opportunity to learn our notes at home before the audition, but because of that, there would be no wiggle room, no excuses, no mistakes. There could only be perfect execution of pitch, rhythm, tone, phrasing, tempo, and dynamics. After all of us had sung once, Shaw started over with another part of the score, going through the line in the opposite direction. I had spent untold amounts of time preparing, and I was shocked at one or two candidates who hadn't learned pitches or melismatic runs (a long string of notes sung on the same syllable).

They're dead, I thought. When will I die too? This, after all, was the big time. No time to be a slouch. God was watching. God was listening.

God was judging. But each time, I sang well to my utter surprise. I did it the best I possibly could, and in fact, I did the opposite of dying. I shone.

A few days later, the letter arrived. I, the person who was invited to sing for Robert Shaw and who didn't fluff the words because they were there right in front of me, was accepted into the small, elite Chamber Chorus too. I had been given the highest of high honors and the rarest of rare opportunities. I was finally where nothing else mattered but the music. Now, I would soar.

I spent ten years in those choruses, and they were the best musical years of my life.

ORLY AND OTHER GHOSTS

Between stimulus and response there is a space.
In that space is our power to choose our response.
In our response lies our growth and our freedom.
—Viktor Frankl

June 3, 1962 was a sunny, cloudless Sunday in Atlanta, Georgia. Across the Atlantic, Air France Flight 007 was crashing on takeoff at Orly Airport near Paris, taking the lives of one-hundred and thirty people. More than one-hundred of the dead were Atlantans: arts patrons, Art Association members, and prominent citizens on their way home after a cultural trip to generate much-needed support for Atlanta's art scene. On the fifty-eighth anniversary of the Orly crash, the dead still survive as ghosts—their spirits affixed in memory, on plaques, in buildings, and in history. They remain with those who were alive in Atlanta then and now, with all who carry their stories forward, and with all who hear them.

————

I grew up in Atlanta, having had ties to the arts all my life. For me, this date brings back a flood of memories and stirs the ghosts that inhabit them. For Atlanta, the impact of this day was, and continues to be, unforgettable, remarkable, and everlasting.

In 1962, I was twelve. Atlanta was booming in some ways. With a population of one-million people, Atlanta was enjoying a cultural push by visionary movers and shakers in Atlanta's arts and political communities unlike any in the city's history. In other ways, Atlanta was still a provincial, small, southern town reticent to accept radical social change. Still segregated, Atlanta was a city of separate water fountains and segregated schools.

It would be another two years before the Civil Rights Act of 1964 would come to be. In defiance of it, Lester Maddox, future governor of Georgia and high school dropout, would take an ax handle known as a "Pickrick Drumstick" off the wall of his Atlanta, whites-only Pickrick Restaurant known for its fried chicken and brandish it at three African American Georgia Tech students asking to be served.

Sandwiched between those two years, John F. Kennedy would be assassinated. On November 22, 1963, my family would once again gather around the small black and white TV in our den to watch

Walter Cronkite deliver horrible news, followed in the days after by nonstop coverage.

Ghosts from that day continue to haunt the memories of all Americans and people across the world: a striking widow in a pink Valentino suit and pill box hat, anointed with the fresh, deep-red stains of a husband's and president's blood; the raised hand of a hastily sworn-in replacement in the suffocating confines of Air Force One; the flag-wrapped casket resting on a caisson pulled in solemn procession. Black Jack, a magnificent Caparisoned horse whose ebony coat shone lustrous in the sun, bore an empty cavalry saddle—sword and boots turned backwards in the stirrups. The funeral cortege, a retinue of grieving soldiers, dignitaries, and family followed behind on slow, heavy feet. A small boy, with shining, buster-brown hair, stood at attention—bare-legged in short pants and a little wool, double-breasted coat—to salute his father's flag-draped casket; a little girl in matching coat kneeled in a cavernous rotunda, reaching under the flag on that same casket lying in state; a striking widow was now dressed in a black Valentino suit, beret, and silk veil. The air was silent, save the clopping of horses hooves, and drums rolling in a slow, steady cadence. A million mourning citizens lined both sides of the street for miles, all the way to Arlington Cemetery, and the light of an eternal flame. The world grieved openly, helplessly, and so did my family, watching it all unfold together in our den in 1963.

The year prior, we had mourned the tragedy at Orly. It was, for all of Atlanta and my family, a most personal loss. For it was on that June day in 1962 an entire family living just three doors down from us, along with so many other family members from all over Atlanta, vanished from the earth.

The entire Frederick W. Bull family was taking off from Orly that day. One of the Bull daughters, Ellen, and I were playmates. They lived on the same side of our tree-lined street in Buckhead. Theirs was a unique house. It was a commanding brick structure painted white, situated on a rise, verdant with English Ivy and manicured lawn. There was an honest-to-God round, two-story turret bulging from one wing supporting a conical slate roof. I always thought of it as an enchanted castle. It certainly was more regal than our red brick split-level down the street.

When the news came that day in June, I could not wrap my adolescent head around the fact that an entire family, including my young, lively friend, would never be home again. The following week their dog was run over and killed, and their housekeeper died shortly after that. To this day, when I drive down Westover Drive and pass the enchanted castle house, I say a prayer for an entire family of ghosts who will always reside there in my memory.

The 2001 GPB documentary, *The Day Atlanta Stood Still*, directly mentioned the Bull family at 37:49 minutes in and showed an *Atlanta Constitution* article written about them by Jack Nelson.

I mention Jack Nelson not because I knew him—I didn't—but because I noticed his article in the video. There was also the six-degrees of separation thing: Jack was a newspaper man, working for the same newspaper as my dad at the time—both of them part of the same journalistic family at *The Atlanta Constitution*. They made a difference in their own way during what some would consider the "heyday" of journalism in Atlanta in the sixties. By his own admission, Nelson was considered a "muckraker" back then. Today, he would be called an "investigative reporter"—a Pulitzer Prize winning one, at that—who went on to expose and report on important injustices. Nelson had a conscience, passion for truth, talent for uncovering it, and a terrific ability to transfer all that to paper. And he was there with my dad, a newspaper ad executive. My father was a "good" Don Draper with his five o'clock martinis, cigarettes, and black, Brylcreemed hair slicked straight back. My dad possessed moral integrity, a social conscience, a lovely and kind spirit, and enjoyed a long, faithful marriage.

Every day at the paper, my dad rubbed shoulders with great men of conscience, like Ralph McGill, who ranks high in the history of the newspaper and Atlanta's civil rights history. While my father never wrote a seven-day-a-week editorial column, or published multiple eloquent books on civil rights, or wrote prize-winning exposés, Hobie lived as a principled man who was an example to his children. It would be in the fall of 1963—only one year after the Orly crash—that our parents would pull Larry and me from a church-sponsored private school in Atlanta. They placed us both at Northside High, the public high school in our neighborhood, because the private school refused admittance to the son of the Reverend and Mrs. Martin Luther King, Jr.

Northside and three other Atlanta high schools had already been integrated two years earlier when Atlanta was at the forefront of peaceful (if not token) integration. Only months prior to that, in December of 1960, English Avenue School—a Black elementary school in West Atlanta—was bombed. And it was two years before

122

that when the Jewish Temple in Buckhead suffered a devastating bombing. While Atlanta media, mayor, and public officials were trying to sell Atlanta as the "City Too Busy to Hate," they knew the KKK—and other hate groups—were still meeting in the shadows and fighting tooth and nail to keep white supremacy alive.

Absent in the 1961 descriptions by newspapers and magazines of Northside's debut integration were any details past the initial niceties of well-intended, well-mannered introductions in the lunchroom; about what it was really like after that for three Black students attempting to assimilate at all-white Northside High that year. Their arrival may have been non-violent, even cordial, but life there was not necessarily rosy for them in the long term. The Black students often felt alone and isolated. It was difficult for them at times—some more than others.

While Northside didn't have a single African American student attending by the time I arrived in 1963, it was free of what my parents considered to be a disappointing, piously hypocritical religious component that was attached to the private school. That's when my folks stopped attending church as well. It would be only one more year until my public school welcomed the first African American students since my arrival.

In 1964, when Black students arrived once again and were in my classes, things were different from 1961. Alfred Wright was elected as a school officer, and Barbara Ross, who arrived a year or so later, became a good friend of mine. I saw no such sadness now in our 1964-1968 lunchrooms like I had heard about in 1961. However, realizing now just how young and unaware I was of my naïve, white privilege at the time, I might not have seen it right under my nose, either.

While Barbara and I often sat together laughing and talking in the lunchroom, passed notes in class, and sang together as tall, fellow altos on the top row of the risers in chorus, I also don't recall ever visiting her house. Not once. I thought we had come so far. We were so accepting of one another at school, but we still had a long way to go; I just didn't know it.

In the sixties, Mom worked as a pioneer helping to establish the Atlanta Arts Festival at Piedmont Park. Dad served on the board of the Atlanta Symphony for a while when Henry Sopkin was the conductor and performances were held in the Municipal Auditorium on Courtland Street—on nights when roller derbies and Live Atlanta Wrestling weren't booked.

It wouldn't be long before the great Robert Shaw would appear on Atlanta's music scene and transform everything—including my life—in the best way possible. All through my high school years, Shaw's focus on teaching young choral singers was influential in my musical growth and that of countless others. It would be years before I returned to Atlanta as a grown woman to join the ranks of a very special family: the ASO Chorus and Chamber Chorus with the incomparable Maestro Robert Shaw conducting. Over ten seasons, Shaw became my musical father. Certainly, when he died in 1999, I felt grief that ranked just behind the death of my dad in '83 and child in '80.

When the Atlanta Symphony Orchestra and Chorus toured Europe with Mr. Shaw in May and June of 1988, we all had the ghosts of Orly uneasy in our hearts and minds. We landed in Paris on June 2—only one day off from the anniversary of the worst air disaster in history at the time. The evening of our arrival we sang the Beethoven Ninth at Le Theatre Chatelet. The audience stood and cheered. Mr. Shaw and the soloists took bow after bow, as did the orchestra and the chorus. It was exhilarating. It was, in a word, magic.

As dynamic as the Paris concert was, it had already been eclipsed several days earlier by our Beethoven Ninth Symphony concert, behind the Berlin Wall in East Berlin.

On May 30, 1988, our troupe of traveling musicians boarded a bus at our hotel in West Berlin and headed to Checkpoint Charlie—the one and only place foreign visitors could cross through the Wall from west to east and back again. After passing through the American guard post, we were stopped at the East German guard post. Dour, well-armed East Berlin border guards scanned the underside of our bus with a mirror attached to a long pole. Then, they boarded to collect our passports and hold them until our departure.

Once through that ordeal, we were cleared to go, and found ourselves in East Berlin—a starkly different place from colorful, modern West Berlin. The Wall was now behind us, but it had an energy, like a constant itch that got under everyone's skin and stayed there, supplying a harsh, ever-present reminder of the continual oppression and captivity of the German people living within its confines. East Berlin was a disorienting time warp: Everything was outdated, old-fashioned; the buildings were all a dull, industrial monochrome; the cars were small, tan boxes on wheels, squared-off two-door sedans called Trabants. East Berlin was all a depressing gray-scape.

But the Schauspielhaus—the venue where we would sing of brotherhood, unity, and joy—was different, incongruous, in fact. It had just been newly renovated, and its new interior of red velvet, white marble, and crystal chandeliers was as plush and opulent as any royal palace in Europe.

We were to perform a late afternoon, weekday concert. In the U.S., a daytime, classical performance on a weekday could be a hard sell. But in East Berlin, we were sold out. The audience was filled with people who had a deep love of music, an even deeper sense of desperation, and a hunger for freedom. They came to hear our music and our message. They most certainly were not free to leave with us, as they were trapped behind an immovable, fortified concrete wall ninety miles long encircling the city, lined with 302 functioning watch towers, each occupied by armed guards with shooting orders. It was a wall that was two walls, separated by a ribbon of space about a hundred-yards wide known as a "death strip" running the entire length. The death strip was furnished with zig-zag barriers that looked like thick letter XXs lined up in rows, and it was paved with raked sand or gravel, rendering footprints easy to notice. It offered no cover, and most importantly, it presented clear fields of fire for the Wall guards. This! In 1988!

We took our places on stage. The chorus was divided. Some stood on the actual stage, and some perched in a balcony just behind and above, which was also shared by the audience as it wrapped around the hall. Those choristers in the balcony were positioned so close to the audience that we could almost reach out and shake hands. We could see the threads in the buttons on their shirts, the lines in their faces, the colors of their eyes, and the tears that flowed from them as we sang to them in their language. They heard the message of unity: "Freude!" ("Joy!") and "Alle Menschen werden Brüder" ("When All Men Are Brothers") without knowing whether they would ever be free.

After the final, rousing notes and chill-bumps rippled over our arms in exhilaration as the tiny hairs stood at attention on the backs of our sweaty necks, the audience jumped to their feet, cheering wildly and clapping with arms raised high. They wept openly. And so did we. There was not a dry eye in the house—not in the audience or on the stage. The applause soon fell into that distinct, rhythmic European-unison clap. These folks were tireless in their appreciation and continued their applause while Mr. Shaw took bow after bow after bow, finally having to lead the concertmaster from the stage. Even after the stage was completely vacated, the clapping continued. It echoed backstage and reverberated down the staircase, all the way through the long hallway of the basement to our dressing rooms.

That concert was an astonishing, transformational experience; magic at a level we had never known. As we were leaving the building through the stage door, people swarmed around us, some for Shaw's autograph, of course, but it seemed any of our autographs would do as well. We were all busy scribbling our names on their programs as a few people tried to secretly palm notes to Mr. Shaw in hopes he might carry them across the border. None of us, especially Mr. Shaw, dared accept the clandestine letters.

The chorus boarded the bus, and the guards returned our passports at Checkpoint Charlie. Turning left onto Friedrichstrasse, we were free. We were absolutely quiet. Leaving those people behind was painful. The day and the entire experience moved us into a reverent, unanimous silence. Perhaps we had provided them a bit of freedom after all, a kind of liberty of the soul that music and human compassion can manage. None of us knew then that it would be only a little over a year until the Wall would come down, and they would have their freedom after all. I will never forget the power of that concert. The ghosts residing in my memories of that day in East Berlin are with me and will remain as long as I draw breath.

My stay in Berlin coincided with our son, Scotty's eleventh birthday on May 26. I called from my hotel room to wish him a happy birthday as Rick was about to take our boys and a bunch of their wild friends to celebrate a rowdy birthday at the Coweta Raceway for mud-boggin.' This, friends, was a perfect microcosm of our married lives together: Beethoven in Berlin versus mud-boggin' in Coweta County. And somehow, we made it work.

Anyway, after our Paris concert and several days after Berlin, we saw Paris—the City of Lights—on a late-night bus tour courtesy of Mr. Shaw himself. We returned to our hotel in the wee hours, happy and exhausted.

We would have no way of knowing that the very next day, the Orly airplane crash anniversary would still have the last eerie word.

On June 3rd, shortly after noon, we boarded a chartered Air France flight, just as the Atlanta folks had done in 1962. No one spoke aloud of the significance and the similarities around this date and time, but they were inescapable. The Orly spirits were with us, and they were restless. The differences were several, of course: We were at Charles De Gaulle Airport, not Orly Airfield; we were flying to Cardiff, not Atlanta; and—in hindsight—we all survived the trip.

But not without incident.

At 12:30 p.m. Cardiff time, we landed safely, and all breathed a collective sigh of relief. Then it happened. As we taxied toward the terminal, the wing tip rolled past the building and sheared off a couple rows of bricks, clean as a whistle. Nothing else—just rows of bricks and a mangled wing tip. No damage to life or limb. The chill we felt disembarking that plane, however, was more than just a reaction to the cold, rainy day. We had been duly reminded. The Orly ghosts were present and stirring. We were hushed for a moment, in reverence for those who had gone before us and in gratitude for everything that had come after them.

Those who visit The Woodruff Arts Center in Atlanta today to attend a concert, play, or to enjoy an art exhibition may sit outside on the circle of stone seats surrounding the Rodin sculpture, *The Shade (L'Ombre)*. Perhaps they will eat an ice cream cone, sketch, nap, rest, or play and take the time to read the memorial plaques installed there. They should know that when it was built in 1968, the building was known as the Atlanta Memorial Arts Center—now known as the Woodruff Arts Center after its major benefactor. They should know that it was built as a memorial to the people of Atlanta who died on June 3, 1962. They should know that *The Shade* was a memorial gift from the government and the people of France.

When visitors find the quiet circle and read the names on the plaques, it is possible to feel the presence of the benevolent ghosts who linger there. They are the people—the families, the children—who in death galvanized Atlanta's arts community, igniting the cultural push Atlanta needed to move forward and imbue the arts with new life.

LETTER TO THE ATLANTA JOURNAL-CONSTITUTION

JANUARY 25, 1999

Mr. Shaw never really knew me personally, even though I sang for him for ten seasons. He must have known my face in the sea of choristers after ten years, but it didn't matter. We had a relationship as profound as any I have ever known. He knew my soul and my spirit because he spoke to it constantly. And I knew him as one knows her own heart.

Mr. Shaw was my musical father. He not only gave me the most meaningful musical experiences of my life, but he saw me through years of my own personal crises: losing a baby, the death of my father, the birth of a new baby, teenagers . . . I treasured our time together for ten seasons and gladly drove one hour each way for Monday night rehearsals and all the grueling concert weeks and recording schedules; for his infamous temper and incredibly moving speeches and letters to us; for a vocal education that far surpassed anything I learned in college; for the most sublime musical and spiritual experiences one can fathom. He gave me memories I hold as precious as my wedding and the births of my children.

After my tenth season with Mr. Shaw, I made one of the most difficult decisions I have ever made: I left the chorus because I knew it was what my children and I needed. I knew my absence made not one difference in his life but would make every difference in mine. Even so, I always hoped, as silly as it sounds, that Mr. Shaw understood.

Now, I am profoundly saddened by his death and will always carry with me the knowledge that he gave me so much strength and beauty, so much music and spirit. I'll be at his memorial celebration Friday. I want to tell him how much I loved him, and that I'm back.

Susie Berta

Therapy

IT'S NOT ABOUT THE VANILLA

"I'm hit, I'm hit!"
"Shut up! We're all hit."
—Lee Marvin, crying out after being wounded as a Marine in WWII, and the voice he heard in reply

I had a need for some therapy in 2007 and I finally got it in 2009—better late than never.

It was not my first rodeo, either. Rick and I had been to a great marriage counselor for a short while after about fifteen years into our marriage, circa the late '80s. I was frustrated, dealing with raising our children and feeling like a single mom. I was sad and compulsively overeating. I added a twelve-step program to my therapy. It helped. Rick was overworked, frustrated, and feeling pulled in every direction. He learned from our counselor about boundaries and actually set some with his clients and employees. It helped, too, although Rick didn't set as many boundaries as he might have, which would bite him in the backside later down the road. Meanwhile, we made things work, not perfectly (nobody does), but we did the best we could. We had some really good times.

Then, after years and years, 2007 lowered the boom, knocking the air out of us both, sending us to our knees. Rick and I were really struggling. I started a journal about it all in 2009 and wrote for my own therapy and posterity, so I would never forget what we both went through from 2007 to 2010. And spoiler alert, *how we recovered*.

Here is that journal, verbatim and written *sicut accidit* (as it happened).

MONDAY, NOVEMBER 19, 2009

I know I am not alone in this. But I feel like it. I feel so alone. I can't be the only person in the world with this heavy weight on my heart, making me feel so sad and lost. But right now it feels like it. I hate myself for complaining. We all have our issues. But I'm putting my inner judge aside in many ways this morning because if she has her way, she won't let me do this thing I must do. I must break free of the chains—emotional, physical, and spiritual—that imprison me and choke the light out of me. I must get out of the Dark Place. I must start telling myself the truth.

I must save my life.

I've had quite enough of the chaos of an over-extended life. Returning to college at age fifty-three and getting that four-year degree damn near killed me. When I finished school in 2007, I thought I would just take a little time off for a well-deserved rest.

Somehow, it is now 2009 and this rest has turned into a two-year depression.

After my college graduation at age fifty-seven, having earned that bucket-list BFA in art, *summa cum laude*, and exhausted from the previous four years, I encountered the perfect life shitstorm. The day after graduation I quit taking the diet pills that had sustained me for years. I went cold turkey. I couldn't have gotten through the last year of school without them, although they betrayed me in the end. In the beginning, they were helpful for boosting energy and weight loss. After so long, they became necessary just to maintain any level of energy and were no longer effective for weight loss. Going cold turkey was a very bad idea too. It set me up for the first step into the shitstorm.

Then, I had arthroscopic knee surgery only days after graduation. Another bad idea. I jumped immediately out of the physically taxing, emotional pressure cooker of school, went into diet pill withdrawal, and then landed right in the emotionally and physically taxing fire of surgery and painful rehab.

Our two young-adult sons also had been having anxiety-producing life issues. One was dealing with the loss of his job, and the other a recent divorce followed by a complicated rebound relationship. My husband was navigating critical issues at his veterinary practice. Coming to a head just two months ago on September 11, 2009, Rick finalized a difficult, messy business divorce, leaving him unemployed and us without insurance, which put us both into a state of terror. Guess you could say we were both flattened by the steamroller of life, and both of us have been depressed for the past two difficult years. At least Rick found another veterinary position at a clinic just this month—thank God. Still, we are stressed.

These past two years have not been easy on our relationship.

Also, between all my singing gigs and my return to college, I've been commuting forty-five miles each way to Atlanta—hard—for over thirty-five years, even harder for the last twenty of those. Throw in raising a family and navigating a marriage, and it has all taken a toll. I am weary, if not near death in spirit and energy. I don't think, however, that finding solace in this dark, do-nothing place is such a great solution, either. Even now, as I write this, I can feel the pull starting. The Dark Place doesn't want me to leave, and it is cranking up the volume like an authoritarian parent: "Go lie down. I'm here for you. I'll pull the shade down now, and you take a nice nap."

The breaking free doesn't just happen. I'm a deny-er. And a forget-er. I am sorry for myself. I am sorry for my husband having to live with a depressed, disengaged spouse. How lonely Rick must be. I am sorry he is similarly trapped in his own pain, and I must live with that loneliness. I want to remind myself every day that this place in which we are both finding ourselves supports me in telling myself lies. It masquerades as my friend. It doesn't want me to know it, but it is killing me, and I am its willing accomplice. I am killing myself here. Not with a gun or drugs. With depression.

I need to remind myself of all of that, *believe it*, and *get the hell out*.

But on rare days like today, when I can see the light momentarily and the Dark Place seems to have relaxed its death grip, I see what's real, and it is overwhelming: I am miserable. I am fat. I hurt. Everywhere. I am tired—bone tired. I am sick. I am depressed. I am intractably sad. I have no desire. I am empty. I feel terribly alone. And I want to be left alone.

I wear the same t-shirt I slept in the night before, sometimes for days. I don't want to do anything. I don't want to leave the house. I spend hours at the computer sitting, reading emails and online newspapers. I avoid mirrors. I can't walk or exercise without hurting. I don't want to leave the house, and so I don't if I can help it. Not even to go to the mailbox. I don't want to be with people. I would rather stand at the window and look out than go outside. Gardening? Too much effort, too much pain. Painting? My studio sits empty. Play the piano or the guitar and sing? No desire. There is no music.

I wake up to an entire day of possibilities and rather than welcome them, I resent them. I do manage to break free when I must, long enough to do what must be done, when pressed. I fake it well. I talk on the phone and sound convincing—like a functioning, happy person. I run the occasional errand or babysit my darling grandson and laugh and enjoy him immensely, or I work very hard during a long, ten-hour shift in the commercial kitchen making product for our cookie company I started this year (2009). More on that later. But for whatever short time I'm able to fake a functional life, it exhausts me when it's over. I must retreat to the solace of an empty house, spending days alone, resting, avoiding responsibility, engaging with no one, and doing nothing.

Somewhere, there must be a place in the Middle, in neither extreme: a balanced, healthy, Middle Place where life has purpose and vitality, and means more than just trying to survive it. Can I recall that place? Was I there once upon a time? How do I get back there?

I must start somewhere.

This moment of clarity is a thin, fragile, crescent, new-moon moment. I will not let it pass unnoticed. I will commit it to memory as an evanescent talisman shimmering with the light of possibility, sure change, and the absolute promise of fullness.

I commit this moment to paper and ink as tangible proof, so when I forget my promise, I can come back and read it again.

Every day, or every five minutes, if that's what it takes, I will choose my moment. Choose what I want. There is always choice. And it starts with the willingness. Just one choice is all I must make. The rest will follow as a result of that choice. Do I choose darkness, or do I choose light?

I choose the light and allow it to invigorate me.

I choose not just to survive but to thrive.

I will read these words I put in ink on the page.

I will rub the metaphorical moon in my pocket, and when I am ready, I will take it out and shine its light on my path ahead. One step, one moment at a time.

Because here's what I want:

I want to leave the Dark Place.

I want to be free to take a nap without wanting to spend the entire day in bed.

I want to stop hurting.

I want to shower every day.

I want to be healthy and lose weight.

I want resilience and motivation again.

I want meaning, people, and energy.

I want to be happy, love life, and feel comfortable in my own skin.

I want my happy marriage back.

I want to live.

And yet, all that scares me to my core. Because I know it will not be easy. Choosing, wanting, surrendering, and accepting is just the beginning. The rest? The rest will be a colossal effort—one day, one hour, one moment at a time. In this moment, I see possibilities.

What I must do right now is be thankful for this flash of clarity and freedom, however fleeting, and get out of my head and into action.

What will it be, Susie? What will it be?

I will take a shower and get dressed. It's a start. There it is. Out on the table. So now, we go forward.

May God, or a therapist, or whoever it is that's in charge, help me. Maybe that's me, but I seriously doubt it. My best thinking got me here in this godforsaken, depressive darkness. Depression is real. I know in this fleeting moment of clarity it will be the hardest work I've ever done. I will call on myself to do my part, and I will seek professional wisdom and support. I know I cannot do it alone. I've tried that. It hasn't worked. Not even close.

I am, right this second, brave enough to move on.

Higher Power and a good therapist it is.

FRIDAY, NOVEMBER 20, 2009

I'm thinking about brain chemistry. I think I need intervention and mood-altering substances of the therapeutic, pharmaceutical kind. Where does one get that, legally, and for free? Our budget is strained now. Rick is surely depressed as well, having left his beloved practice that had become a place he no longer recognized. He is at loose ends. We are both in a distorting hall of mirrors, bumping into ourselves and bouncing off one another without truly connecting.

We are both too self-absorbed to comfort the other. Maybe I can get help, and bring some wisdom and grace home to share with him.

I am going to a consignment store in Atlanta today to try selling some of my expensive diva gowns I purchased years ago for musical performances. Maybe I can help our flagging budget that way. Maybe I can manage a shower before this trip.

God help me. I don't want to leave the house.

LATER THAT DAY:

It took some kind of miracle to blast me out of here, but I went. And now I'm back to tell the tale. What an afternoon!

I had decided I just wasn't going to Atlanta today, least of all on a Friday afternoon. What the hell was I thinking when I made that appointment a month ago? Years ago, I swore off being in Atlanta on Fridays, when the traffic is at its worst, and so is the road rage amongst a tired and cranky commuterati. When I called the consignment shop today at noon to reschedule my 2:30 appointment, I got a recording. Still sure of the fact that I wasn't going, but finally sick to death of myself, I got in the shower anyway. I figured I'd call again when I got out and talk to someone then about rescheduling.

Post-shower, I had clean hair, shaved legs—the works. The hot water felt damn good. I smelled damn good. I even dressed in my nice corduroy fat-lady-big-as-a-damn-tent top and my one pair of nice, dark stretchy fat jeans and dress boots. Why waste a good shower on crappy clothes, even if I had sworn off Atlanta for the day. I could still run my local errands to the bank and not look like a bag lady for once.

When I called again at 1:15, a lady answered and said they had no more openings for the rest of the year. It would be now or never. I swallowed hard and promised to get there. Now the good news was I had already showered and dressed. The bad news was I needed to leave at that very moment in order to arrive on time, but I had not yet pulled the dresses from my closet upstairs.

I am unable to maneuver stairs like I used to. I hurt—a lot. No wonder I avoid them. I don't even sleep upstairs anymore. The stairs require me to deal with what is unpleasant and real. The reality is I am nearly disabled, and while I can't do anything about my arthritis and my pitiful post-surgical knee, I could jolly well take a load off by losing weight. And I don't. I hate that. So, I avoid that whole stairway scene as much as possible. But, like so much of how I live my life these days, the circumstances forced me to go there. I lumbered up and down clumsily, painfully, one leg, one leg, one leg at a time—my arms loaded with heavy, expensive gowns encased in cumbersome, over-sized plastic garment bags. After three trips, hurting and sweating and taking care not to trip, I was done and in the car. I didn't know it at the time, but it turned out it would be the highlight of my trip.

The upscale consignment shop, Fantastic Finds, is in a well-heeled North Atlanta/Sandy Springs suburban shopping strip just a few doors down from Van Michael's Hair Salon where the Atlanta glitterati go and pay commensurately. The shop had me lug all my stuff in and assessed it piece by piece. They wouldn't even consider taking my three long, stage performance dresses.

"Gorgeous gowns but not for our clientele," they said. "Too fancy, too showbiz, and over the top," they said.

I didn't know it was possible to be over the top in this place.

And by the way, may I take this opportunity to say that paradoxically, while I was clean and fresh, these beautiful, stick-thin European women with thick accents and dressed to the nines had B.O. that could make a goat wince. But they held all the power in this moment—hygiene notwithstanding. They rejected the three most expensive dresses I had most hoped to sell. The others were accepted, however, and I was in for a serious dose of shock and awe when monetary values were assigned. If the clothing sells, I will share only half the sharply discounted sales price. HALF.

My total consignment-assigned value means I stand to make less than one-tenth of the estimated original purchase price. Oh God . . . this is a hard lesson. Why, oh why, did I spend so much money on those clothes? What on earth was I thinking? And not only that, I am reminded of my darkest secret of all: In seven years, I had worn almost none of it.

In that moment, I glimpsed the extent of my selfish and self-indulgent behavior. Time to repent and reorder my priorities.

I begged them for a recommendation for the diva performance dresses they didn't take. Did they know anywhere that might accept them? The young girl who sat at the computer told me about Le Dress in Buckhead. I am sure I visibly winced when she mispronounced it, "Lay" Dress. Sue me. I thanked her for the tip and left. Fantastic Finds had not been so fantastic for me. But, like it or not, it was finished. And I was moving on.

War-torn and battle-scarred from my first consignment foray du jour, I forged my way through the ever-mounting Friday traffic to fight the next good fight at the corner of Piedmont and Peachtree. Up until I approached the freeway exit, I was waffling, trying to decide whether to go there or go home: *Am I too tired to deal with this? Can I stand fighting the traffic that worsens every minute I am there? Will this place be a huge disappointment? Will they turn me away? Will my dresses be fully appreciated?* I forced myself onto the ramp and committed. *Sound the battle horn and say a prayer. Here I go. Sweet Elvis, help me.*

I found Le Dress. From the outside, it did not look promising. Its location was inside one of a forlorn, little strip of shops that runs alongside a large commercial property anchored on the front by the ever-popular Container Store. But Le Dress sits hidden away at the bottom of the drop lot, flanked by two unoccupied spaces, and fronting an asphalt down-ramp that most folks use more as a shortcut out of the Container Store parking lot rather than a shopping destination. Its only parking consists of one short row of parallel spaces along the curb and directly in front of the shop. I parked, took a deep breath, and went in.

I entered the store and was instantly awash with relief. On display were racks and racks of gorgeous gowns—both wedding and evening gowns. Mine would not look out of place here. They had a chance. My heart leaped. The proprietress—well groomed, well spoken, cordial, and odor free—agreed to look at what I had. Hopeful, I fetched my gowns from the car so she could assess them. As soon as I took them out of their bags and began arranging them on the rack, two women walked by and audibly gasped—ooh-ing and aah-ing over my exquisite dresses. The gowns looked so incredibly beautiful. I was again flooded with hope. Turns out that hope would be short lived.

Ms. Proprietress fingered the goods: a fiery red, Helen Morley couture satin gown with a daringly low, scalloped neckline, long sleeves, fitted bodice, and toe-length slim skirt with a long, regal train in back. I'd purchased it years earlier off a clearance rack at Bergdorf's in New York. It had been "a steal" on clearance for—wait for it—eight-hundred dollars. Ha! Imagine eight-hundred dollars being a steal! Had my head been on straight, I never would have even considered it. Had it been years earlier, I could not have afforded it, either. But I had inherited some money from my mom, and I was flush. I knew my next big classical singing solo gig would come, and I had to be ready. I remember how I felt that day in Bergdorf's: I was thin and in great shape, slipping that dress on so effortlessly, like Cinderella's slipper, gliding from the over-sized dressing room into the opulent parlor. I wanted to model it for my husband, who was trying hard not to fall asleep in the comfy, overstuffed upholstered parlor chair.

Shopping in the same parlor were two long, lean Manhattan matrons, impeccably dressed in designer togs. One doyenne carried a tiny, long-haired pooch in the crook of her arm. The other sported a floppy, wide brimmed hat, her shiny bracelets clanking on her bony wrist as she flipped through the full-price racks of exquisite clothes. As I stood on the plush oriental carpet in the center of the room, facing the mirror, turning and twirling, swishing and swaying, I was a vision. I was in Bergdorf's! Me! I was a princess!

Upon my return to the fitting room, the store seamstress was summoned for a few minor alterations. She was a tiny woman straight out of central casting: heavy accent, black hair pulled back in a tight bun, dressed in black pants and a crisp, long-sleeved white blouse. A cluster of straight pins stuck out of the cushion attached to her wrist. She went expertly about her job as she transferred the pins from the cushion to her tightly closed lips and then to the fabric. The service and attention to detail were so very old school and so very rare. So very once-in-a-lifetime New York. I adored it all.

"Ze drress vill be shippt as soon as next veek," she said, smiling with the slightest curtsy. "I hope you vill enchoy it!" Then she turned and vanished—gone before I could open my mouth to thank her.

I remember opening the large, flat box when it arrived and finding ze drress—MY dress—inside a sturdy zippered garment bag, carefully, expertly wrapped in tissue, the train padded with extra tissue in the fold so as not to crease the beautiful, red satin fabric. I tried it on again, and it was perfection. Exactly where I would wear it, I wasn't at all sure yet, but when the time came, I would be ready with one helluva knockout gown. I carefully arranged it back on the sturdy hanger, catching the little straps sewn into the inside of each shoulder around the hanger's hook to keep the dress in place. I mindfully re-padded the train with the tissue and attached it to the clips on the second hanger. Back in the long garment bag, it was hung reverently on the closet rod. And there it stayed. *Forever.* Until this day.

I'd also brought two other floor-length, formal, stage dresses—both purchased in Atlanta for an outrageous price I cannot bring myself to disclose even now.

One gown was black velvet and covered in sequins. It was so spectacular and theatrical I had convinced myself I would surely wear it on stage. I could imagine myself standing there, audience before me, orchestra behind me, as I made my graceful bows. I had no such gigs arranged, however, and none were on the horizon. But I had done a one-woman show at the Rialto, I reminded myself, and there would be the sequels to it coming up at some point. I had planned one show per decade, three in all: *All Grown Up* was the epic show I had already done for my fiftieth birthday. I imagined *All Dressed Up* for my sixtieth, and *All Washed Up* for my seventieth. If not one of those, there would surely be something else, and I caved into the fantasy. But the years passed. I lost my singing voice, never did the other two installments of my show, and it turned out the theoretical had once again overshadowed the practical reality. The dress came home, and like the red satin dress from Bergdorf's, it found its place of honor on the closet rod never to be worn again.

The third dress was a heavy, midnight-green, velvet Stephen Yearick couture gown—the neckline and sleeve cuffs encrusted with sparkling stones. A breathtaking, beautiful, fairy princess dress for sure—my absolute favorite—that in eight years was the only one I ever actually wore. *Once.* In 2001, I knew I would be singing the mezzo-soprano solo in the Beethoven *Mass in C* with the Coastal

Symphony on St. Simon's Island. I would need a diva dress. And I found it. In spades. It fit my body perfectly and was more flattering than any dress I had ever had on in my life and more beautiful than any gown I had ever seen or could even imagine. Indeed, it was perfection. My gig was a hit, I got standing applause and "Bravas!" from the audience, and I felt stunning in the dress. Who knew that on the evening of my one chance to be a real diva princess, not one photograph taken by my husband came out clearly? The memory of that night, in that dress, however, is etched in my brain forever.

Flush with my mother's inheritance in 1999, there had been real power in my bank balance. That money helped pay for my first (and only) one-woman show in Atlanta at the Rialto in 2000. It helped pay for our son's destination wedding in 2002. It helped me through my four-year return to college in 2003. It fenced our yard. It renewed our furnishings and put granite counter tops in our kitchen. It also paid for a bunch of high-priced gowns I wish to God now I had never bought. While I was appalled at the outrageous prices, I convinced myself it would be a one-time self-indulgence (read: validation) I deserved and would cherish forever.

Ms. Proprietress at Le Dress priced the gowns at a tiny fraction of their cost.

"Priced to sell," she said glibly, smiling, "and you never expected to get anything out of them in the first place when you bought them, so whatever you do get will be gravy, right?"

In that moment, I was enraged, though silent. In the next moment, demonstrating an exceedingly rare self-restraint, I caught myself before I said something rude I would regret, and then I just gave up. I surrender. How could I explain to this woman that she had no idea what she was talking about; no idea of the significance these dresses had in my life; the extraordinary power they possessed; the expectations I had wrapped up in each one; the realized and the unrealized career possibilities, and the devastating loss they now represented—both monetarily and symbolically? This was a bitter end: each dress was going to net less than three percent of their original price. I would essentially be giving them away, and I would now be forced to face the dysfunctional, pitiful reality of what I had done and what I hadn't—what was, is, and would now never be. I had hung up the singing for good, and unless I received an invitation to a royal ball or the Met Gala, I would never have reason to wear these dresses again. This was an epic failure on my part—on so many levels. How could I explain all of that to this woman? I could barely comprehend it myself.

Instead, I lowered my eyes, poised my pen over the paper, and told her quietly, "I had hoped for more, but you know best."

I signed the contract, got in my car, and drove home through the awful, rush-hour gridlock, sobbing all the way.

SATURDAY, NOVEMBER 21, 2009

In the aftermath of yesterday afternoon's Massacre at the Consignment Corral, I am licking my wounds, assessing things, and trying to take a philosophical approach. It's not every day a girl gets to face what a complete nutjob she is.

While I'm pissing and moaning about buying and having to sell my couture clothing, there are people who are naked, penniless, starving, and dying in other countries. Hell, there are naked, penniless people starving and dying in my country. I risk being one of them at this rate. I also risk coming off as a vapid, pompous, narcissistic idiot to those who would judge me as such. But I remind myself this is a time for therapeutic truth-telling and not for judging. There is little anyone could call me that I haven't already visited upon myself. But this is my story, and this journal is my truth—warts and all.

I'm still hurting over the enormity of my shame and mistakes, brought sharply into focus by yesterday's events. My eyes are still red, swollen, and hot from all the tears. I cried all the way home and into the night. What exactly did those dresses signify? And why did they hold so much power?

My voice has left me, at least in a way that I would not feel remotely comfortable inflicting on a once receptive audience. Hormones? Age? Early menopause? Acid reflux? I had all that checked out by specialists. Indeed, I was prescribed Nexium for significant acid reflux before I started having vocal problems right around the time of my one-woman show in 2000. High and low ranges were getting harder to achieve. After that, the quality of my vocal production in general was deteriorating year by year. After four years in art school and not singing in public much, my voice just took a hike—"exiting stage left," as the old saying goes. Efforts to revive it proved futile. Now, it's over.

My friends tell me I still "have it," but they have no idea. I most assuredly do not. What I have is the inability to sound like anything but a gravelly old woman who can no longer produce a pure tone or sustain any kind of vocal production without coughing or croaking like a frog. They do not believe me. The very idea I wouldn't sing? Unbelievable.

I know how my friends feel. I never thought I would stop singing, either. But they want what they want: my voice as it was, not how it is now. They chide me, like I am withholding intentionally or something. They miss my voice. Well, guess what? I do too. One thing I know for certain is I am aging. Looking down the barrel at sixty years of age, I have lost my singing voice and must accept it. This. Hurts. Like. Hell.

Voicelessness has been foisted upon me, and I am clueless about my identity now. Who am I without my voice? The voice that for my whole life was my therapy and talent. It was my expressive, beautiful, clear-as-a-bell gift—my "person-ness." This is my sadness, my grief, my pain, my loss. I must deal with what was and what is to find out who I am now.

Will being the veterinarian's wife be enough, now?

I never had the big, famous career those dresses commanded and deserved. I am past the time now when I could create one, even if I wanted to. Indeed, my career was a small pond, but it was real, for what it was. I am silent now—old and frumpy and fat and tired and debilitated.

Other than that, Mrs. Lincoln, how did you enjoy the play???

WEDNESDAY, JANUARY 6, 2010

As I sit propped up in my bed with my MacBook on my lap, recovering from the holidays and a nasty, week-long battle with the flu, I read a friend's status update on Facebook: "I'm on the plane to NYC!" the friend crowed.

The last time I was on a plane to NYC was last year in March of 2009 when Rick and I teamed up with my brother and his wife on a whirlwind trip to the Big Apple. I had gained so much weight it was, to my surprise and absolute horror, the first time I would have to ask for a seatbelt extender on the airplane. I made Rick take a blood oath of silence. I was also pissed he didn't need one. Not that he wasn't fat. He just has a man's ass, which is no ass at all, and could place the seat belt low, under his round belly. I've never told another living soul about this.

I'll never forget that moment of shock and shame when I couldn't get the buckle together. I literally could not believe it. Talk about denial. I had NO concept of my size (never have), and no clue my body had grown so much—even though I had seen it every day in obvious ways, like clothes that didn't fit anymore. Even after that eye-opening trauma with the seat belt, my need not to "see it" gave rise to creative solutions: I simply surrendered, threw in the towel, and disappeared. I wore the same uniform every day: loose, long-sleeved black t-shirts and fat jeans, accompanied by fewer and fewer glances in mirrors. I started staying to myself, not leaving home unless necessary. Sometimes not even then. I think that one episode on the plane may have been the final straw, the thing that finally pushed me over the edge and into a very dark abyss.

I've been watching the PBS three-part series, *This Emotional Life*, as well as another show the title of which I don't recall exactly but was about the plasticity (adaptability) of our brains, narrated by Peter Coyote (who for some reason annoys the hell out of me as a voiceover talent, but that's a discussion for another day.) Anyway, *The Brain Show*—I'll call it—caught my attention as it discussed the amazing ability of our brains to rewire themselves and to regenerate neurons where needed in the face of strokes, other injuries, or simply in response to "active learning." In addition, there's the negative brain training in which we engage through bad habits and negative self-talk, both of which we repeat over and over and over. It's like wearing a persistent rut in the road in our brains. But guess what? If it's possible to create a negative rut, it's also possible to create a positive one, and that's the great news. The lesson is, if you want to "change it," you must engage in the change repeatedly, intentionally, purposefully, and regularly over a period. It takes time to build a road. That new road will rise eventually and become the new default. It's time for me to make some positive changes. Time to build a road.

Nobody says it's easy—just possible.

Then, out of the PBS show, came stories of people with PTSD, phobias, and depression. Those who succeeded in rising above were those who didn't avoid the memories but faced them head on, talking about them and acknowledging them, eventually taking their power away. Also, the hippocampus evidence rages, as science begins to prove that those of us with depression have smaller hippocampi; that medication can cause regeneration of cells in that organ. And, like the PTSD patients, those with phobias and depression are taught not to fear their anxiety but to acknowledge it, accept it, allow it, and then move past it, taking away much of its power. Feelings are just feelings—not immutable facts. The old "feel the fear and do it anyway" thing is true. And out of the whole PBS special emerged the most wonderful reminder and mantra: "If you can change your thoughts, you can change your feelings."

That's it. It's about education. It's about training my brain. Isn't that what cognitive behavioral therapists do for people? I've been trying to change my feelings with feelings and comfort food instead of retraining my brain to make different choices and behaviors. What I need to do is to change my thoughts and reorder my thought process by assigning feelings to their proper place—no more, no less. It's always been the feelings that stop me, overwhelm me, and fail me. Enough of that. I'm approaching this thing as a business model... train my brain with new thoughts and actions. Literally, change my mind! Time to get to work, be methodical, intentional, and as efficient as possible—take it seriously and tackle this project. The satisfaction of a job well done awaits.

Disclaimer: Now, with all of that said, I say again my best thinking got me into the mess I'm in today. There's a very good possibility that perhaps I should never assume I have anything figured out. Ever. Best advice: Get out of my own way and leave it to the professionals. Which reminds me, I need to find one and make that call.

A few more thoughts: This week I ran across a YouTube video of Mr. Shaw conducting the ASO Chamber Chorus singing the "Hallelujah Chorus"—in 1987. At 0:07 seconds in, there I was—upper right, two o'clock. *Gawd, I was young!* As the camera continued to pan, I saw Larry Higgenbotham, now dead; Hugh Deen, now dead; Dr. Forgot-His-Name, devilish smart ass, now dead; Caroline Shaw, now dead; Mr. Shaw himself, now dead. Nola Frink is, thankfully still alive but retired and gone to live in Florida and dearly missed. There stood other chorus friends now MIA in my life: Laurie Swann, Judy Rogers, and others.

There I was in that video—the living, moving, singing embodiment of my thirty-seven-year-old self. *That was twenty-three years ago.* And the thought struck me: What will I be like twenty-three years from now? I'll be lucky to be alive then, at age eighty-three. It's a frightening new perspective that comes from the awareness that one has more time behind them than ahead of them.

I thought about the realities of that time too: The music transported me to a place of unbelievable bliss. My commitment and sacrifice gave me an incredible education and deep satisfaction, as well as validation as a musician sharing my gift entertaining audiences. But there were those people in my life who suffered because they were left alone many nights. I hold dear the investment I made in the music, and I also honor my decision, after ten seasons, to quit in favor of my responsibilities to—and love for—my family, husband,

and children. I think what I miss most right now is the passion for something—anything—that I once had. And what gives me the most pause is the very real probability that the passion I once had may have been selfishly detrimental to those I love the most.

Even after I quit the ASO, there were long periods of creativity that commanded my attention and consumed my time away from family. I kept pursuing the music. Because I had to. It was who I was. I had so many music gigs over the years. I worked as a music teacher. I had a habit of forming small, elite singing ensembles with clever names like The Treblemakers and Mid-Life Crisis. I co-wrote a musical show, *Old Friends*, and performed it locally to sold-out audiences. There were years of group and solo performances at the local civic clubs, and schools, and churches, and weddings; all those Sundays in Newnan churches where my children sat in the congregation as I sat in the choir loft. And then I spent ten years singing at St. Mark—a wonderful church in midtown Atlanta. Then, there were special concerts, weddings, funerals, and church holy days. There were cabarets, benefits, guest solos at other churches, in homes, and the occasional concert hall. The time-sucking, stressful preparation for, and execution of my one-woman show, *All Grown Up* in 2000, and the odyssey of returning to school in 2003 were big—really big.

Was this all about having a career, or was it selfish indulgences? Or neither? Or both? How could I ignore my calling as a musician? Did I sing at the expense of my children? My husband? Myself? Did I know we would live an hour from Atlanta when I married and we settled down into what I thought would be a small-animal career— Rick in a white coat, us living in Atlanta? Did I juggle and spin all my plates, or did I drop some and hopelessly shatter them? How many? Do they resent me now? Do I resent me? Should I ask? I'm afraid to know.

I feel sure there's truth here inside some dysfunctional, "all or nothing" bullshit rattling around my brain that is doling out the guilt and doing me no good.

MONDAY, JANUARY 11, 2010

Since before Rick left his practice in September of last year, things have been so distant between us. Finally, I had a long, overdue post-holiday heart-to-heart with Rick. Things were confessed tonight that were not easy to hear, but I am grateful we talked at all. The man has been the living example of still waters running silent and deep.

With silence broken, finally, Rick's feelings surfaced tonight. Still I am unsettled, smarting, and not at all sure where we go from here.

Rick has this notion that I'm the only one who needs fixing. He said I need to go to a therapist. I didn't disagree. I suggested that same thing myself, weeks ago. Obviously, I am a hot mess and have been for some time. But then I made another suggestion. I quietly proposed that when I go, he goes with me. The notion that he, too, could benefit from some help came as something of a surprise to him. After all, we had done therapy together once before years ago and it was a marvelous help. Surely we could do it again.

That the events of the past year might have had a profound effect on him—and by extension, on us—and to what extent he might have brought about some of the unpleasantness at his practice through his own conflict-avoidant process, Rick received as something of an odd concept. After all, this conversation was supposed to be about what a mess I am and how he has been so long suffering. What was it he said? That I had become a stone around his neck, and he was not able to carry us both. At that moment I wanted to slap him, and I wanted to hug him. I thought of him having to function every day through his depression and mine—me having no such restrictions on my life and time. I could be a dysfunctional hermit while Rick had to suck it up and be out in the working world, no matter how much he felt like hibernating.

Oh my God, based on how he feels about me and our relationship there is little left to salvage.

I remember our friend talking about his wife in the same way after she killed herself. He said he loved her, but her absence was a huge relief from the burden she placed on him with the chaos of her alcoholism and mental illness. He'd been sorry to say it, but she had done him a huge favor. I also thought about my mother, who managed to kill the affection I had for her through her constant criticism and harshness. While I deeply mourned for her as a daughter mourns a mother, I felt a huge sense of relief at her passing. I would be forever liberated from her persistent critique and negativity.

Have I done the same thing to my marriage? Have I killed it? Or has it been a joint process? Is it truly dead, or can it be resuscitated?

Admittedly, I've done a good job of contributing to the stress in our relationship, but I'm too chicken to kill myself. I'm too young to just keel over, so we must work this out. I'm staying here, and I'm hanging in. I'm not the only one here who's got issues. Yes, I desperately do need to see someone on my own. I also want Rick to get help for his issues, and for us to come together to address our problems as a couple. I want to salvage what's left and rebuild. I want him to want that too. And as usual, historically, I'm the one to make the first move. It's going to be about me going and his benefiting from my lessons. That's what has happened every time we have entered any kind of therapeutic situation. I blaze the trail, and he follows. At this point, I'm willing to do what it takes.

All this drama about me being a problem came, paradoxically, on a night when I had bothered to dress, done the laundry, ironed the napkins, made dinner, balanced and reconciled the business checkbook, and paid the sales tax. Rare, I know, but ain't that somethin'. But wait. Because I am committed to looking at my fifty percent, maybe he's on to something here. Maybe that minimal "Participation Award" I just bestowed on myself is a low bar. I want to contribute consistently to our relationship and live life at my highest and best—blue-ribbon style.

To do that, I will need some assistance of the professional kind.

TUESDAY, JANUARY 12, 2010 – SOME PRODUCTIVE THINGS

I called my doctor's office for the name of a psychiatrist. I should get points just for making it through their phone system without hanging up. I got a kick out of the recording that repeated over and over and over: "Our nurses are currently assisting other patients. Someone will be with you shortly." That one alternated with, "Your call is important to us. Please remain on the line and someone will be with you momentarily."

God help me. Define "shortly" and "momentarily."

They might as well add, "If your condition has resolved by the time we answer, great, lucky you! Hang up and have a nice day. Otherwise, well, you know the drill. Someone will be with you..."

My patience was eventually rewarded with a real voice attached to a real human in my doctor's office who then passed on the name of Dr. Price, a psychiatrist in Newnan. The only psychiatrist in Newnan, actually. Maybe Rick will be proud of me for following through. Maybe he'll say so.

I also scheduled the next two Wednesdays to work at the industrial kitchen Rick and I used to schlep our cookie dough. This I congratulate myself for even though I do not look forward to the next two Wednesdays.

147

The cookie business Rick and I started is much like the paper route I signed us up for in hopes of not starving to death when we first moved to Newnan and Rick had zero clients. Sensing impending doom again last year with Rick's work situation at his practice and in combination with my overwhelming sense of spender's remorse, I made another desperate attempt to be productive and help with income. Thus, Good n Gracious LLC was born in May of 2009. Our cookie-making business is anchored by one and only one product: Rick & Susie's Scrumptious Little Ricotta Cheese Cookies. These little bites of heaven are the Christmas cookies we have been making for years, earning consistently rave reviews from friends and family. "You could sell these!" they all said. So we did.

We began by baking in our kitchen, selling online and at some far-flung, outdoor popup markets. Then, we discovered the city's restrictions banning home cooks from selling commercial products out of home kitchens. Rick and I went legit, applied for a business license, and searched for a commercial kitchen. Because of insurance liabilities, local restaurants, churches, and caterers were not able to accommodate us. We found only one place that would work: Shared Kitchens in Suwanee, Georgia—seventy miles and one-and-a-half hours away up I-85. Determined and undaunted once a week Rick and I trekked up the road for brutal ten-hour shifts in the windowless kitchen. It meant Rick having to sacrifice his Wednesdays off. It meant, too, that I was right there, really working and not hibernating at home. I wanted to be active and present in our efforts to survive, both financially and maritally.

When Rick left his practice in the fall of '09, he was bound by a non-compete clause in his business divorce that said he couldn't work within ten miles of his clinic, nor could he initiate any advertisement of his services. This made local job prospects difficult, and it was nearly impossible to get the word out to old clients as to his whereabouts.

Luckily, within a few months, Rick found himself hired for a part-time position at a local veterinary clinic just outside the non-compete boundary; he no longer had the headaches of ownership but could just enjoy practicing veterinary medicine. It only took a month for them to take Rick on as full-time, although with no benefits or insurance.

If the cookie business never makes us a dime, it will still serve as the saving grace of Rick's career. Every Saturday, we have made appearances at the local market day on the square in Newnan. Inevitably, each week an old client sees us and pops over to say hello. Also, inevitably, they say they miss him terribly and hope he is enjoying his "retirement." Then, they always ask how he is occupying himself. And always, it is Rick's pleasure to respond that he is not retired.

They respond, "Wow, what a surprise, Doc! That's not what they told me at the practice after you left. They said you retired! Where are you now?"

In response to their question, having initiated nothing in defiance of his non-compete clause, Rick happily informs them he now works at a different veterinary hospital. The response always comes, "That's great to hear, Doc! I have really missed you. I will come and see you there!"

So our market day appearances became our unwitting PR machine, without Rick having to instigate a single advertisement or conversation. We continue this cookie business in the hopes of making a buck, but if we don't make a dime, it's been worth its weight in other ways. I may be depressed, but maybe I am not a complete fuck-up after all.

It is not lost on me, however, that if we are working in the kitchen on Wednesdays, Rick's only day off, we cannot exactly be sitting in the chair across from a counselor receiving therapy together. How we work this out remains to be seen. I'm open to suggestions. I may have to do that part on my own.

I called the two consignment shops that have my dresses and guess what: They aren't selling! Aside from the one red Helen Morley from Bergdorf's that sold right away, the rest are languishing on the rack. After all the handwringing about letting them go for pennies, now I must come to grips with the fact they might not sell at all! Then what? Do I leave them there to be donated to charity? Or do I fetch them and try to sell them elsewhere? Do I bring those things back into the house? That seems a bit like a step backward, somehow. Is my ultimate goal to make a much-needed buck or to shed the clutter and psychological baggage? If I can't do both, which is more important?

FRIDAY, JANUARY 15, 2010

I had my first cognitive therapy session with my new therapist yesterday.

I've done the best I could with what I had. Now it's time for some direction. And as Yogi Berra says, "If you don't know where you're going, you'll wind up somewhere else."

Today, I close and lock the door on the darkness, leave the building and walk into the light. Real life. It is bright and very scary out here.

While this departure/arrival is a good and joyful thing, nobody said this process from here on out is simple, easy, or fast. I'm being given tools now, and I must work hard to learn how to use them. It will take practice. I must learn how to forgive myself when I fumble and press on. Yes, it's about pressing on no matter what.

I feel exposed and anxious. No hiding in the light. And no retreating back to the dark. That door is locked. No wimping out. I am not alone. I've got resources—a therapist. This can be done. I can do it.

First day's always the hardest, isn't it?

THERAPY TAKEAWAYS:

1. **Helpful vs. Not Helpful**: A thought is just a thought. Same with feelings. They are not dictators—like little Hitlers or Castros. I shouldn't assign them that kind of absolute power. I needn't allow a thought or a feeling to dictate my actions. I need not obey a thought or a feeling. It's just a thought. It's just a feeling. It's either helpful or not. I get to be aware of it, mindful of it, evaluate it, and then choose. If it's not helpful, I can acknowledge it as such and then step over it and keep walking. Or I can choose to change it by substituting a helpful, positive thought in its place. Thus, I change a dysfunctional belief system one thought at a time. Not necessarily easy. Just possible.

2. **Three-Legged Stool:** There are lots of threes in psychology and therapy. Geometry was never my strong suit, but I know a triangle when I see one. Here's what I want to say about geometry and triangles now and what it takes, according to my therapist, to get me better:

   • **Medication:** I'm starting on the antidepressant Wellbutrin, or rather its generic, because the pharma companies are greedy as hell, their prices are sky-high, and they don't care, but let's not go there now.

   • **Meditation:** It will get me out of the mind rut and into a mentally calm, at ease, healing place. I have no idea how to do it.

- **Cognitive Therapy:** I am working like hell on recognizing and changing negative and unhelpful thought processes and behaviors.

THURSDAY, JANUARY 28, 2010

My assignment this week is to journal each day about the actual thought that precedes a dip in my mood. This is not going well. While I can prattle on endlessly when the fancy strikes me, it appears I don't do so well on command. I am either a rebel or constitutionally incapable of getting to the thought at that very moment. Apparently, my psyche has strong boundaries. What's that Frost poem about good fences making good neighbors?

The phrase, "You don't want to know," is haunting me. Also, "You can't handle the truth." Tough nut, I am. Emphasis on nut.

I'm having a hard time with this. I don't like the fact that I lack the ability to be aware of "the" exact thought, but I am becoming more aware of how I feel about that, and maybe this is a skill that is going to take some practice. Historically, I don't like to do things that I'm bad at.

One thing I do know: I don't like feeling stupid or failing. I don't like hurting. And I don't like being fat and ugly. I hate exercise. I don't care for crowds. I am happy to isolate in my home for days. And I hate stuff I can't figure out.

Sticking to the assignment here, I've managed this meager offering for the week, which follows here:

Yesterday was "work our asses off day," involving our standard all-day trip to the kitchen in Suwanee. We left home at 9:00 a.m. and got home at 11:00 p.m.

IN THE CAR TO SUWANEE:

Thought: *This business is financially failing. We are working our asses off in the kitchen, but I'm not smart enough as a businessperson. It's my fault, and I just won't take the extra initiative to make it successful. If it fails, I have failed—again. Now, I'm trapped. I see success stories of women who take their recipes and create multi-million-dollar conglomerates—Mrs. Fields and her cookies, Sister Schubert and her rolls, Geraldine Cunningham and her cheese straws, Angela Logan and her apple cakes. Truth is, I'm conflicted. I want success, but I just don't know how to be a businesswoman. I'm a math-challenged, right-brained creative, dammit.*

Feeling: Worry. Sadness. Anger at myself. Confusion. And ultimately, overwhelmed. Don't know what to do? Do nothing and take a nap.

Thought: *I know the only way out is through. But I am so tired. I want to stay in bed in my house and rest. But I know that's inappropriate. That's bad.*

Feeling: Frustration. Shame: I am literally embarrassed for myself. A glimmer of a reminder, though, of the good feelings engendered by our being present on the square selling cookies and how it has helped Rick's clients find him again.

LATER IN THE DAY:

I was tired of scooping little dough balls onto parchment-lined sheet pans. My back was in knots, burning, and stabbing. My legs, knees, and feet hurt.

Thought: *I'm not trying hard enough. I still don't know how to meditate. Not sure I will ever learn if I don't try harder.*

Feeling: Fear. I'm afraid to spend all this money on therapy and not try harder.

Thought: *I should give myself credit for what I have done, for what I've gotten right. Or is this letting myself off the hook? Is it rationalizing? I didn't do the things I needed to do, but look what else I have done? Good for me? I was not conditioned to think this way.*

My mom was a writer and an editor. She had a red pencil in her hand for a living. She was trained to find the mistakes first. That's how I was brought up. The mistakes were always a bigger deal than the accomplishments. Or at least it felt that way. As a musician, I carried on in the same tradition, always looking to improve, never satisfied. Maestro Shaw had a red pen, too, but somehow his criticisms were different from my mom's. Did I respect him more? Did I take his words less personally? After all, he was my "musical father." But she was my mother.

Shaw was famous for his perfectionism and his tireless quest for it. He would berate his world-famous chorus in rehearsals, sometimes shouting, "People! You're so close to singing the right pitch, you might as well just sing it!" If we rehearsed the *Coventry Carol* once—"Lully, Lullay, thou little tiny child"—we rehearsed it hundreds of times. Hundreds. He'd stop and scold us again, and again, and again to rephrase or reinterpret the slightest musical nuance, accent, breath, word, or syllable, patiently explaining, at first, that we weren't singing sensitively enough.

Finally, when Shaw had had his fill of our ham-handed incompetence, he would explode. "People! You're putting the baby to bed with a goddamn hammer!" He would yell, throwing his glasses, running one hand frenetically through his hair wet with sweat, squeezing his eyes closed in concentration while his other hand shook his baton frenetically in tortured desperation. Shaw lambasted us until we not so much understood what he wanted, but with each tiny improvement we were inspired and moved by what we heard, finally able to bend to his tireless will, and produce a transcendent result. He was always right. Always. And when we got it right, his countenance morphed into ecstatic approval, and he praised us with blown kisses and a hand on his heart.

Looking back now, my mom was usually right too. Why couldn't I take it from her? Maybe, historically, I almost always got sent back to the drawing board and always fell short of a transcendent result, blown kisses, and heartfelt approval.

Feeling: That feels like an "aha" moment. I am sad. And I am tired now. Really tired.

THERAPY TAKEAWAYS:

- **Why Am I Tired and Unmotivated?** The simple answer is *depression*. Hello! Honest to God, I still need to be reminded that depression is a thing. It is real—with real, significant, physical, and emotional effects. Give the medication some time to work. The other parts to that answer involve action: preparing for that moment when the medication starts working, so I have the best chances at success. Taking action—whether I feel like it or not—will get me primed, practiced, and ready to move forward.

- **Action** = Structure and a Plan. I will implement some structure and accountability to my day. It doesn't necessarily mean I have to go all out. No need for a three-piece pinstripe suit, heels, and a leather briefcase. At least not yet. On second thought, how about never.

- **Start Small and Build on That.** I will do something proactive every day in each of the three areas: business, personal relationship, and diet.

- **I've gotten the big picture.** Therapy is not for sissies, and it's not a passive enterprise. Slackers will lose at this if they expect to be magically anointed with answers without doing the footwork. This whole process requires a person to dedicate themselves to recovery and work like hell.

SUNDAY, JANUARY 31, 2010

It occurs to me after another uncomfortable exchange with Rick today that sometimes things aren't always about my deficit. I beat myself up for saying, feeling, and responding to something a certain way when maybe it's not just about me. Rick can be wonderful, dutiful, and hardworking. He can also be moody, resentful, and passive aggressive. Welcome to the human race! Could it be I'm not the only one in this relationship who is fully human and has foibles?

These are questions I take to therapy, and I am thankful for the opportunity to work through them with a wise professional in their right mind.

Perhaps the last straw in an emotional day came as Rick and I watched Dateline on TV. There was a segment about newbie medical residents and the challenges they face on their way to becoming doctors. They had to learn how to deal with their patients but also the families of patients. With no warning, the show profiled a young couple whose twenty-four-week preemie, delivered alive hours earlier, could not be saved. There was a quick camera shot of the parents hovering over the incubator, stroking the tiny, dying baby followed by a shot of the grieving parents after their baby had expired. I suppose I was in a vulnerable state already and primed for an emotional reaction to this. While I might have weathered it better on another day, this one wasn't it. With tears in my eyes, I rose swiftly from the kitchen island without a word and emptied my dishes.

The guilt washed over me as though it were yesterday—our own situation thirty years earlier when our twenty-six-week fetus died in utero. There would be no saving her. She would never breathe a breath. I never saw her after I finally delivered her—a full month after being pronounced dead inside of me. Grief-stricken, overwhelmed, and not knowing quite what to do, we made the best decisions we could at the time, but I have never come to terms with what we did. Rick and I left her in the hands of the hospital. We did not pause to hold her, bend over her, or tell her soft goodbyes. I was drugged and tranquilized into oblivion during delivery, but I could still hear. The memory of the horrible, heavy thunk of something still and silent falling into the stainless tray is seared into my brain. To this day, I do not know exactly what happened to her or how the hospital handled her. I was never told. I will never know.

Although it was a decision we had made after much debate and with the advice and consent of our doctor and our priest, I have lived with deep regret, guilt, and sorrow ever since. We were young, and I was afraid to look. I didn't know what to expect, since this was, after all, a fetus that had been dead for a month. What would that look like? Exactly what was it at that point—a blob or a baby? A miscarriage or a stillbirth? I didn't want to take the chance I would be haunted forever by the sight of it, the sight of her. How could I know then what I know now: That instead, I would, for the rest of my life, be haunted by and ashamed of what I didn't see and didn't do.

Rick later tried to describe to me what he saw which was a tiny, macerated body—a miniature dark red and purple floppy alien weighing less than two pounds; not the fat, bouncing baby we had hoped for. This was a tiny person. Our person. I wish someone had told me how important it would be to look upon her and say goodbye. We should have had her body cremated. We named her Sarah Kate. And then we abandoned her. I vowed to volunteer in a hospital nursery or NICU so I could see what a twenty-six-week fetus looks like and somehow make amends through service to others, but this I could not ever bring myself to do.

It has been thirty years. I'm always surprised when the guilt, shame, and sadness resurface—even after all these years. I have, over time, tried to forgive myself. I have done the best I could with that too. But I never, ever forget.

After I arose from the kitchen island so abruptly, Rick asked me, "Did that upset you?" I replied, clearly shaken, "Yep, sure did." He made no effort to comfort me—neither with action nor word. After a long silence, he turned and said he was taking our dog, Porter, outside. Standing alone in the kitchen, I felt weary and decided to go to lie down in bed. It was only 8:00 p.m.

Reading a book, I heard Rick come inside with Porter and head back to the kitchen television. We would stay in our separate locations for the rest of the evening. And when it was time, Rick came to say goodnight. Bending over, he gave me a peck, said goodnight, and turned to leave to sleep in another room. It was as though nothing happened this day. No acknowledgment of a tough day. No addressing the issues. No apologies. No requests. No resolution. No closure.

No, Rick and I would leave all the events of the day unresolved, just hanging in the air—like a smelly fart no one wants to claim—and we would not speak of any of it again this day.

Or any other day, no doubt.

MONDAY, FEBRUARY 1, 2010

Despite Rick's and my recent set-tos and difficult interactions, I feel like the medication is helping. Now, I need practical help navigating our rough places, understanding more about both of us and why we respond the way we do to each other, and ultimately, how we can BOTH work together to make it better.

THERAPY TAKEAWAYS:

1. Now that the medication seems to be starting to work, the pathways of my brain are open to rerouting. We must work very hard now to create new, positive, constructive pathways and reinforce them.
2. I must teach Rick what I need. Equally as important, he must learn to do the same.
3. Show Rick DR. P'S FIVE SECRETS OF EFFECTIVE COMMUNICATION E.A.R. CHART and understand it together. Ask if he will help me by going over it and implementing these things together.
4. Use these phrases in times of conflict:
   - "I know you love me and want me not to hurt, but can I tell you what's going on and what I need?"
   - "It's not your job to fix this, but I need a hug. That would help."

The underlying thing is PAIN. Rick needs to be informed about me in a way that doesn't sound critical—and vice versa.

My session with my therapist has given me one of the best gifts: learning how to communicate with Rick. We are both consumed with our own pain. We need to talk to each other and understand what the other is feeling, sensing, and going through. That's getting our heads out of our own asses and being attentive to our spouse's pain in addition to our own.

SUNDAY, FEBRUARY 14, 2010 - VALENTINE'S DAY

There would be no gifts or special efforts between Rick and me this year—not heart-shaped pancakes, doilies, red hots, chocolates, or flowers, not even a card, or a kiss. No, this year is all about practicality and austerity. We had agreed ahead of time we would not be celebrating or buying anything, but the day still felt out of kilter. Kisses and pancakes are absolutely free. Why could we not at least muster up some of that spirit?

It was just another morning. Rick made breakfast without waking me and was sitting down alone to eat just as I awoke and came in to join him. We ate, talked, and read the paper. There was no anger or stress or negative energy. For that I was grateful. But it was almost too benign. I wished then we could possess the spirit to engage, at the very least, in the small endearments, the special, little gestures and playful conversation that cost nothing. Maybe that would take time. We finished breakfast, and Rick took Porter for a long run, leaving on Valentine's Day morning and returning at noon. I wondered just how much time it would take to get us back on the same page or if it was even possible.

Truth be told, we had already done one thing special. We had bought a gift for Harper, and we were both excited to give it to him. Rick gets all the credit for this. He had come home on Friday with a tip from one of his coworkers about a cute, little toy she had purchased for her grandson. Rick and I made the trip to Dillard's on Saturday and found it. Then, on Sunday, after Rick returned from Porter's run, we sat together at the kitchen island, hand decorating the brown paper we would use to wrap Harper's gift. I drew little hearts, and Rick colored them in with crayons. There we sat, thoroughly enjoying our simple, little project, and it hit me—we were engaging in small endearments, special, little gestures, and playful conversation. It was exactly what I had been wishing for earlier that day. With those simple efforts, we enjoyed each other's company in a way we hadn't in a long while. This was the answer to my question of how long. It would take as much time as it takes, and it's up to us to make it happen. And it did seem possible.

We spent Valentine's Day afternoon at Harper's house, playing with the Twilight Turtle we bought for him. Who knew this small toy—with the little star-shaped holes and a crescent moon punched in its shell, a light source inside, and an on-off switch and three buttons that change the color of the light inside the shell—could provide so much entertainment! We all piled on his bed in his darkened room and turned the turtle on. Stars in constellations projected magically all over the ceiling and down the walls; Harper was entranced. We were thrilled. And it was fun. Imagine that—fun. What a gift.

THURSDAY, FEBRUARY 18, 2010

Dr. P asked me, "Do you give compliments?"

I said "Yes, but why?"

"Just make that your assignment. Try giving more compliments, and you'll see," he replied.

MONDAY, FEBRUARY 22, 2010

It was a wonderful, memorable weekend. The mid-February weather was rare . . . in the sixties and sunny. We kept Harper all weekend, and we celebrated my sixtieth birthday (a few days early) on Sunday. We had my most favorite foods for dinner: Rick made baked brie and fried green tomatoes while Nick, who graced us with his presence, cooked a lovely rack of lamb.

It was a weekend filled with activity and two-year-old laughter, smiles, innocence, and fun. Imagine it once again—fun! We three camped out on air mattresses at bedtime in the darkened den, laying on our backs watching what seemed like a million magical stars from Twilight Turtle projected on the ceiling. Rick, Harper, and I listened to a sweet lullaby CD until sleep overtook us all. The next day, we ate s'mores and the word "goopy" elicited giggles and laughter; we made a graham cracker house cemented together with Nutella and covered it with sprinkles; we had playtime inside and out, playing rhythm instruments to Peter, Paul & Mary's *Mommy & Me* CD, cookin' on the toy BBQ grill, toiling at the play tool bench, shopping with the toy grocery cart and checking out with the toy cash register, playing in the playhouse and the sandbox and running, running, running in the backyard.

Harper and I played with the water hose while Grandad pressure-washed the brick columns clean; we transplanted the hydrangeas in the backyard and cleaned out the window boxes on the playhouse; Harper played and splashed in the bathtub; we read books; we took trips in the car, went shopping for toddler jeans and a booster seat for our kitchen; we talked and laughed and hugged and kissed. There is nothing quite like the moment when your grandson comes running into your arms, flings his arms tight around your neck, and says "Gamma!" or "Grandad!"

We threw open the kitchen doors on Sunday during a perfectly beautiful day, and the house was refreshed, open, and airy. I took off the covers on the patio chairs, and we ate lunch on the back porch with Harper snugged up to the table in his highchair—happy as a spotted pup in a wagon rut. When his dad arrived during lunch, Harper was glad to see him, and they kicked the soccer ball in the backyard, and lobbed tennis balls for Porter-pup to fetch, playing together while Rick and I got a few chores done. I did some house cleaning and then blew the leaves in the backyard. My body was tired, and my back, hips, and knees burned, but how satisfying it was to do normal things—like clean up the leaves off the lawn—as our son and grandson played in the backyard and Rick puttered.

When I took a short break from blowing leaves, Rick asked me if this was the scene I had pictured when I began to rehabilitate and redesign our backyard all those years ago. I answered unequivocally "Yes!" This was exactly what I wanted, what I envisioned, and what I dreamed of. It is precisely what I have spent the last ten years preparing for, landscaping, gardening, and working toward. With all that and the playhouse now accomplished, my vision came to life this weekend: Our toddler grandson ran full tilt in the backyard, laughing and playing with his dad, and loving being here with his grandparents who love him so much. I don't know who was happier this weekend. I suspect it was a three-way tie.

MY HOMEWORK: THE LIST OF COMPLIMENTS

The list isn't exactly long. Maybe it's more important to engage in quality rather than quantity here. I don't know exactly what my therapist had in mind, either. Maybe just the process of complimenting people changes the endorphins in my brain. On further consideration, however, Dr. P knows that for me to give compliments I must interface in some way, shape, or form with people. Real people. And not only that, but I also must get outside of my own head and deal with others. Damn, I do believe he knows what he's doing. I trust him enough to do what he says and be glad.

I told the greeter at BJ's Discount Warehouse she had on a pretty sweater. She smiled, clearly pleased, and said "My sister didn't want it so she said I could take it."

"Well you made a great deal!" I replied. It was such a brief exchange, but it felt good. I liked telling her that, but I liked her response even more. A spirit-lifter.

I said to Rick, "You are my best friend. That may be the nicest birthday card you have ever given me. I love it. I love you."

"You're my best friend too. I love you, babygirl."

I made it a mission to look outward at others and see them in their light—free from the shadows of my own inner darkness. I saw people, friends, strangers, and loved ones with fresh perspective. I told friends, "Your friendship means so much." And I meant it.

I am finally cultivating gratitude. I'm opening to others. I'm moving forward.

There's a closeness with Rick that's returning, and it feels damn good. The walls have come down a bit. And I'm getting out of purgatory, step by intentional step.

TUESDAY MAR 2, 2010

Yesterday, my therapist dropped off a book in my mailbox, *Try Giving Yourself Away*. We talked about it today. How kind and thoughtful was that? A perfect example of the lessons from the book: Practice random acts of kindness and cultivate gratitude.

I had a lovely girls' day out with my dear friend, Leanne, on Saturday afternoon: A trip to Anne Irwin Gallery to see David Arms' current artwork was a true gift, inspirational, and invigorating. That's where I got my free, priceless "IGBOK" bumper sticker. I knew I had to give one to Dr. P. "It's Gonna Be Ok" is a phrase Arms put on bumper stickers, and the gallery was handing them out for free, along with a large, signed IGBOK poster with an image of a bird's nest bound in ribbons. Arms' symbolism and weird juxtapositions are magical—his birds suspended in the sky on little swings made of string and, say, a carrot, fork, twig, or an asparagus stalk. He's the artist who inspired me to paint my only painting of 2009 and my best, *Spring Totem*. I hoped he would inspire me again this spring.

Dr. P and I discussed loss, with respect to my singing. It was brought to the fore again over the weekend at a memorial service Rick and I attended. Whoever that girl was singing, she was beyond awful, and that's not me being critical or tacky, that's just the God's honest truth. So there I sat in the pew feeling bad that I didn't offer to sing, having pangs because they didn't ask me, either, and then wondering if I wasn't deeply relieved no one asked me. I also remembered—duh—I'm telling people I'm retired. And the reason for that is because my singing sucks now too. And that is a painful thing to accept. Sometimes I forget to read my own memo. I am stuck between denial and acceptance.

Dr. P took the stance that maybe I was premature with this decision to retire from singing; that it's so all or nothing: "Like giving up walking just because you can't walk well anymore," he posited. I knew where he was going, and I told him this was not about perfectionism. And walking is not the same as performing unless you're a dancer. A limping dancer who performs poorly is no more likely to satisfy an audience than a singer who sounds terrible. God help me. I will not visit my limping voice on a captive audience. Period.

I'm always incredulous at the loss, though. It's surreal—kind of like when you just can't believe someone important has died. They were just there a second ago. Suddenly, they aren't. Acceptance about this has been a tortuous process. It has not come easy for me or for those who try to convince me I still have it, even though they haven't heard me sing and therefore can't possibly know. "You're just out of practice," they say. "Your voice has just changed to a different sound," they say. It's true; I am out of practice, and my voice is most definitely different. But I'm afraid there's more to it, and it's more permanent in the way death is permanent. Nobody wants to accept it. Including me. And I grieve. I am stuck in the grieving process without wanting to accept the death. Not helpful.

Then, there's the selective memory issue of singing: remembering the wonderful times to the exclusion of the less-than-pleasurable aspects of performance life—the stress, time, preparation, pressure, commute, and leaving family and friends. Truth be told, this retirement issue is about more than the voice. I'm also tired of dressing up. I don't want to be on display. I don't want to work that hard anymore. I don't need the stress in my life. And I certainly can't say I miss the pressure. Still, I forget to consider these things when the pangs of indecision and doubt fill me and, like a stuck record, return to torture me repeatedly.

I'm conflicted for sure, and it is all...*not helpful!* I must unite these divided sides of myself, let some things go, and proceed with my life in peace.

THERAPY TAKEAWAYS:

- Getting your feelings hurt isn't the end of the world. It's OK. It needn't last. IGBOK.
- Making things about me when they needn't be is a BRF (big red flag). The fact that I'm still feeling egocentric at times tells me I'm not out of the hole just yet.
- I still beat myself up a lot. It would be good to give myself some breathing room and just relax a bit.
- Goal Dichotomy: relaxing into change versus making change happen. Be gentle while purposeful.
- Let it Be versus Make it Happen: two ends of the pendulum, with IGBOK sitting right in the middle. Dr. P likened it to a metaphorical Serenity Prayer.
- Enjoy the process, not just the goal.

SUNDAY, MARCH 14, 2010 - AN UNFORTUNATE SET-TO ABOUT VANILLA

At least we started the day well—breakfast together, chatting over coffee and the paper. Then, Rick took Porter for his two-hour run. Upon his return, we had lunch and then Rick appeared in the kitchen with the cookie racks and the extra eggs, ricotta cheese, and butter from the basement fridge. Time, he had decided, to make a couple batches of cookie dough before going up to the kitchen on Wednesday, since some of our ingredients were expiring and it would, in theory, give us a leg-up on getting enough cookies made for May Day at Serenbe—our next big event.

I thought we were doing okay; I really did. And then it happened. It came out of left field.

After completing the first batch of dough, Rick said, "If we're going to make another batch, we're going to need more vanilla. We're out."

And there it is, boys and girls, the beginning of the end. Trying to be helpful, I said . . . wait for it . . . "Are you sure?" I opened the spice cupboard, rotating the circular shelf around. "Did you look up here on this shelf?"

He responded testily, "I told you I looked everywhere."

Still clueless and still trying to be helpful, I looked in another cupboard, asking again, "What about here? Did you look here?"

Again, the response was the same—only more intense and louder, "I *told* you I looked *everywhere*."

162

"Wow, that's not exactly what I asked you. Could you please just answer me? Maybe we'll find it in a place you haven't thought to look."

The response was the same, only this time ramped up yet another notch. "I TOLD you I looked EVERYWHERE."

I was irritated by Rick's obtuse, obstinate responses. I was only looking because I wanted to help him and to save him a trip to the store if I could. I knew of a few places there might be vanilla lurking, and I didn't think he knew about them. It was then I had the audacity to find a bottle of vanilla on the upper turnaround. Apparently, he hadn't looked everywhere. Imagine that.

"Hey, here's a small bottle, but it isn't the brand we normally use. It says, 'double strength.' Huh. What's up with that?"

A few quiet moments from the man who was so sure we were out of vanilla and who was certain he'd looked everywhere. Rick asked curtly, "Do you want to use it?"

I wish I hadn't found it. Honest to God—I wish I hadn't even tried to be helpful. What's that saying? "No good deed goes unpunished?" Ah yes, I was living it at this moment. And so I wish I hadn't said the following: "I'm afraid to experiment on a double batch of cookies with a brand of vanilla we've never used, and one that says double strength at that. If it has an off taste, we'll have wasted a lot of dough." It was just about then I was going to say we did have a choice, however, and we didn't really have to make the second batch today if he didn't want to go out. But Rick beat me to it.

With a swirl of his jacket, Rick shoved an arm sharply through each sleeve with a huffy sort of air, wordlessly opened the kitchen door and left. I guessed he was going out for more vanilla. *Or he could just go to hell.* That whole thing was just so mean. Why did he have to behave that way? Bastard! I had that sinking feeling one gets in their tummy when they've been spoken to harshly, especially when it's undeserved. I didn't deserve it, did I? What had I done that was so awful? Was Rick really mad at me, or was I imagining it? I asked him when he came home.

"Can I just ask you something? Were you mad at me when you left?"

Rick's head dropped. He was thinking. His lips tightened and he said, low and slow, "I just didn't want to go out again."

I tilted my head instinctively, like a dog who can't figure out what his human is saying. I replied, "I'm sure you didn't. But were you mad at me?"

"Yes. I was mad at you. I told you I looked everywhere. I felt like you were telling me I didn't know what I was talking about and that I was being doubted."

This really made no sense. From whence came all this vitriol being spewed my way? "I was just trying to help you," I said, "and I did actually find some vanilla, so I guess you didn't look everywhere, did you?" Uh-oh—maybe that was not a smart thing to say at this juncture. But there it is, I said it, and I'm not sorry.

"But we didn't use it!" Rick barked.

Oh dear, sweet Mother of Elvis. Were we really having this conversation?

"That is beside the point," I said. This was deteriorating rapidly. And by now, I was really getting mad. Rick was mad at me for no reason and taking it out on me. I was over it. I stood slowly, carefully reached for my purse and said, as calmly as I could muster, "I really don't think my feelings are going to serve us very well right now, so I am going to leave for a little while and take a drive. I'll be back." I walked quietly to my car with—I am proud to say—not a single slammed door or a tear shed. However, *fuck you* was spoken loud and clear on the inside.

I didn't know where I would go on Sunday afternoon at 3:10 p.m. I thought maybe I'd catch a movie. I headed that way. Then, it came to me—I'd go to Walmart and shop for some workout clothes so I could go to the gym and start working out, lose weight, feel good about myself, and look great. Then, I could divorce Rick's ass and live free of his moods and temper and maybe find myself in the process. Two hours later, I emerged from Walmart with a superstore hangover and way more workout clothes than I needed. My plan was to try them all on the next day in the peace and quiet of my own home and return whatever fit the worst.

When I pulled into the garage, Rick was out in the back by the shed, and I could hear the chainsaw going. Guess he needed to go outside and do a therapeutic man-thing. To each his own. I had driven away and shopped; he went outside and chopped something down.

The kitchen was just as I had left it. Rick had clearly deserted it all when he decided to go play with his chainsaw—the butter still on the counter, the canisters of flour and sugar still out. I set about to cleaning up, putting the rest of the cookie-making paraphernalia in its place, washing the measuring cups and bowls, loading and running the dishwasher, wiping all the sticky residue off the granite counters and polishing them shiny clean. I sat in my chair at the computer and was still there when Rick came in. I didn't speak. Neither did he. As a matter of fact, Rick walked down the hall, through the dining room and the front hall, and up the stairs so he wouldn't have to walk past me. I decided to retire to my room and journal about all of this. I can hear him back in the kitchen now, TV on, doing something that sounds like a project . . . sanding something, perhaps? I'm staying put.

So here we are, in separate rooms, not talking. Ridiculous. I've been home now for a good four hours. The way these scenarios always play out is we'll start talking when I make the first move. Guess what. I'm over that too. Not gonna happen this time. As much as I want to settle this, I am going to make it different. Rick is going to have to make the first move.

No doubt, Rick's problem is something he's not talking about. Like money. He did just pay the bills last night. Maybe we're about to be really broke, he's stewing about it, and he won't tell me. That's his pattern—not talking about what's on his mind and then letting it come out in passive aggressive ways. He just stuffs it, feeling powerless and victimized.

It's after 9:00 p.m. when I hear him going back upstairs. All is dark and silent. This is serious. And I'm not crying, goddammit, I refuse to cry.

I just got up and went to the kitchen for a bite. I turned on the light and saw nothing that looked like a sanding project. Then, I saw the kneepads on the counter—the kneepads I had placed in the guest bath earlier today in preparation for my grout-cleaning project. I looked in the guest bathroom and saw what the sanding sound actually had been. It was the sound of a brush scrubbing the tile floor. The tile and grout were sparkling white.

It has also been Rick's M.O. to let actions speak when he cannot. I am touched, but I am still going to make him come talk to me. Because nothing changes if nothing changes. And this has got to change.

MONDAY, MARCH 15, 2010

Rick left this morning without saying goodbye. I didn't exactly rise to greet him either.

I spent the morning doing the usual household chores and reflecting on our weekend dysfunction. I wondered how long it would take for Rick to talk to me.

I fixed dinner in preparation for his arrival. Would he speak to me? Would he talk to me yet? I was anxious but determined to let him take the lead. When he walked in, he was silent. So was I. Rick managed a clipped, quiet "Hi" as though he were trying to say it as briefly as humanly possible. It sounded like a depressed kind of hello—I should know.

I responded with a "Hi" I thought wasn't too terse and kinder in tone.

In that moment, it occurred to me maybe Rick has been depressed and angry for a longer time than either of us has been aware. Just because he stays busy and goes to work every day doesn't mean he's not depressed. We handle it differently: I shut down, isolate, and go fallow; Rick busies himself with nonstop projects and physical labor to distract himself, pushing his anger down. It bubbles out in other ways. I've seen it over the years and lately in his debacle with his practice and partners, in his mercurial moods, with his temper, over-sensitivity to perceived criticism, and anger just under the skin. Maybe it's time Rick saw a therapist too.

As the evening progressed, we spoke more, even thawed out to a kind of "situation normal," but we never spoke about the vanilla elephant in the room.

Because I had given up taking the initiative on this one, I knew we never would.

THERAPY TAKEAWAYS:

Dr. P's suggestions for what to say given our recent dysfunctional encounters:

- "I'm glad we could talk about this. Thank you."
- "I hear you are upset. Help me understand?"
- I should have asked, "Do you want my help finding some vanilla?" Or "Would you like me to help you look?"

THINGS TO REMEMBER:

- We don't understand each other's viewpoints. Neither one is right. The truth is somewhere in the middle, *and "right" is not the objective anyway.*
- I am the one in our relationship who is the catalyst for initiating change and growth. I can piss and moan about it, or I can accept it.

ABOUT THAT BATTLEPLAN TO VISIT THE YMCA:

I made myself turn my car in, park, and walk into the gym. With a deep breath, feeling like I was about to step in front of a bus, I told the lady at the desk I was thinking of joining but needed to try and see it first. "I'm pretty insecure," I admitted. "Could you help me?"

She said, "We have a seven-day free pass, but I don't have access to that here. You'll need to print that yourself and bring it back in."

I inhaled before letting out a sigh. I spoke as a timid child—wide-eyed and innocent, "You mean I have to go all the way back home and print the coupon and then come all the way back?"

"Yes," she said politely, having no idea why I would have a problem with it. Had she never met an exercise-averse neurotic before? I contemplated this and decided I would start fresh on Thursday. Navigating highway traffic two extra times in one day, and this late in the day at that, simply was not happening. So I thanked her and told her I'd return. I just didn't say when.

WEDNESDAY, MARCH 17, 2010 - IT'S NOT ABOUT THE VANILLA

I'm starting to love the time Rick and I have in the hour-and-a-half drive in the car on the way to Suwanee. Yes, even last week, when I was hearing things I didn't want to hear, it was still a time when we were together without distraction and trying our best to communicate and understand each other.

It would hold true on this day, as well.

Armed with my new bag of tricks from yesterday's therapy session, I was ready when the question came. "How was your session with Dr. P yesterday?"

I started carefully. "I want you to know, first, that my sessions with him are not spouse assassinations. It's not about throwing you under the bus. It's about learning what's helpful and not helpful with our interactions and trying to change them. I need to ask you if you want to work on that with me and make things different."

Rick nodded. "Yes."

"So," I continued, "our learning how to change things through therapy is going to have to happen one of two ways: Either I take the lessons and bring them back and share them with you, or you go with me."

"I can't go with my schedule," he said quietly. "You'll have to bring them back."

"OK. Then here's where we must start: We must first agree, you and I, on a basic premise in order to go forward. We must agree that we love each other, and when our interactions go south, we do not intentionally mean to hurt one another. Do you agree with that?"

Rick was nodding now with sincere purpose. "Yes," he said emphatically, "absolutely."

"Me too," I said softly. "We are having problems communicating. When things aren't going well, neither one of us is to assume we are right, and the other is wrong. The fact is that we are both a combination of right and wrong. And further, being right or wrong is beside the point. The goal is to figure out the bigger picture. And so when things go downhill, we must agree to stop the madness by disconnecting from the moment and connecting with the bigger picture—what's really going on. Sunday was not about the vanilla. Any time we get bent out of shape, so completely out of proportion, it's a sure bet it's not about the particular thing but something else.

Our goal is to figure out what that something else is. That may not happen right away."

Rick took it all in and then spoke quietly. I had the sense to shut up and give him his time. "It has taken me days to figure this out," he began solemnly and sincerely, "but that vanilla thing on Sunday would have been different if I hadn't lost the patient I saw the night before. A woman brought an animal in on Saturday for an emergency visit, saying it was having difficulties, but when I saw it, I couldn't find anything wrong. The animal was behaving normally. I did a full exam—nothing. I sent it home. But when I called the next day to give her the lab results, she told me it had died. Whatever the problem was, I missed it." Rick's eyes were brimming with tears, his lips tight, the pain registering on his face.

Now, we were getting somewhere.

I was hurting for him, but it was also a balm on my soul to hear him speak so honestly from his heart.

"Thank you so much for telling me," I said, overflowing with love and relief as tears came to my eyes too. "I can't tell you how glad I am you are talking about this with me. I'm so proud of you. This must be so painful. You are a really, really good vet. You care so much. And you lost one. Nobody bats one-hundred percent—not even Dr. House on TV."

He smiled. We talked about it for a long while.

"It's really difficult emotionally, to be a vet," Rick said. "Imagine the emotion going from one room where you just put down a beloved family pet to the next room where excitement is in the air over a brand-new puppy. Being able to deal with grief and sudden, great joy is like emotional whiplash. I will either drive myself bonkers with what I cannot manage, or I will accept what I cannot change, change what I can, and learn the wisdom to know the difference."

We were on our way.

WEDNESDAY, MARCH 24, 2010 — TWO DOCTORS AND ANOTHER GIFT

There I sat this morning in a small, cramped area of my family doctor's waiting room—six chairs jammed together arm-to-arm against the wall in groups of three at right angles to one another with the obligatory low table in the corner. A woman and her toddler approached, finding a seat in the chair on the end of my row. The little girl was darling, quiet, and well-behaved. Her hair was partitioned into sections—each one gathered tightly and encased in clear beads, strung together like pearl necklaces. She wore jeans and a pink, ruffled top and sneakers. Her mother—a heavy-set woman, shrouded in dark clothing and a bulky jacket—sank into the chair, bowed her head, and leaned forward with elbows on her knees and her head in her hands, completely covering her face. The woman was obviously distressed as she wiped tears away quietly. Her body language left nothing to the imagination. It said very plainly, *Leave. Me. Alone.* The little girl was doing her best to wait patiently, but toddlers will do what toddlers do, which is to do something at all times. She sensed her mother's distress and asked sweetly, "What wrong w'you, Mommy?"

The more the mother ignored her, the more her daughter demanded her attention. After the little girl's third inquiry, the mother pleaded with her, talking low and slow through the hands still cradling her head, "Please. Leave. Me. Alone."

I scanned the area for entertainment options. On the table were only two magazines: a copy of *Lifestyles* and a six-month-old *Good Housekeeping*; the only other item on the table was a plastic holder filled with pamphlets about healthcare—not exactly kid friendly.

I stood and walked around the corner, looking at the rest of the large, communal waiting room. There it was: a children's area with a few manipulatives that looked promising. I retrieved one and brought it back to our little section, placing it on the floor in front of the little girl. It was a wooden box with things to explore on each side—geared wheels to spin, colorful, swirly metal rods upon which beads and buttons slid back and forth and all around, rows of twirly wood rectangles imprinted with letters of the alphabet and a corresponding image. The little girl was a moth to the flame. She lit up and started spinning the geared wheels before quickly settling on the alphabet blocks. Turning them on their stiles, she stopped one and pointed to the image on the "P" block.

I said, "What is that?"

To my everlasting surprise and joy she looked up at me, smiled, and replied softly, "Panda."

"Yes!" I replied quietly, smiling at her, "That's right!" We continued to play that way for five or six more letters until I was finally called inside to see the doctor.

So this was my gift. I realized in that moment that I am getting better. I had come out of myself and extended a kindness. I had cared for a couple of strangers by helping each one in a small way to ease their pain. I was reminded I do, indeed, have compassion, thoughtfulness, and the ability to contribute to those outside of myself. In doing so, I was healing myself too. God, that felt good. It was such a small, simple gesture, but it was such a large gift—for all three of us.

Inside the exam room, it was my turn to be cared for. I told my doctor, "I've been in the deepest, darkest depression of my life. I'm seeing a therapist, and I'm coming out of it. Now, I want to lose the weight. And you know what they say: 'Consult your doctor before beginning an exercise program.'" He was kind and affirming. Once I am cleared for takeoff, I will get my sweet ass to that YMCA. I plan to make myself get into that pool.

THERAPY TAKEAWAYS:

The way one lives life is a conscious choice: You can surrender to anxiety and depression if, and when, they present themselves, or you can acknowledge them and move on through them.

Sometimes, people need medication to help them execute the choice, but it's the choice that must be made first.

Dealing with real life means occasional depression and anxiety, but "everything in moderation" is a great yardstick.

There has been no moderation for the last few years—school was full-bore, aforementioned husband and kids' problems, health problems, and constant anxiety for four straight years. After that, exhaustion.

Like I said, I tried to take a well-earned, two-week vacation, and it has turned into a now three-year depression. I have had enough.

TUESDAY, MARCH 30, 2010

Dr. P: "Give yourself a timeframe to get something done. Create deadlines for the stuff you want to do."

I pissed and moaned my way through my session today about how I still wish I woke up feeling more motivated with more desire to do things. What I have come to decide now is I cannot wait for the feeling. I must decide on something to do. Just. Do. It. That's what healthy grownups do. They are responsible. They resign themselves to do things they don't necessarily like doing in order to get the things they want. I remember being that person. I want to be, and I will be her again.

Tomorrow, we have a cookie baking day. I will rise. I don't have to shine, but I will do the job for the day. Then, on Thursday, I will rise and get myself to the YMCA to sign up. I am committed. I will do this. It is a decision. It is my decision.

THERAPY TAKEAWAYS:

- I have learned so much on this journey.
- Feel the fear and do it anyway.

TUESDAY, APRIL 27, 2010 - A CHANGE OF SCHEDULE

I went to therapy today without my laptop. What??? Yep, I entered the session feeling strong and decisive. Notes not required. My idea: stretch out my sessions to one every four weeks. Why? This is expensive. I'm feeling better. It's time. Dr. P agreed. Rock on!

My goals between now and then are to watch my diet and add some physical activity. I am starting small: gardening, just moving. Adding the gym will come once I've lost a bit more weight and can tolerate the workout.

WEDNESDAY, MAY 12, 2010 - FINALLY, LETTING GO

Kitchen day. I finally remembered to take my iPod with a speaker gizmo. It made the scintillating task of scooping endless dough balls onto baking sheets for hours on end much more tolerable. One exception, however: I had a here-we-go-again emotional moment. I selected my "classical mix" and listened to a beautiful soprano singing the Schubert "Ave Maria," Bernstein's "A Simple Song," and "In Trutina" from Orff's *Carmina Burana*. The pain washed over me quite suddenly when I instinctively tried to hum along for a few bars, reminding me my voice is gone. GONE. Jesus, not this torture again. I instantly saw myself standing in front of an audience (There were so many audiences.), singing so confidently, expressively, and beautifully. At that moment, the grief I keep locked away snuck out. I felt a rush in my head as my stomach flipped, eyes watered, and heart physically hurt.

The truth was in my face yet again, and it was unbearable. I have lost my voice. I am no longer beautiful in that way. The music that once poured out of me is no more.

I finally accept it now. It's a conscious decision to accept it. I cannot wait for my feelings to convince me. I will revisit this torture no more. It is finished. But I think it's okay to say I miss the magic and always will.

TUESDAY, AUGUST 9, 2010

I've lost thirty-four pounds since my highest weight ever back in February. That groove is firmly in place now, and it feels really swell.

Rick and I are talking, but it's not just that—we're communicating. He and I are cherishing our talks together. Gone is his need to lash out. Gone is my need to feel sorry for myself and hide. Gone is the emotional armor both of us wore. It's been replaced with true openness, gentleness, and willingness to reveal what we're really feeling and what's really happening. His profession has called on him to ride on a fast-moving emotional seesaw. Giant, arcing, dizzying ups and downs come quickly—sometimes only moments apart, many times a day. Rick's defense mechanism of shutting down becomes rote and tiresome. Too many veterinarians experience burnout and depression. Some even kill themselves. It's a harder profession than most people realize. So all during this emotional time, Rick put on his armor and couldn't take it off when he got home. Now, because we are working hard, Rick brings his thoughts and fears and feelings home, we talk about them, and he feels better. So do I. Now when there is a conflict, whether professional or personal, we can admit what went wrong and what we can do better the next time. Thanks be to therapy—and grace.

We're all hit. It's what we do with it that matters.

———

TUESDAY, FEBRUARY 16, 2021

Well, here we are kids—a decade-plus later. I want to finish where I left off on August 9, 2010.

My therapist, Dr. P, moved on to another journey—sort of an *Eat, Pray, Love* adventure as I gathered. I was ready by then to fly and find another therapist to see only on occasion.

My therapy appointments with my new doctor are only fifteen to thirty minutes once every six months now—mainly just for tune-ups and prescription refills.

I'm still on my medication and probably always will be. Brain chemistry is a thing. Depression is real. Life is good now, and I'd like it to stay that way.

I swam every day at the "Y" for a good long while until I strained my back and quit altogether. Apparently, like spelunking, I'm not built for swimming, either.

I had total knee replacement surgery in 2018, and Rick took two entire weeks off work to care for me, doing a damn fine job. He knew then he would semi-retire because he enjoyed staying home with me. I was delighted, and so was he.

Rick and I went on after our rough patch to not only survive that season but crush it. Therapy was a game changer, of course, and as we continued to practice what we learned, we learned how to practice it. We continued to let go of demons and we communicated. As a result, Rick and I are closer than ever. We have always loved each other and were both lost for a while in a dark place, but we were worth the struggle and the perseverance it took to exit that place. We were blessed with what I can only say is a final moment of grace. We got better and better over the years, but the pinnacle of our personal renaissance came during the sudden loss of two of Rick's friends' wives and the occasion of my fiftieth high school reunion. It was a jolt that electrified us. Out of nowhere—or maybe as some cosmic, beatitudinal, *gratia plena* for all our hard work—grace flew in and finished sweeping us both clean. It renewed us and imbued us with deeper gratitude for life and love for one other, greater than we have ever known.

We cherish each day as never before.

In August of 2011, the cookie business died a natural death after we finally admitted we were not then, nor would we ever, have a successful venture with a product that brings us zero monetary profit. Rick and I were also tired of lugging tents to markets in the heat and the freezing cold. Our little venture, while a financial failure, had been a boon in its own way by giving Rick his lifeline to his clients and making lots of people happy with his veterinary care and our delicious cookies.

I never sold the rest of those diva dresses, and yes, they are back in the closet. They'll tell me what to do with them when the time is right. So far, they've been silent. And they've lost all their power, anyway. I just don't care anymore.

I still go up and down with my weight, (thanks, especially to the year-long pandemic) but I am no longer tortured. At my height, I have no need to be a size two. I'm pretty sure I'll never see a size twelve again. I will lose my pandemic pounds eventually when I'm good and damn ready.

Rick and I aren't particularly proud of some of our behavior during our darkest times, but I share it so others can find hope and perhaps see themselves in parts of it and know there is hope when the trees are too close to see the forest.

I asked Rick if he was okay with my including this journal since it puts both of us in in a very poor light at times.

"It's okay," he said.

"But it makes us look like assholes," I whined.

"I was!" Rick countered with a laugh.

"Me too!" I confessed.

It's honest. It's real. And still scares the hell out of me to share it.

It's how we learned, however, the only way out is never circular but straight through the difficult, messy, goddamn middle.

Feel the fear and do it anyway.

Dogs

THE POWER OF THE DOG

Rick's favorite poem

There is sorrow enough in the natural way
From men and women to fill our day;
And when we are certain of sorrow in store,
Why do we always arrange for more?
Brothers and sisters, I bid you beware
Of giving your heart to a dog to tear.
Buy a pup and your money will buy
Love unflinching that cannot lie
Perfect passion and worship fed
By a kick in the ribs or a pat on the head.
Nevertheless it is hardly fair
To risk your heart for a dog to tear.

When the fourteen years which Nature permits
Are closing in asthma, or tumour, or fits,
And the vet's unspoken prescription runs
To lethal chambers or loaded guns,
Then you will find - it's your own affair, -
But ... you've given your heart to a dog to tear.

When the body that lived at your single will,
With its whimper of welcome, is stilled (how still!),
When the spirit that answered your every mood
Is gone - wherever it goes - for good,
You will discover how much you care,
And will give your heart to a dog to tear!

We've sorrow enough in the natural way,
When it comes to burying Christian clay.
Our loves are not given, but only lent,
At compound interest of cent per cent,
Though it is not always the case, I believe,
That the longer we've kept 'em, the more do we grieve;
For, when debts are payable, right or wrong,
A short-time loan is as bad as a long -
So why in - Heaven (before we are there)
Should we give our hearts to a dog to tear?

– Rudyard Kipling

DONATELLO

Donatello was in trouble. It was the dead of winter in 1998. It was snowing and had been for several days. He lay in the backseat as his owner drove into the parking lot of Rick's veterinary clinic and parked her luxury car.

In the treatment area down the hall Rick could hear the receptionist utter a loud whisper all the way up at the front desk. "Is that a Jaguar?" She was looking out the window as the dog's owner ushered Donatello out of the backseat and through the front door.

As soon as the lady pulling on Donatello's leash brought him into the lobby, all attention was on the dog. He hobbled in on three legs, holding his right front leg up. His lower leg was bright red, bloody, dripping, and raw. The owner was sophisticated with perfect hair. Multiple shiny gold bracelets clanged together on her slender forearm as she brushed off wet snowflakes and a few dog hairs from her designer suit. Donatello hung his head as he whimpered in pain. His fur smelled like wet wool. And why not? He had the long, luxurious coat of a magnificent Afghan Hound, who at this moment was sopping wet, utterly bedraggled, shivering, matted, miserable, and anything but magnificent.

The woman volunteered her name, Judith Smithson, and explained breathlessly that her dog had just gotten his leg caught up in a chain, and she had brought him in as soon as she found him. He gazed upward, his dark, eyes squinting as he continued to whimper. The front desk staff audibly gasped. A technician took the leash, gently ushering the dog to the back while the receptionist got paperwork from the woman. The woman gave the receptionist her business card with her contact information, indicating she was a psychiatrist.

The technician brought Donatello to the treatment table where two vets took a closer look and shook their heads. "Dear Lord. He will need to stay with us for extended treatment. This is really bad. I don't know if we can even save this leg, but we will do our best. This dog is a sweetheart. What's his history?" Rick queried the vet tech.

"Owner says he got a chain wrapped around his leg, just recently," the tech sighed, both hands curling her fingers into air quotes, "and she brought him in as soon as she found him. Riiight," the tech said in a sardonic tone. The tech knew as well as Rick did this was no one-time, recent wound. The fresh, dripping blood may have been from the dog's encounter with a chain that very day, but there was plenty of damage too extensive to have been accomplished just this once. "So the woman said 'Do whatever needs to be done. Anything, anything for Donatello.' And now she is leaving the building."

Outside, the front-desk staff heard the sturdy, padded thud of an expensive car door closing and the purr of a fine-tuned engine. Judith was gone.

On examination, multiple areas of Donatello's lower leg had pressure necrosis so severe he was in danger of losing his leg. This was definitely not a fresh wound. Much longer without treatment, and Donatello could've died. It took two months for him to recover at the clinic after rigorous rehab, including daily antibiotics, pain medication, bandaging, debridement, and a lot of love. Thanks to excellent care, Donatello kept his leg, and when he had recovered sufficiently, it was time to go home. His eyes were big and bright now; his thick fur clean and dry, shaved, and groomed. Nobody was happy about returning him to Judith, his abuser. The employees at the clinic had bonded with him and he with them. There was talk of not returning him and filing charges.

Happily for everyone, and best of all for Donatello, he was not returned to her. When it came time to contact her, Judith had gone radio silent. AWOL. Calls to the number on her business card went unanswered. The clinic checked with the police for possible missing persons reports, and the mystery was solved. She was in custody, in the hoosegow—the county jail—for fraud.

The woman had said she was a psychiatrist. Sure looked like one with that fancy car, fancy clothes, and fancy dog. "Judith" was a straight-up con artist. We discovered she had five or six aliases and as many false credit cards. She also passed bad checks. As a matter of fact, she wrote a bad check when she purchased Donatello. Judith traveled and wasn't home a lot. Her neighbor said the woman had a habit of tying up the dog outside on a chain while she was away. For quite a while. Even in the snow. The con artist was buying the house she'd been renting, and when her check bounced, the owner charged her with fraud. Inside the house was a grand piano and two brand new water heaters—both purchased with bad checks. Nothing else.

That evil woman had made the colossal mistake of abusing an animal, one of the sweetest, most beautiful dogs in the world at that. *Not on our watch, lady, not on our watch.* The clinic filed an abandonment letter addressed to the owner at the Coweta County Jail. Rick took possession of Donatello and brought him home.

When one brings a new dog home, there's always an initial adjustment period. There was already another younger dog in residence which we feared might be an issue, but the two dogs got along from the first howdy-do. They couldn't have been more different—Donatello with his elegant, blond mane, and royal agency compared to Jack (AKC registered, "That's a Fact Jack") who was our midnight-black Labrador that hunted fields with Rick, flushing pheasants and quail like a pro. Jack knew instinctively how to zigzag expertly in the wind, working the scent, narrowing it down to a central focus, pursuing his winged prize until his master could take the shot. Sometimes he circled like a cinnamon roll. Sometimes he flew straight forward—an ebony missile shot out of a cannon. Whatever he did, Jack did it with singular purpose and intent. Rick prized and adored him. Jack returned the love with a dog's unbridled devotion for his master.

Donatello's breed as a Sighthound, originally from Afghanistan, should have qualified him as a fast-running hunter too. However, after years of breeding selectively for hair coat and temperament rather than hunting talent, Donatello would become a modern companion animal and not a pursuer of prey. No longer a hunting dog, Donatello was a sweet, loving pushover. He even let the housecat whip his ass. While Jack toiled dutifully in the field with Rick, Donatello accompanied me in the garden and lay serenely, quietly on the grass at my side as I worked the soil, planted flowers, and pulled weeds. His previous owner had given him his name, and we kept it because he was used to it. The name fit him though. Donatello was truly a refined beauty, worthy of the name.

Donatello knew he was safe and loved. He was right at home—comfortable from the get-go. But we had never had a dog his size in our home. He was massive. Not as brawny as Jack, Donatello was leaner, taller, and longer. His feet were round, over-sized string mops. Sitting in a regular desk chair, I could look him straight in the eyes when he stood facing me nose to nose. He was sweet and affectionate. And heavy. Unaware of his magnitude, one horizontal stride forward ensconced him effortlessly on the sofa, head nuzzled in my lap, barrel-chested body stretched across the entire length of the cushions. What was once a four-person sofa became a two-person loveseat. Me and him. Once in position, Donatello was immovable. There was no getting up on my part, either. Pinned to the sofa, I was happily comforted by his warmth and mutual affection. He was one with that sofa, as though it gave him his cosmic life force. Years later, when his sofa went into our yard sale, he sat on it faithfully and resolutely in the driveway until someone bought it.

Every night, Donatello slept soundly between Rick and me in our king-sized bed. Inevitably, someone woke up each morning balanced at the precipice, on the last inch of mattress, having ceded a large area of prime real estate in the center to Donatello as he stretched his muscular legs and pushed us aside during the night. Jack stayed close too, but he preferred to curl up on the floor on Rick's side of the bed, for which I was grateful. One sheet-stealing, bed-poaching canine was enough.

Donatello loved us immediately, just as we loved him. But it wasn't long before he showed some insecurities.

Rick took him out on a Sunday morning for a walk down the driveway to get the newspaper. When Rick picked up the rolled paper, Donatello immediately backed away afraid, pulling hard on the leash and whimpering. We knew then his con-artist owner or perhaps a bad boyfriend had also abused him in other ways.

A morning shortly after that, one of our sons arrived at home wearing a camo cap and shirt, which sent Donatello into a frenzy, barking, growling, and showing his teeth. We checked "box number two": The abusive boyfriend must have worn camo. Once Donatello got past his initial reflexive terror and recognized our son inside that camo, he calmed down and was fine.

We checked "box number three" when Donatello snapped at strangers approaching him directly, getting too near without giving him time to acquaint himself. If they reached a hand out to pet him too quickly or too soon, Donatello considered that an invasion of his space, assuming it was a move to abuse him, we conjectured, like the boyfriend of his past had so aptly taught him every time he struck him. It would take time and patience and an abundance of love to heal this dog's emotional wounds. Fortunately, we had all three.

Funny thing, though: When gay friends of ours came to visit, there was none of the barking, snarling, fear, or backing away. Donatello greeted them immediately with a waggy tail and a distinct body language, signaling total acceptance and affection. After that discovery, Donatello had a new nickname: "Stud Finder." We can't definitively explain his talent, but if you believe dogs can smell ethereal essences we humans cannot—fear, illness, evil, goodness, love, acceptance—we would agree.

The years were good with Donatello. I joked that snuggling with him—his muzzle resting on me, and my arm draped over his warm body stroking his fur—was better than a date. He loved to relax on the flat top of a grassy slope in front of our house, in majestic repose like one of the iconic lions, Patience and Fortitude, flanking the entry to the New York Public Library. He was blonde and beautiful, regal, and resplendent in the sun, situated atop his verdant plinth at the Berta House. The neighbors used to comment on his stately beauty after they drove by and saw him there.

As the years passed, Donatello did what dogs always do. He aged, weakened, and eventually died. In 2003, he was lying on our kitchen floor as he let out his last breath. I sobbed as I draped myself over him, burying my face in his fur.

A mere two hours later, I had to dress up, put on makeup, drive to a church, and face a different kind of music. As a professional soloist, I had been hired to sing "Ave Maria" at a wedding that very afternoon. It was too late to cancel. They had paid me well, and I had an obligation. Sometimes being an adult sucks, but we do what we must do. I did it. But goddammit. That was hard.

I still have Donatello's bright red collar and metal tag. It's affixed permanently now around the neck of a cute, brown and white spotted papier-mâché dog I bought at an art sale and brought home. It was love at first sight because the paper dog touched my heart and made me smile, even laugh out loud. Still does. He is an anatomically correct, expertly crafted, three-dimensional, irreverent beagle-sized pup who is hiking his left rear leg in mid-pee. We named our adopted, urinating yard dog Buster. It would be impossible to find Donatello's equal—real or not—and I didn't want to anyway. Too painful.

Buster stands guard at the entrance to our formal living room looking like a Georgia yard dog instead of a New York Library lion. He wears the classy, red collar, though.

I smile, reverently, every time I walk by.

JUNIOR

Heading his truck out of the parking lot at Bubba Doo's World-Famous Burgers and Oil Filters in Luthersville toward his next call in Grantville, Rick heard the pager in the truck cab buzz to life, interrupting his lunch midchew. Rick placed the partially eaten Bubba Doo burger on the bench seat, stopped, turned around, parked, and went back inside to place a call, still chewing. Finding a phone was the only way to communicate then. It was still in the early years of Rick's new, large-animal practice, and a mobile radio like the one he had grown accustomed to at the equine practice in Virginia was not in our fledgling budget just yet.

As a newly minted, solo practitioner starting out on his own in 1977, the truck, fancy fiberglass veterinary insert in the truck bed, his equipment, pharmaceuticals, and supplies were the limit. The extra bedroom at home would have to do as an office for a while. And I, the ever-supportive wife and new mother, would serve as jack of all trades: secretary, accountant, telephone operator, office manager, wonder-mom, and wife in charge of the domestic home fires, cooking, cleaning, diapering, and bottle washing. All for zero pay.

Rick dialed home, still chewing. "Yep, it's me. What's up?"

"Hi," I said, smiling. "You eating something?"

"Why yes, how could you tell?" His mouth was full, and he was displaying the slightest tone of impatience mingled with a good-natured attempt at humor. Rick swallowed with a gulp, cleared his throat and said, "I'm enjoying a gourmet lunch. And I'm also on my way to see a cow at Mike and Debbie Smiths' place in Grantville. What do you need?"

"Howard Hurley just called you with an emergency request."

"Mm, mm" Rick mumbled, "so what does a small-animal vet want with me?"

"Doc Hurley said his client's German Shepherd just limped home with a leg-hold trap on his leg. The owner tried to take the trap off, and the dog bit the hell out of him."

"Ohhh . . . Do I really want to hear what's next?" Rick asked.

"Probably not, but here it is. Howard wants to know if you'd go out there and take that trap off the dog's leg ASAP. Their name is Jackson. They live in the parsonage next to the Methodist church in Roscoe where he's the minister."

So young, naive, and feeling a rush of adrenaline mixed with concern for a dog in an emergency pickle, Rick hurried back to his truck and nosed it in the direction of Roscoe. Finishing his rapidly cooling Bubba Doo burger, he drove the twenty extra miles out of his way to the small, pastoral community north of town.

"Hey there, Mrs. Jackson," Rick greeted the woman standing on the porch as he parked in the drive and got out. "I'm Doctor Berta," he said, introducing himself, "I understand you have an emergency. Your dog caught in a leg trap? And I hear somebody got bit. Hope it's not too bad."

"Yessir, Doc Berta," she replied, blowing out fast breaths. "My husband did. Last I saw him, he was holding a bloody paper towel to his arm and hightailing it to the hospital. So here I am with our poor dog. I sure do thank you for coming. No way I could get Junior in the car and over to Doc Hurley's office. He said this problem was above his pay grade anyway and you'd know what to do."

Rick couldn't decide whether to laugh or cry over being anointed the sacrificial practitioner risking his limbs and livelihood for another vet's client. But it was about the animal. And the owner was a man of God, after all. Rick couldn't refuse on those terms. He found the dog lying on the porch whimpering with a large metal trap clamping down on his leg. In his inimitable way, Rick began calming Junior. He approached slowly, speaking in a soothing voice. In his closed hand, he hid a roll of gauze.

"It's OK, Junior-boy, we're gonna make you better," he intoned, low and slow. Junior was still snappy and fractious. He almost caught Rick's arm a time or two with his long, sharp teeth, but eventually the dog calmed down enough to allow Rick to wrap the gauze gently around his snout as a makeshift muzzle. From his shirt pocket, Rick pulled a syringe he had already filled with sedative. With a firm grip on Junior's collar, he inserted the needle subcutaneously in the dog's shoulder.

"Night-night, bud," Rick whispered, as sweetly as a dad tells his son goodnight. "Sweet dreams. Let's get this trap off you."

Rick explained to Mrs. Jackson that the hardest part of removing a leg-hold trap was first getting hands on the animal. Second, the removal involved knowing the right technique. Rather than pulling on the trap, which is instinctual but also ineffective, the correct thing to do is to step on the trap's lever to release it. Demonstrating, Rick stepped, and the trap popped open—and lo, the angels of the Lord shone round about him. The trap was removed, and Junior's leg was free at last!

"Oh Praise the Lord!" Mrs. Jackson sighed as she expelled a long breath of relief.

Rick thought: *The Lord only gets half credit for this, but okay.*

He charged Mrs. Jackson thirty-five dollars for his trouble. Rick had been a valiant vet who delayed his day to save a dog's leg and was feeling virtuous. Leaving to go to his original call, Rick was behind schedule, though, hoping to finish his day before the moon and stars came out. Even so, he felt good about himself because he had, after all, done a good deed.

Dr. Hurley called Rick later at home.

"Want to thank you for all you did to help my client and Junior. I had no idea how to get that trap off, and I don't make house calls either," Howard admitted. "Really appreciate your willingness to go out of your way."

"Thanks, Howard. It put me behind, and I was late the rest of the day, but I was glad I could help a minister and his wife and their poor pup," Rick said, sincerely. "So what happened after they brought Junior in to see you once I left?"

"Good thing he was still sedated," Howard said. "He's a big boy. I had to take some X-rays, then put a cast on, and give him antibiotics."

Rick knew better than to ask, but he did it anyway. He was curious, as he had only charged the Jacksons a small fee for the favor of detouring his day for a non-client and risking injury from an angry, snapping small animal in pain.

"How much did you charge him, Howard?" Rick asked.

"I let him off pretty easy," Howard laughed, "I had pity on the guy, so I only charged him one-hundred and fifty bucks."

Rick spit his coffee back into his cup. "Well you did good, Howard!" Rick laughed. So did Howard.

Rick hung up the phone and thought about his day. Howard had taught him a valuable lesson. Valiant deeds are well and good, but one also needs to know his own worth and what it takes to pay the bills. Rick knew to his core that a good heart and a sacrifice now and then have value and their own rewards as well. Not that Howard had overcharged—quite the contrary. Dr. Hurley was an excellent, business-savvy vet with overhead and bills to pay too. Rick had no problem with Howard's fee structure and understood full well that Howard had also adjusted his price. Between large- and small-animal veterinarians, fees are relative.

Perhaps Rick and Howard both saw their adjusted fees to the preacher and his wife as a kind of tithe. A kindness. A sacrifice. That's the kind of vet Rick wanted to be. And that is exactly what he was and always has been. Kindness doesn't pay the bills, but it does come back to you in unpredictable ways.

As long as bills get paid, one need not want for luxurious things. They sell for pennies on the dollar at your estate sale anyway. I should know. At least that's Rick's motto. Most of the time, it's mine as well. I admit to some blatant bouts of recidivism on my part over past years, reviving bad spending habits at times that drove Rick to distraction. Yet he retains his sense of humor, and jokes that if it weren't for me and my decorating and gardening skills (and purchases), we'd probably be living in a plain, concrete block outbuilding on a dirt lot with no class or beauty whatsoever. Rick also says I would've picked a better color of tar paper for our shack. He knows the truth: That would happen over my dead body.

Kindness has always been Rick's option. I used to prod him to charge more, but he charged according to his conscience. To this day, he stays and talks with a client as long as necessary when he could choose to roll and stroll them in and out on a conveyor belt. Rick never pushes unnecessary treatments. He is fair and caring. There was and will always be a special place for Rick in the hearts of many, many clients, and of course, in mine forever.

SCHATZI AND AUGUST

We were fortunate enough to have a couple of sweet German Shorthaired Pointers in our lives—Schatzi and August. Schatzi was a beautiful gray and white brindle. August's coat was a dark, silky, liver color. We'd had them since vet school days when we lived in that corrugated sardine can along with my family's pup—a lovable little black and tan mutt named Perro. Spanish-speaking people should chuckle (or groan) over that clever name. We all lived in crowded harmony, as they were most assuredly beloved members of our family.

The dogs made the move with us to Virginia in 1975 and again back home to Georgia two years later. By 1982, Rick had established himself well enough to build his large-animal clinic. Nothing fancy, it was a metal Butler building on the corner of a wooded lot at the intersection of nowhere and nowhere else. Really, it wasn't that far out of the city limits—only about five miles. It just looked like it was.

When we built it in October of 1982, there was nothing there except a Georgia Forestry building down the road, a few other small storage facilities, and a concrete plant. We were, as they say, ahead of our time. About fifteen years later, the county would build the Coweta County Fairgrounds and Conference Center, which is a lovely building complex on eighty grassy acres on the other end of Pine Road to house large events like the county fair, summer camps, 4-H competitions, and horse shows. In 2021, it hosted 20,000 fans at an Alan Jackson concert to benefit our little town after the F4 tornado destroyed a swath of Newnan.

We needed Rick's new clinic building in '82, since I was pregnant and due to deliver in December. We finished it just in time to get the office out of our extra bedroom at home and turn it into a nursery. I was drywalling and painting right up to the clinic's grand opening in late November. My own, very personal maternal grand-opening celebration—complete with the ultimate neonatal, eight-pound door prize—came on December 1, when Nick was born.

One day, Rick was at the new Pine Road clinic and had both Schatzi and August with him. They were usually good about romping around outside and sticking close, but August was suddenly not present. She had disappeared. After calling her to no avail, Rick went looking. He searched behind the property, up through the woods, and into an area clear-cut for a power line. To Rick's horror, there she was, yelping, caught in a leg-hold trap. There was no permit medallion on the device, and the trap certainly did not belong to Rick. He quickly released August's leg, carrying her back to the clinic to dress her wounds.

Once he tended to his dog, Rick returned to the trap and smashed it with a sledgehammer. He wrote a note, placing it in a sealed baggie, and used a zip-tie to attach it firmly to the largest crushed fragment. It said that the sorry bastard had caught Rick's dog in his trap, and if he came back and Rick caught him, he would kill him. Nothing was heard from the trap owner again, and the broken pieces remained in place, untouched for a long, long time.

You do not want to hurt Rick's dog. Just don't.

Rick came home that day, carrying August in his arms, and he told me the story. He was fuming and hurting for her. After a while, Augie-dog was up and walking normally, chewing happily on a bone, and Rick had calmed down after having dinner and a couple of stiff, adult beverages. Rusty Nails (Scotch and Drambuie) have always been his go-to.

It was then he told me a joke—blame it on the Rusty Nails.

"Did you hear the one about the two raccoons, baby doll?" Rick said, smiling into his glass as he prepared to swig another sip. He was a bit tipsy by now but still coherent and only slightly impaired. Perhaps slightly anesthetized would be a more appropriate assessment.

"No," I said sweetly, "what is it?" I knew he was gearing up and there would be nothing I could say that would stop this joke. So I sat back and let him run with it.

"Well, there's a raccoon that's an Alabama fan and one that's a Georgia fan. They're strolling through the woods, and they both step into leg-hold traps at the same time. Now, they're trying to figure out what to do. They hear hounds coming. So Georgia says, 'Come on, Alabama, you gotta chew your leg off and get out of the trap!' Alabama replies, 'I can't do that, man! I just can't!' So Georgia chews his own leg off, frees himself, and heads down into the woods. At that moment, Georgia has a fit of conscience. 'I can't leave Alabama. I gotta go help him.' When he returns, he finds Alabama and says, 'Come on, man! You can do this! Chew your leg off!' Alabama replies, 'Hell, I've chewed three off and I'm still stuck!'"

Rick reared back in his chair and laughed so hard tears came to his eyes. I couldn't decide if I was appalled or amused, but I gave him a little chuckle, my eyes reflexively moistening too. I reached over to tenderly pat his knee. I decided that joke, as twisted and stupid as it was—along with his laughter and those tears—served as a much-needed release for him. It was an outlet and a cleansing of sorts, a way to wash away the anger and pain from the reckless deed of another human being who hurt an innocent dog—his dog.

Later, as we got in bed and turned out the lights, I held Rick close as we snuggled together. I told him he was a good man. I told him I was upset, too, about what happened and sorry he was hurting for our pup.

I also said, "But please don't kill anybody. I love you, and I need you—so does your family."

He said, "OK, babygirl, but I sure was mad enough that I wanted to."

Stroking his hair gently in the dark, I whispered, "I know, me too."

And just like that, Rick was asleep. I moved my arm from under his head, found his face in the dark, and kissed his cheek, finding it moist. It would be the last tear before he would wake in the morning refreshed and repaired. I knew, despite the raccoons' gruesome fate in the dopey joke he had told me the night before, Rick would never harden his heart to the real pain of real pets. It was the people who harmed them that worried me for him. Perhaps I needn't have worried about that, either, since wanting to kill and doing it are two different things.

There are other ways to deal with abusers without sacrificing one's aching soul to the devil. Beyond legal retribution, when there is nothing concrete left to be done, belief in Karma helps. Sharing your pain with your loved one, letting go, and kindness are the ultimate therapy.

GABI AND PORTER

My dear, longtime friend, Leanne, inherited her sweet Cocker Spaniel, Gabi, when Leanne's dad died. When Gabi came to her, the dog was already a young adult, not a puppy. Leanne doted over Gabi, who was an entirely deserving, dote-able dog in the first place. Gabi had big, bright, wet eyes that melted a person's heart. Always wagging, always happy, Gabi was sweet-tempered and adorable. She loved snuggles and running after the ball outside. She was everything a dog owner could want in their dog. She was also the last connection Leanne had to her dad. And she was loved commensurately—what a bond those two forged.

As part of her job, Leanne had to travel periodically, so I would sometimes keep Gabi at my house until she returned. Gabi was no trouble. She loved our house, Dr. Rick, and me. Rick was attentive to her, especially if she encountered any problems. Over the years, as she aged, Gabi did indeed begin to have problems. Thank goodness for the doctor in the house!

One sunny weekend afternoon, Gabi was enjoying herself in our backyard, running full tilt up and down the length of the grass chasing a ball while I sat on the garden bench watching her. Her coat glistened in the sun, ears and wisps of dark hair flying in the breeze as she extended her strong legs with every stride. Then, she pulled up short, stopping dead still after a quick, sharp yelp. I ran to her as she winced in pain. I called Rick to quickly join us outside. He ran out to us, took a quick look, and said, "I think she's torn her ACL. Cockers have this problem as they age." His face was stern. "But we can take her in and have a look-see. Call Leanne."

I placed the call. Leanne was, of course, worried for her pup, but she reassured us she trusted Rick and me implicitly to do the right thing.

There still is no fear like the panic one feels when they are babysitting a friend's child and the child gets hurt under their care. It was nobody's fault Gabi came up suddenly lame. But damn if it didn't weigh on me as though it was somehow in my power to prevent. Logic has nothing to do with the moment a child (or pet—same thing) is hurt. I felt so bad for everyone. Eventually, I calmed down and came into my senses once Rick took Gabi to the clinic, and I spoke with Leanne again. Gabi got the care she needed, and all was well.

As time went on, Gabi was declining as she moved into old age. Her eyes faded gradually, contracting glaucoma until she was blind. She could no longer hear. Leanne took the best care of her possible, spoiling her with homecooked meals, visiting specialists, purchasing expensive eye drops and other medications, and paying for surgeries. Gabi was a warrior, just like her mom, and held on through every single challenge. Eventually, the inevitable happened. Gabi lost control of her functions and the light in her eyes; while still alive, it was obvious she was ready to go.

Leanne raced from Atlanta to Newnan to deliver poor, fading Gabi to Dr. Rick's care. Leanne already knew what was coming, but if this was the end, she wanted it to be with dear friends and Gabi's beloved Dr. Rick in charge. I got the phone call from my tearful friend asking me to meet her at the clinic. I was in the car, driving across town, and standing by her side in the exam room in record time.

Rick confirmed Gabi was no longer there. Although she was breathing, it was time to let her go completely. It is horrifically painful for an owner to put a pet to sleep—just as it is also impossibly difficult for the vet to be the one to end a life. Rick never hardens himself. Each and every time when the injection is performed, his pain is palpable, his eyes moist, and his face grim. Leanne held Gabi in her arms after Gabi breathed her last and sobbed into her fur. I put my arms around Leanne and cried along with her. Rick left the room so he could compose himself and continue his job in the next exam room without falling apart.

———

It was much the same story with Porter, Rick's Brittany Spaniel. Porter was Rick's shadow since puppyhood. This dog had the natural instincts of a hunter, and Rick trained him to go hunting and chase the birds. Porter was a constant companion, even though he refused to retrieve. Rick joked about it, saying Porter could sniff out any quail and point like a pro, but forget about asking him to retrieve—not happening. Rick didn't hold it against the dog. They were fast buddies no matter what. Still, it would've been nice.

Porter had been something of a surprise—not that I didn't know we were getting a puppy. I had already witnessed Rick's long quest to find the right pup during long sessions on the phone with various people. When he told me he had finally found the right person, I was delighted to hear it. What Rick didn't exactly tell me was we would be acquiring the pup on the very same weekend as our son's destination wedding at the beach in '02. It was only after the wedding was done that Rick shared that detail.

Our friends had all departed, and I was ready to rest. Devoid of energy and purpose, I lay prostrate on a chaise, relaxing in the sun by the swimming pool at the rental house.

"I'm going to drive up to north Atlanta now and get the new puppy," he said. "I'll be back tonight."

I opened my eyes, barely able to even do that, while I shaded the sun with one hand. "What did you just say?" I mumbled. "I swear you said you're going to pick up a puppy. Now? Right now? But we're still in the middle of recuperating from the wedding. I'm exhausted! How can I have a new puppy running around too?" I whined. "And that's a twelve-hour drive round trip! Are you serious!?"

Never let common sense interfere with a man and his soon-to-be puppy.

"I can't help mother nature," Rick laughed. "The pups are exactly eight weeks, and I have to pick mine out now, today, or I won't get the one I want. Besides, I have some very concrete reasons. One of which is I must take my fishing boat back home to Newnan now so when I return to the beach, I can hitch up the eight-foot covered trailer I bought for all your plants. So after I drop off the boat in Newnan today, I'm just going to swing up to north Atlanta—Demorest to be exact—and pick up the puppy too. See, I have my reasons. I'll be back to the beach before you know it."

"Ok," I sighed, "but how do we get this puppy home? Our cars will be filled to the brim. Even the passenger seats will be full of stuff. Not another inch available for a dog crate—even a small one."

Rick winked, "He'll be tiny, sweet, sleepy, and adorable. You can keep him in your lap while you drive, can't you? And if you like, we can trade laps halfway. How 'bout it?"

At that point, I knew I was toast. I knew I would fall in love the moment Rick brought that little pup into the house, no matter how much I didn't want to. I also knew we would manage no matter what. By the time Rick returned to the beach with the new dog, he'd already named him "Porter" for Porter Springs, an exit on I-85 Rick had rushed past on his way to pick him up.

As infuriating as it was to be blindsided by the dog, it was in my best interest that Rick didn't tell me ahead of time. He did me a real favor by waiting because otherwise, I might have had to kill him and spoil the entire wedding. This way, I needed him to get everything back home, and I didn't have another ounce of fight left in me. As it turned out, Rick also did us both the greatest favor of all by bringing that sweet pup into our lives.

We had Porter for many years, and he was the sweetest, most loved, rusty-red and white-spotted pup in the world. We adored him, despite the buckets of white, wispy dog hair he left on the furniture and our clothes every day and the constant grit that was always underfoot on the hardwood floors, carried in on his paws after Rick took him for his runs out in the countryside.

When, after thirteen years, Porter contracted cancer—the kind that doesn't end well—it fell to Rick to put down his own dog. Oh Lord, no one should have that horrid task.

Right before Easter in 2015, Rick made the difficult decision that it was time. We silently loaded Porter into the car. I drove while Rick held him in his lap. I could see Rick as I drove, loving on Porter, holding him, petting him softly, and whispering words of comfort all the way to the same clinic where Gabi had met her final day—along with so many other clients' animals. Only this time, it was Porter's turn.

We arrived after closing time when no one else was there. Rick and I had peace and quiet for Porter on his last day. As tears rolled, Rick and I prepped him, and I gently stroked the fur on his head with my hand, telling him how we loved him so.

Rick took the syringe in hand, and without a word, he ended his dog's life. It was over. Porter's fur was wet with our tears. We wept. Porter was still. He was gone, set free.

There was a huge void in the house afterward—a painful, intractable silence. It's hard to explain how silence can echo so loud in a void where a living thing once occupied space and time. Rick still cannot speak of Porter without tears welling in his eyes. Such love for a dog.

Porter was our last and final dog. At this age, Rick says he doesn't want another dog he might have to abandon because it will outlive him. However, Scotty owns Porter's rusty-red and white long-haired Brittany doppelganger named Pilot, even though they're of no relation. Scotty purchased him as a pup from a different owner a couple of years before Porter left us. Porter functioned as a mentor to Pilot, teaching him the hunting ropes—with one exception. Porter, our non-retriever, could not teach Pilot to retrieve. Pilot would have to rely on instinct if he were to acquire that skill.

Pilot now satisfies Rick's need to run and hunt a dog. Rick always loved to watch the two dogs run full tilt—their coats shining, long hair rippling in the breeze, feathery white hairs on their legs and tails flying straight out. Even when they (and now, just Pilot) found stinking, dead things in the woods and rolled in them good and proper, they always returned energized, wagging, smiling, tongues hanging long, panting, and damn proud of their accomplishment. Rick would hoot over their rancid smell, expel a few expletives accompanied by a reflexive gag or two, followed by a hearty laugh, and then pile them in the back of the Jeep for home. He knew it was only a matter of some soap and water for them to be as good as new and ready for the next run. Wash, rinse, repeat.

It's the perfect scenario now: Grandpa Rick gets to play with the grand-dog, and then he takes him back home to his parents and the boys to enjoy and deal with all the dog hair and grit on their furniture and floors.

And the best news of all? Pilot retrieves like a pro.

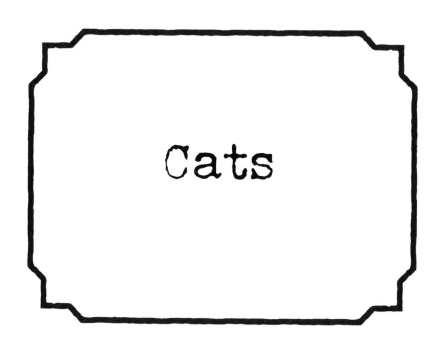

Cats

MRS. VANDERHOOP'S CATS

Mrs. Vanderhoop was a quirky, unassuming, chatty lady. In 2010, she began bringing in her cat—sometimes a couple of cats—for Rick to treat for one thing or another.

There were the occasional skin conditions or respiratory problems with Mrs. Vanderhoop's cats, but nothing out of the ordinary. She was very proud to be a cat rescuer, and so she often brought in new cats for treatment.

Rick was amazed at her dedication after hearing how she was fearless in her mission. Mrs. Vanderhoop would go anyplace to rescue a cat, even restaurant garbage bins where strays appeared, and she brought them inside her home to care for them. During Rick's exams, as she chatted away about anything and everything that came to her mind, she spoke often of her husband whom, she said, helped her with the cats; and her son, a young man in his early twenties who, incidentally, took ballet classes.

Mrs. Vanderhoop often hotly protested to Rick about how the girls in her son's ballet classes were too large, complaining that he had difficulty lifting them. "Maybe they were local farm girls," she conjectured, "drinking milk from the cows they treated with too many hormones, and that's why they were so hefty." Rick was often amused by her logic but too busy (or polite) to reply. But he always mentally filed them away in his "Things That Are Weird" file and shared them with me when he got home.

My thoughts? *Are oversized ballerinas a thing?* No sturdy, big-boned farm girl I can think of would aspire to show up as a ballerina in a room full of mirrors wearing pink satin shoes, size eighteen pink tights, and an XXL tutu. Please. Someone prove me wrong. Like I said, Mrs. Vanderhoop was quirky for sure.

Over time, however, there were some things happening that raised some BRFs (Big Red Flags) for Rick. Unwanted pregnancies in some cats shouldn't have been happening if Mrs. Vanderhoop had been separating the males from the females, getting them neutered, and doing all the right things rescue groups do with rescued cats. She was traditionally late for her appointments because she said she was always cleaning up after all the cats, which she said took a lot of time and effort. Then, Rick started seeing more respiratory problems, which is indicative of shelter problems. Mrs. Vanderhoop began bringing in more cats—new and younger animals that should not have been there as rescues. Her chats included more desperate personal stories of her woes which included her husband having moved away for an out of state job, leaving her with the care of the rescue cats.

What we didn't realize until later was that Mrs. Vanderhoop had so many cats she was taking all her cat litter and dumping it into the storm drain at the curb on her street in her subdivision. At one point, she complained because she had a broken water pipe in her house, and her husband, who had returned, was now living in the backyard in a tent. Her son was living in the garage. She bitched about how she couldn't get a plumber to come fix her broken water pipe. Rick hadn't quite grasped the magnitude of her obsession until then. He thought she had been rescuing cats and finding homes for them. As it turns out, Rick would soon discover she was keeping them all. Every last one.

Rick started seeing FIP—feline infectious peritonitis—in Mrs. Vanderhoop's cats, which signified there was a very big problem in her house. More and bigger BRFs. Just as Rick was addressing all this with her and delving into what exactly was going on, animal control officers descended on her with a surprise visit to her home. There had been multiple complaints, including those from neighbors *and her own husband.*

It was then, and only then, the whole horror story unfolded.

After entering Mrs. Vanderhoop's house, animal control found a mind-boggling number of cats—*two-hundred and sixty*—not all of whom were alive. The house was uninhabitable, filth and excrement everywhere. There were dead cats under sinks and inside cupboards. Some cats were so sick they had to be euthanized. Turned out the reason she couldn't get her pipes fixed was because the plumber wouldn't step foot in the house. Mr. Vanderhoop and his son were sick and tired of every square inch of their house being occupied by cats, living and dead, which explained the husband's tent in the backyard and the son living in the garage.

When animal control went through the house, our friend and veterinarian who worked with them was in attendance. She called us afterward.

"OK, you guys, I don't want to freak you out. The cats are scary enough but get this—Mrs. Vanderhoop has papered the wall of her garage staircase with the lids from the boxes you sell your cookies in. There must be at least twenty-five of 'em tacked to the wall."

My blood went cold. Our best customer, who had bought more boxes of our Rick & Susie's Scrumptious Little Ricotta Cookies than anyone else, was a cat-hoarding psychopath. We had thought maybe she was buying our boxes of cookies as gifts. Now, we wondered if she fed those cookies to her cats—or maybe to the ballerinas in her son's ballet class. We could only wonder why in the world she saw fit to tack the box lids with our labels to her garage staircase.

I could only assume Mrs. Vanderhoop was obsessed with Rick as well as her cats.

I had a sudden vision—it was like a standard scary movie plot where the disturbed weirdo is obsessed with a person and plasters pictures and clippings all over the walls of their secret hideaway. Our hapless hero, Rick, attempts to investigate and descends the dark, creaking stairs to the basement (Why do they always go down the stairs to the basement? Alone?). It's then he discovers a room located at the darkest, most remote spot in that basement. The door is cracked slightly. Slowly opening the creaking door to the room, Rick is shocked and terrified to see one single light bulb hanging from the ceiling, illuminating the mayhem covering every inch of wall space: paper clippings, photos of Rick, letters, old vet bills, maps to our house, crayon drawings of hearts and cats, cats, cats. Cue the sudden staccato violins. Then, Rick notices shelves of lampshades and vests and chaps sewn from leathered cat-skins with his name burned into the leather like a cattle brand. The camera zooms in on Rick's horrified face—pale and sweaty, eyes wide, mouth agape. Run, run, run away before the weirdo returns to kill you, Rick!! Annnd scene!

Of course, this did *not* happen, but I swear to God, it felt...Just. Like. That.

In reality, Mrs. Vanderhoop was indeed a troubled person—no doubt about it—and a cat murderer. What she needed was what she got: someone to find her out, turn her in, and get her out of that horrible situation. Rick had been close to uncovering Mrs. Vanderhoop's sickness but knowing her only through her clinic visits made it harder for him to see the big picture. He regrets he couldn't have seen through her sooner. We are thankful her family turned her in. She was clearly trapped and overwhelmed, having lost all perspective. Charges were brought against her, and we believe she paid some hefty fines and served some time, too, but don't quote me on that. After we recovered from the initial shock, Rick and I weren't concerned with following her punishment. We were happy it was over, and she was no longer doing harm.

We hope Mrs. Vanderhoop got help, and we believe she moved away, which, I'll admit, made us all sleep better at night. All I know is that one disturbed woman was stopped, and I hope to God she never rescues another living thing. Except herself if she hasn't already. That would work. I can only hope she did.

Little Surprises
&
Inside Stories

LITTLE SURPRISES AND INSIDE STORIES

2021

Rick tells me often about all the weird things animals eat that are, technically, inedible. So many foreign objects in their tummies or intestines make for a whole lot of sad critters, human headshaking, and emergency surgeries.

The animal usually presents with vomiting. Rick asks the owner if they are missing any items, toys, food, or objects—anything the animal might have ingested. Understandably, their reply is usually shoulder shrugs and "No idea." Pets have eaten underwear, pieces of towel, and round rubber balls from leftover birthday party favors. And that's just the short list. Whatever is lying around seems to be fair game. One poor dog ate a tube of expandable glue that made it into the stomach before expanding into a perfect mold of his organ. Surgery was successful, but what a chore. In another case, a cat ate twenty-one rubber hair ties, all of which were retrieved in surgery. Our dear friends even brought their sweet dog in because it had eaten the sand they dumped from their pool filter.

Every year, there are contests in the veterinary journals detailing the most bizarre ingestions by animals—knives, pieces of fiberglass, fishing line, fishing hooks, Popsicle sticks. Truly, these cases give meaning to "exploratory surgery." Yep, surgery awaits all these hungry little hippos.

One memorable case for Rick was Daisy—a sweet female beagle, fifty-days pregnant, who came in for an X-ray so the owner could see how many pups were to be delivered. In addition to Daisy's eight pups showing on the radiograph, she had what looked like floral wire in her stomach. Surprise! Delicate surgery would be required, but careful calculations were needed too. Rick had to calculate whether the pups would survive Daisy's abdominal surgery. If they did, could her incision hold during labor and pushing? Rick made the decision to operate, taking all the care possible.

Rick and his surgery techs masked Daisy down to anesthetize her. After making his incision revealing her abdominal cavity, they put wet lap pads soaked in normal saline all around her. To get to the stomach and the obstruction, Rick needed to move the burgeoning uterus full of pups out of the way. Ever so gently, as though they were handling a live explosive, they raised the dog's uterus completely outside the body and onto the wet pads. When they got into Daisy's stomach, they found their surprise: There was a floral wire as expected, but it was also wrapped around cloth connected by two elastic bungee-type bands to a stuffed animal. Once Rick removed the obstructions and stitched the stomach, they put everything back in place with all the puppies still alive inside the uterus.

Ten days later, Daisy had her puppies, and all was well. That makes a vet have very happy feet for sure. Rick's eyes tear up just recalling the tense surgery, his worry for the momma dog and her pups, and the happy outcome.

Rick has racked up so many of these stories over the years I've lost count. They're always fascinating—no matter the number— yet disturbing and ever puzzling. What possesses an animal to eat inedible things?

One evening, Rick barreled through our kitchen door after work— his voice strong and his face flushed. "Well, I got another one for the books, babe! Actually, this one should go in your book!" he declared, dropping his briefcase in the kitchen chair, dirty smock in hand and heading to the laundry room.

"Oh my," I smiled, "OK. I'm all ears."

He plopped down in the chair across from me, as I sat at my computer, like I do every day when I finally have some peace and quiet in the house. Grandchildren have been babysat and fed, picked up or dropped off, and chores done. I am finally alone and still have a few neurons left to fire and the energy to type.

"This really sweet dog came in today," Rick began. "History was sudden vomiting, but the owner couldn't offer any reason. The owner was pretty scruffy. Fella said he had very limited funds, offering as how he had just gotten out of prison."

With that, like a seasoned stand-up performer, he paused for my reaction. And, of course, I gave him one.

My chin jutted forward from my neck like a silly goose, and my eyes bugged open. "Do tell."

"Well, it's really quite un-funny, but I couldn't resist the Johnny Cash opener."

"So in addition to prison and a hound dog, is there a train, alcohol, a funeral, or a pickup truck in this story? How 'bout his momma?" I teased.

"No, but it sure is a curious mystery." He cleared his throat. "If I may . . ." He settled into the chair, ready to hold court.

"Please, Sherlock," I pleaded, "continue with your story of *The Case of the Ex-Con's Vomiting Dog.*"

"Well, he did, indeed, arrive in a beat-up Ford pickup, so you can check that box," Rick smiled. Returning to his concerned doctor-face, Rick went on. "The owner gave us a limited history on the dog and shrugged his shoulders, indicating he had no more insight to offer us. We decided to do some tests. Again, the client was concerned since he didn't have much money, but we did our best, discounting as much as we could—even finding him funds from a charitable group. After the X-ray showed little in the way of results, a barium swallow was indicated, which we performed."

"And what did that show?" I asked, curious.

Rick continued. "Wait for it. There were two perfectly smooth oval, balloon-like objects stuck in the intestine. We told him surgery would be his only option and quoted him the cost. It was at that point the man said he would pay us in cash for the tests, but he would take his dog elsewhere for surgery. So he pulled cash out of his pocket, handed the money to the receptionist, got his dog, and left."

"Wow, that's a pretty hasty exit," I puzzled. "Why?"

"Cost, mostly. I felt for him. And it was an emergency, remember. He said he could get it done cheaper elsewhere at a rescue place he knew in the next county. He told us he had taken the dog there once before and said that's what he would do now. We agreed the dog could wait long enough to go elsewhere, but only if he promised to go directly to the shelter and have the surgery."

"So you never got to find out what was inside the dog?" I sighed, disappointed.

"Well, not so fast, missy." Rick smiled. "After the owner was long gone, one of the vet techs took another look at the barium X-ray and said, 'Wow, those look like condoms. Is this dog a drug mule, perchance?'"

Again, I did my astonished-goose impression, mouth agape this time, slapping both hands on my knees. "Oh no, are you kidding me?"

"That had us going," Rick said. "The tech said before we let him go we should've called the K-9 drug police to come give our ailing patient a sniff, if such a thing was possible. Talking about the possibilities after the fact, we weren't at all sure a dog could smell drugs inside of another dog anyway. And that would've taken precious time the patient didn't have. We thought maybe someday we'll invite the police K-9 drug dog unit to give us a demonstration when we aren't having a real emergency. As soon as that idea came forth, it was squashed. We realized it would be impossible since we couldn't, in good conscience, provide another dog as a drug-mule guinea pig for demonstration purposes.

"Anyway, about an hour later, we called the rescue clinic where he took his maybe drug-mule dog to follow up on whether they did surgery and what they found."

Rick paused for dramatic effect.

"Well, out with it, man!"

"Wait for it," Rick said again, theatrically, "wait for it!" His face turned dark as he took a deep breath, stood, raised his finger, and pronounced in mock-Sherlockian over delivery, "It was . . . two hacky sacks!" He exploded with laughter.

Rick waited a beat, gathering himself and heaved a huge sigh of relief.

"And the dog is just fine! Case closed."

Rick reared his head back, lips stretched wide in a smile. "I'm SO glad for that dog, above all," he said. "I'm happy the guy took it somewhere that could help him for less money. We would've, too, if we could have. It was understandable from the money angle, and as it turned out, he clearly cared for his dog. Our suspicions were totally unwarranted."

"See," I admonished, "that's what you get for jumping to conclusions. Rough-looking ex-con in a beat-up pickup and drug-mule dog, indeed. Perhaps we could all learn a little something about pre-conceived biases and profiling from this case, Sherlock, hmmm?" I smiled, giving him my best stink-eye.

"It's all the vet tech's fault," he joked, heading to the fridge for a beer. "She said it first. I never would've thought of it, frankly. After she said that, we all sort of went down the rabbit hole with the idea. Guess I'm an innocent, naïve guy. I didn't even consider a condom full of drugs. Gotta show me, I guess."

"I think you're from Missouri and never told me," I teased, rising to hug him and receive him properly. "Welcome home, Sherlock. Now, put down your pipe and call off the hounds. It's time for dinner, a glass of wine, and some "us" time."

Rick put his big arms around me, kissed me right on the lips, and whispered, "With pleasure, my dear Watson. With utmost pleasure."

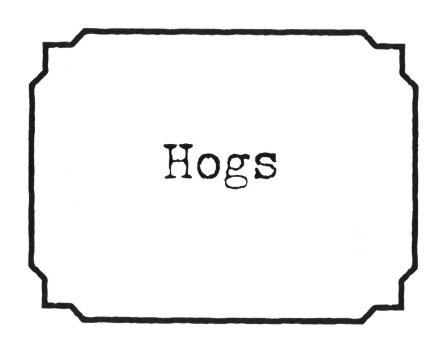

Hogs

WHEN PIGS FLY

Pigs can be loud. To stand near a big ol' hog screaming, (Rick would remind me pigs don't scream, they squeal.), is a sensory experience like no other. Add to that a bunch more pigs and the sound becomes a mind-melding, out-of-body experience. If you stand there long enough, you might even meet Jesus. To me, screaming is a better word for pigs. Squealing is when babies delight in smearing peas on their highchair and in their hair. Screaming is way more than a couple of levels past squealing. So, screaming it is.

My most memorable experience of pigs screaming was when Rick was in vet school. There was no reason for pig screaming, really, at least not in my mind. But behind those pink, round eyes in their little porky brains I guess they were terrified of us—two strange, city-humans standing at the opening to their pen, politely attempting to coax them into walking up a homemade loading chute and enter a dark horse trailer where they were to be hauled off to become bacon and picnic hams. How did they know? Go figure. Pig's ain't dumb, turns out. And they doth protest a lot.

Rick and some fellow vet students had raised these pigs from little shoats. They had formed a co-op, finding a volunteer to house, feed, and water the pigs until they got to optimum size for a little trip down the road in the horse trailer. The undergrad school had a facility to teach handling and processing of live animals, which was their ultimate destination.

On the chosen day of departure, Rick and I stood by the pen under a shed roof at the barn when the pig screams commenced. He and I stood facing one another, nose to nose, then lips pressed to ears, hollering at each other while those pink porkers out screamed us at stratospheric decibels. We could no more hear each other than if we were truly deaf, which, I imagined, might be the end result of that all-out aural assault. Rick gave up trying to talk to me and forged in there amongst 'em to help get the job done. Rick and his student pals persevered, however, managing to load the trailer and hit the road to the processing plant.

Pigs off to slaughter, pig pens finally deserted and quiet, I went home to our tuna can trailer and put an ice pack on my aching head. The only sound left in my ears was a jolly good case of raging tinnitus, which lasted for hours.

But there would be good news on top of good news. By the time the meat was processed and picked up, we would have delectable pork to eat for a good long while, and perhaps even better, everybody fully regained their hearing.

A year or so later, Rick was working a summer construction job in Tuskegee between semesters at vet school. The job superintendent approached Rick and told him he owned a hog farm and had a nice, fat hog Rick could purchase and take to the processing plant himself. Eager to pack our freezer with economy of scale, Rick thought this a grand plan. However, unbeknownst to me, our horse trailer was out of commission and unavailable.

What happened next, I can't explain even now, other than the obvious: Rick is a man. Let's start with that. He's also a man of ingenuity, not to be daunted. In the absence of a proper, pig-carting conveyance, he thought it a wise idea to place the pig in the way-back area of our passenger SUV—a Chevrolet Blazer—if she would fit. Apparently, solid geometry was Rick's only consideration, size his only criterion. So while I was driving home from my job at the bank in our little VW bug, Rick drove our Blazer over to the man's place to assess the situation and hopefully pick up a fat, fine, and very much alive, sow.

This thing was gargantuan, weighing three-hundred pounds if she weighed an ounce. Rick was determined. Because we had dogs, Rick had already constructed a sturdy dog barrier in the vehicle, like an oversized baby gate, suitable now for a young porcine Godzilla riding in the cargo area behind the backseat (Was Godzilla ever a baby, or did it just show up a full-grown monster in the movies?). Based on his visual assessment, the sow would, indeed, fit perfectly—sideways, that is.

In that moment, Rick thought back to his grandfather's story about the pony the old man needed to move off his farm in the late 1940s and was without a proper conveyance. Just so happened Rick's uncle drove up Grandad's driveway in his brand-new sedan at just the right time.

And lo, the angel of imagination shone round about Grandad, and a brilliant idea was born.

Rick's grandfather and his farmhand visualized the perfect space for his pony: in the back of Rick's uncle's car. They envisioned it'd fit if the seat was removed, its head stuck out one window, and its tail out the other. Grandad was never one to be denied, and so it was done.

Likewise, since we've decided now that it must be genetic, Rick would not be denied either. The owner had a decent loading chute, and the sow did not protest too much. With some shoving and prodding, the pig slid perfectly into the back of the Blazer, snout breathing steam on the window on the starboard side, tail brushing like a curly windshield wiper against the port side. And they were off.

Now, Rick had not counted on the late hour. By the time he loaded Miss Piggy into the car, the processing plant was closed for the night. So Rick just drove home. The backseat passenger-pig would stay in the car, secure for the night.

The door opened to our little sardine can trailer while I was cooking dinner. Rick appeared, grinning like a mule eating briars. Hands on hips, like a superhero, he puffed his chest and announced joyously, "Ta-daa!! Well, baby, we got us a pig!"

"Great! Good for you, Superman! How did it go?" I laughed, totally unprepared for what was coming.

"Oh, it wasn't too bad," Rick said, aw-shucks-ing it. "But . . ." He paused, looking at the floor.

"But what?" I inquired, now curious. "I know one thing—you sure smell like a hog!"

"Yep. Well," he said, looking back up, "maybe I should just show you."

With that, Rick slid back the curtain at the small kitchen window overlooking our parking area. The moon was full and glistened on the roof and hood of the Blazer.

At first, I did not see it. "What?" I asked, confused.

"Look inside," he urged, hushed but proud, like he had the answer to all the problems of mankind, and they were inside that car.

I bent a little lower and squinted so I could see clear through the vehicle, front to back. The moon shone through the car and over the top of a rounded, dark, unmistakable silhouette of . . . of . . . a pig's back.

"OH DEAR GOD!" I gasped. My hands snapped reflexively up and over my mouth, eyes wide, then blinking fast. "Is . . . that . . . what I think it is? WHAT HAVE YOU DONE? AND WHY?"

The male brain is a curious thing. Rick had not assumed for one minute that a pig, squished perfectly into the back of our best passenger vehicle for an entire night, would present any kind of problem. He had not thought past his brilliant engineering prowess.

Only that the pig was secure for the night, and that meant all was well. One need not be a rocket scientist nor even a vet student to know pigs don't "hold it" until they can find a bathroom. Our vehicle was a carpeted, mobile pigpen riding on a Chevy chassis now, and the pig would operate and function accordingly. *This was the genius I married. What the hell have I done?*

"Well . . ." Rick paused to explain himself sheepishly, realizing all really wasn't well before stopping short of a long excuse and opting for the bottom line. "It is what it is, babe. Sorry. The place was closed. No choice. I'll take him in the morning to the processing plant just as soon as it opens."

And so he did.

And so I forgave him. Eventually.

And so we had a freezer full of pork.

And so I decided just to be grateful he hadn't let the pig ride shotgun.

Getting the smell of pig shit out of the Blazer, however, was epic and virtually impossible. Never, not in a million years, would the demon essence of swine excrement that possessed our car be completely exorcised—no matter the soap, detergent, bleach, ritual incantations, disassembly and reassembly of every part, nut, and bolt in the back of that Blazer.

"Not even when pigs fly," I said, "will this car ever be right again."

We sold it on a sunny, dry day when the car smelled almost normal. We fessed up in full disclosure to the buyer that there had once been a pig in there but assured the buyer we had done everything we could to clean it.

"Smells ok to me," he said.

I dismissed the urge to cross myself. Rick and I flashed a look at each other in disbelief at our good fortune, feeling virtuous in our honesty while also suffering the sharp pangs of guilt. We had stood by our sales pitch, "Low mileage. Only one pig carried." We had not disclosed what else we knew, however: That the pungent, demon odor was guaranteed to awaken inside that vehicle on the first hot, humid Alabama day to come his way and every humid day thereafter.

"Well, then," Rick said, "it's yours!" The man paid with cash and drove the beast away. Rick and I turned to go inside. "Whew, glad that's over," he sighed, relieved.

"You're an idiot," I said laughing, "but enough with the compliments." I took his hand and wove our fingers together as we walked. "You're my idiot, and I still love you and always will. Just don't ever pull another stunt like that again, ok?"

"Promise. Guaranteed," Rick replied, smiling, squeezing my hand.

I didn't believe his man-genes would render him fully capable of carrying out such a promise for a lifetime. In fact, I was one-hundred percent sure he couldn't. But at least he was sincere in his intent. And I appreciated him for trying. If we were to stay married, we would encounter plenty of occasions requiring conflict resolution and forgiveness for both of us. This was good practice, I reasoned. How right I was!

Almost fifty years later, I have lost count of the opportunities Rick and I have given each other to practice our skills and learn even more skills. And by the way, practice never makes perfect. No such thing. But practice does make for improvement and experience—and there's absolutely no substitute for experience.

We never heard from our buyer again—thank you, sweet Mother of Elvis—but I still wonder, even now, how that poor man fared on his first rainy day after the sale when the gawd-awful fumes of porcine-past most certainly came out to haunt. While death and taxes are two certain things in life, I'm here to firmly attest to the fact there's at least a third, forever-thing to add to that list: Eau de Swine Shit on a rainy day in, or on, anything thus anointed. Guaranteed.

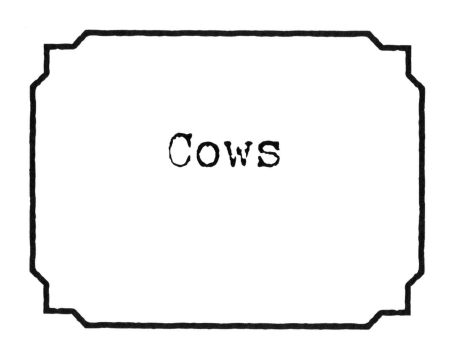

Cows

MR. TRAMMEL'S COW

1980S

I dunno, Doc, she just won't get up. She's down in the pasture, purty as you please.

The Trammell family had a long, respected history in the Luthersville area in Coweta County. Mr. Trammell, Sr. was a dairyman who knew a lot about cattle and farming. His grandson had a beautiful, eleven-hundred-pound, gray, part-Brahma, show heifer.

When Rick arrived at the Trammell farm, the heifer was resting on the grass like a proper lady who could've had a flower in her straw hat and a patent-leather pocketbook on her arm. Back legs neatly folded under her, front legs likewise, she looked normal for all the world—pretty and poised. The problem was she just couldn't get up. She wore a halter. As a show heifer, she was used to being handled so she wasn't crazy or wild. Rick examined her, listening to her heart, lungs, eyes, breathing. All were normal. Her temperature was normal, and her rumen was gurgling normally. She had sensation when Rick pinched her legs; she just couldn't get up. Thus, Rick determined, all other things being normal, there was a neurological component to be investigated.

Rick started thinking outside the box. He considered polio encephalomalacia—a vitamin B-1 (Thiamine) deficiency which is one of the most common problems in animals raised on grazing-beets out West. Beets aren't necessarily the only cause, but they do tend to cause the vitamin B-1 deficiency. This was a show heifer, though. She was raised in the rural south, cared for with the best of the best feed and getting everything she needed to look "bloomy," as they say in the show-cattle biz. She had good body tone, coat color, and everything. Plus, she was out in the field with all the other cows— none of whom exhibited any symptoms.

Stumped, Rick made an educated guess and administered his "kitchen sink treatment": steroids, antibiotics, B-1 vitamins, and prayer.

Again, the cow tried to get up, but this time she lurched backward, stumbling as far as the edge of the creek, which was about as wide as her body. She fell lengthwise into the creek, facing upstream, blocking the flow of water. Terrified, Rick quickly sized up the situation. As the water started rising, it was clear the cow was going to drown if something wasn't done to change the inevitable.

In the middle of that horror, Rick also realized he was supposed to be home soon so I could go with my carpool up to chorus rehearsal in Atlanta. If he arrived late, Rick could expect more horror when he got home. He was running out of time—on so many levels.

Luckily, Rick had on high boots and immediately waded into the creek to grab the cow's halter and lift her head up. Mr. Trammell, Sr. ran to his tractor and drove it down to the cow. Together, they put ropes on her hind legs and pulled her out, landing her on the bank. By then, the cow was facing the stream, perpendicular to the water, and the men figured if she tried to get up and she lurched backward again, at least she would launch herself away from the stream. It was a small comfort, maybe, but practical at the very least.

At that point, Mr. Trammell turned to Rick. "Go to the house. The boy's mother will pay you," he said in a low monotone that unmistakably communicated *I could've gotten any other veterinarian within four counties, and I got you.*

Rick flashed back to the memory of a lecture by the dean of his vet school, Dr. T.S. Williams, who said, "Gentlemen, if you don't come up with a diagnosis, somebody else will."

Still, Rick wasn't sure any other veterinarian could've diagnosed this cow's problem, but he sure could've done without the drama in the creek. This cow could've had any number of neurological problems including rabies, encephalitis, a brain abscess, or an infection. In those days, if you took a sample and sent it off to the diagnostic lab, you'd get the results back a whole week later if you were lucky. There were no in-field diagnostics. For Rick, this was "what the hell can I come up with... right now?" All in all, what Rick came up with was his considered, educated choice of his "kitchen sink treatment." And all he could do after that was hope and pray to God it worked. Having just endured some unexpected bovine melodrama, he had made the Trammells mad, embarrassed himself, and left defeated and demoralized. What else could Rick do but hope and pray?

When he arrived home, wet to the bone and weary, poor Rick could not get a break. He got "the look" from me for being late. That meant I would be tardy to rehearsal—an offense for which our temperamental maestro, Mr. Shaw, loudly and publicly excoriated and humiliated anyone for committing. Plus, if a singer committed too many of those sins, they could be excommunicated permanently.

How could I have begun to understand what Rick had just been through? There was no time for discussion—just comings and goings and feelings. Looking back, knowing the whole story now, I feel deeply for the guy. Back then, that night, not so much. After Rick's late arrival, I initiated a new line-item in our budget: babysitters. It was a marriage saver. That, and a whole new concept: talking.

To Rick's credit, he called the Trammells the next day to inquire about the cow. They said enthusiastically, "Well, Doc, she's up and running and doing great!" Rick felt relief pulse through his body. He knew then which part of his treatment had been the cure—the B vitamins. The diagnosis had to be polio encephalomalacia, a condition caused by a B-1 deficiency that damages the brain. Nothing else would've responded to the kitchen sink that quickly.

Still, there were questions: How the hell did she get it? Was all forgiven, or did they scratch it off to *Well, it sure wasn't his skill, so he just got lucky!?* At this juncture, Rick didn't care. He was singularly overjoyed the cow was better. And he knew in his heart it was skill and a lot of luck thrown in for good measure that made it so.

Rick was called back to the Trammells' place numerous times over the years, underscoring the forgiveness in the saying, "All's well that ends well."

Rick loves the joke he got from my dearest friend, Smith Pass's daddy—a fine man who farmed his whole life in Alabama, may he rest in peace:

Farmer has a cow down and calls Dr. Jones out to see about it. Farmer asks the field hand, "Grubby, who's the better veterinarian, Dr. Jones or Dr. Berta?"

Grubby says, "It's Dr. Berta."

Farmer says, "How can you say that in front of Dr. Jones?"

Grubby laughs, "Dr. Jones, he comes out to treat the cow, and I gotta carry food and water to it for a week before it dies. Dr. Berta comes out, it's dead the next day."

Rick's other favorite joke has a man standing on the corner, head down and looking forlorn:

Friend stops. "What's wrong?"

Man says, "Daughter got sick. We called the doctor, he came out, but she passed. Then, the family milk cow got sick. Called the vet out. He killed her."

Sometimes, being a veterinarian is like a Rodney Dangerfield punchline, "No respect. I don't get no respect." But laughter makes a good man's tough job a bit lighter some days. Knowing his own worth and ministering to sick animals no matter what it takes does the trick too.

LIGHT AND THE STOCKYARD

2021

Rick was enlightening me recently about the effects of light on the animal world and how it affects their seasonal reproductive habits. "You mean like humans respond to daylight saving time?" I ask dumbly.

I enjoy these kinds of conversations with him. He doesn't roll his eyes or make me feel stupid. Rick engages me as a professor might teach his class—without judgment or ridicule. I am always grateful, and it allows us to continue freely. Besides, I am a naturally curious soul who wants to learn. He lets me ask more questions than a professor should endure.

"In August, I was out walking in a field," he began patiently. "I noticed a locust tree. That's a tree with big ol' monster thorns, and the deer love 'em because they can rub the velvet off their antlers in preparation for breeding season."

"Why do they have to get rid of the velvet?" I asked, inquisitively. "Can they not walk and chew gum at the same time?"

"Because breeding season means fighting amongst the males for superiority," he continued. "They have to have sharp horns. No velvet."

"Ok, so what about the light?" I asked, getting him back on task.

"Well," Rick began, settling back in his chair for what would obviously be a lengthy session. I swear had he possessed a pipe he would have lit it and prepared for a long, leisurely smoke, like he was reading The Night Before Christmas with children at his feet. "The light influences the testosterone levels of the males and the estrus cycle of the females. The gestation period for a deer is five months, so they want to breed in the fall and deliver in the springtime when there is abundant food to feed the babies. In the fall, the male deer's neck starts to thicken. Once gathered in little pods, or male groups, like fraternities, they now begin to separate and fight for territory. Full rut culminates in early November. When Georgia lost almost all their deer to over-hunting, they brought in white-tailed deer mostly from up North. Whether they were from Wisconsin or Iowa, those deer had shorter breeding seasons because of the light hours up there."

"What? Seriously? Did they manage to evolve to match the Georgia deer population?"

"Yes, eventually. It's just interesting that the folks who study these things noticed different estrus cycles at first." Now, he was on a professorial roll. I imagined a smoke ring floating into the air. "Goats and sheep are on the same cycle—breeding in the fall and delivering in the spring. Horses are different. They ovulate in the spring and deliver in the spring, since gestation is eleven to twelve months. So deer respond to shortening of days, and horses respond to the lengthening of days. The stallions' necks thicken anyway, but they don't change up and down like deer do."

I kept my mouth shut and just let him go. It was interesting, and he was clearly happy to expound.

"They regulate chickens with light too," he continued. "They control their laying by light hours. Ever seen a big operation's chicken house with lights on at night?" he asked.

"Uh, not personally, but if you say so. I don't get out much around commercial chicken houses," I joked.

"Well, they do that so the chickens will lay more eggs," he replied patiently.

I interjected, "So the point of all this is animals are affected by light, and so are humans. Circadian rhythms or biorhythms or whatever it is, right?"

"Right, but we don't get thicker necks, and leaving lights on in the bedroom doesn't help at all," he laughed. "Chocolate and wine work better." We were both laughing now, enjoying his bon mot breaking up what was becoming a class whose bell needed to ring soon and adjourn.

Then, I thought of yet another question, and class was back in session. "Do other animals respond to light and circadian or bio rhythms?"

"Interestingly, cows do not." Rick revved up again with renewed vigor.

"So cows, do they have a season?" I asked.

"Wild buffalo respond to light hours. Elk do too. They breed in the fall. Because of the way man has genetically altered cows, they will breed year-round."

"Wait, what? Anytime you want to breed a cow is a good time? And how has man genetically altered cows?" I asked, astonished.

"Through selective breeding. In cattle management, what some people try and do is have the breeding cycle of the herd all the same, so they all calve in February or March. That way, by the time the calf is old enough to eat grass, it's available in April or May. In some places, they have poor breeding programs. The bulls are in with the cows year-round, and calves are dropping all the time. They're out in big hundred-acre pastures, unmonitored, and impossible to catch. Or in the case of small operations, they're just let loose without enough room to separate them because there's no room for separate facilities or pens. Bad management. Good managers time things out, introduce bulls only at certain times, and then remove them. As calving time draws near, good managers move their herds closer to a work facility, especially their first-calf heifers, to monitor the pregnant cows and help with the delivery if there is a problem.

"This is so far from most peoples' idea of cows and gentleman's farming," I said. "Oh, let's get some cows and put them out on our one-acre lot and be farmers!" I quipped. "It ain't so simple when you know what you're doing, is it?"

"There is nothing wrong with backyard farming," Rick assured. "However, backyard farmers can't expect the same results as large, managed farms. If they do, they're not being realistic."

"The business end of it is fascinating," Rick went on. "As a large, well-managed operation, you can sometimes pre-package your entire calf-crop to sellers for a premium price. Whereas, if you take them to the stockyard one or two at a time, you are at the mercy of the buyer. They will pay you as little as they can get away with."

I remembered how years ago in the late 1980s, Rick worked as the stockyard vet in La Grange one day a week, and I asked him to tell me what that was like.

"That was quite an education!" Rick drew in a long breath and exhaled, giving him a moment to recall those exhausting days. He worked grueling hours in stinky pens, being jostled and bruised by huge bovines in chutes while doing the Brucellosis testing—a screening program required and run by the state. It paid Rick poorly, but it was a steady income at the time. He always came home smelling strongly of cow poop and stockyard grahdoo. I could almost tell he was home before he hit the door.

"There were buyers and there were cowboys working the sale barn. Some were rough customers," he said, "like Timmy."

"A guy named Timmy was a rough customer?" I joked.

"Oh yeah," he said. "Timmy was a cowboy who worked the aisle where the animals came charging through after they had been bought in the sale ring. Timmy snorted cocaine and was always wired. One day, a four-hundred-pound bull calf came roaring down the aisle and knocked Timmy off his feet. He flipped up in the air while the bull calf raced underneath. Timmy landed on his feet, eyes wide, stupid grin stretched across his face, and said, "Holy shit Dude, that was a helluva ride!'"

Rick was on another roll.

"The buyers' room was off to the side where men went to relax while their cattle were being processed," he began, smiling. "I often went in there to get a moment to sit down after Brucellosis testing a million-and-one cows. One day, a buyer brought in a dildo, brandishing it in the air and then turned it on. Like silly schoolboys, they were all tittering, pointing, and joking around until the door opened. A woman who worked the sales office across the hall came in for a glass of water. With no time to turn it off, the buyer quickly lowered the dildo and sat on it while it was still vibrating." Rick roared. "There was not a single dry eye in that room, except for the woman, who had seen just enough and chalked it up to stupid men. She got her water and left."

Rick launched another story before I could even take a breath.

"There was a scoundrel buyer named Red," he said, "who had a place over near Centralhatchee in Heard County. Red had his own herd of cattle he kept at his place, but he also frequented the sale circuit and bought up other cattle, bulls, cows, calves, heifers, bull calves, and anything he could resell. When he got enough for a truckload full, he approached me for health certificates. Red would tell me he had eighty, three-hundred-weight steers going to XYZ feed lot in ABC state. I'd look them over and see the animals in question. All would be in order, and I would issue his health certificate. What I didn't know was that after the health certificate was issued, Red took the liberty of adding more animals he had bought from any number of places—whatever he wanted to put on the truck—and sent them out. These were the animals he took to be sold. This was, if you hadn't guessed, highly illegal. First, because some were breeding age, they should've been TB and brucellosis tested, which they weren't. And second, they were not the animals as stated on the health certificate."

"Did you know that was happening at the time? Did you get in trouble for that?" I whispered. "I don't remember your getting in trouble for that."

Rick laughed. "Nope. And neither did Red. His driver would inevitably drink too much and have a wreck or get a flat tire and get pulled over. The officer would take one look at the paperwork, the animals, and Red's name on the health certificate before hauling Red in front of the Department of Agriculture for a hearing. They'd ask him, 'Did you do that, Red?' And Red would say, 'Yep, sure did.' After which they'd slap him on the wrist, fine him, and Red would go about his business. Turns out Red was a huge source of their ongoing income, justifying a full two-thirds of their budget. If they put him in jail, there would be no budget. They needed him, and that was that!" Once again, Rick guffawed, pitching his chair backward.

"Hilarious," I laughed. "So back to the stockyard," I said, trying to pull him back. "Tell me more about what it was like."

"Oh," he said in a long breath, "yes, where was I? There was a veritable Market Day Swap Meet in the parking lot where people sold stuff. There were the 'pinhookers' who tried to buy cows straight off trailers in the parking lot before they even went in the sale barn."

"To what advantage were these pinhookers doing this?" I asked.

"Kind of a fast lane crapshoot," he said. "A trade-off bargain if you will. No guarantees to the pinhooker that the cow would be healthy. That would be his gamble. But it would be a matter of expediency for the cow owner. And the pinhooker could buy the cow much cheaper because the farmer could avoid the hassle of waiting to sell inside the barn, and he could get out of there faster." Rick's eyes closed as though he were seeing it all in his mind as he spoke. "That whole parking lot scene was a kind of circus. Until," his voice rose, his eyes popped open, he leaned forward, and a chuckle flowed as he spoke, "somebody sold a gun at the Swap Meet and it went off. BANG! You can imagine the mayhem—frightened animals balking and bucking as people dove for cover under trailers and behind trucks. After that, there were no more Swap Meets."

He continued, settling back in. "There were pens in the back where farmers unloaded their trailers, and then the animals were fed into a chute about three-feet wide. Once in the chute, each would receive a sticker with a number. Then, the animals would wait to be funneled into the brucellosis testing chute I manned. I remember the day a monster Angus bull who was waiting in the sticker chute reared up and fell over backwards, landing upside down. There was no room to right himself, and he was like a fifteen-hundred-pound cockroach on his back. He was going to die if something wasn't done—and fast. Nobody was back there except me at the time. I ran into the barn and got some burly cowboys. We roped that monster around his neck, and all of us tugged with every ounce of energy we had. By God, we pulled him through the chute into the pen where he was able to right himself. It's a wonder I didn't hurt myself. Well, maybe in the long run I did. My back hasn't been the same since." Rick joked. I laughed, but I remember very well the day he came home after that incident. He walked bent sideways at the waist for days.

True to form, Rick had morphed from light affecting animals to stockyard stories, and I was entirely okay with it. He was entertaining and had clearly inherited his mother's tendency to go off on tangents in her storytelling. This day, it was utterly charming.

"Then, there was the client of my partner, Dr. Morris. This man was a farmer hauling his bull to the Carrollton stockyard in his horse trailer. About at the intersection of Dixon Street and Temple Avenue, right near our little starter house on Dixon, the bull leaped right out the back opening of that trailer and onto the pavement. Somehow, unhurt, the cow began to book it down Dixon Street. The owner got all the way to Whitesburg before he was stopped by a Georgia State Patrolman."

Rick said he was told later the patrolman asked the driver, "You missing something, sir . . . like your bull?"

Rick heard that the farmer bolted from his truck, ran to the back of his trailer, and saw it was empty. Horrified he was missing his passenger, the farmer asked the patrolman where it was, and the officer told him.

"We got a call there was a bull running down Dixon Street. Said it came out of a trailer headed west. So I tracked you down. Thought it just might be yours since you're headed in the right direction . . . and your horse trailer's empty as a church on Mondays."

The farmer called Dr. Morris from the nearest pay phone. "What do I do?" the guy begged.

Dr. Morris replied, "That's Dr. Berta's neighborhood. He can take care of it!"

Rick almost pitched over telling me, his hearty laughter filling the room.

"Well, did you go?" I asked?

"Oh yeah, I went," Rick said, "and by the time I found the bull he was down in some woods. He wasn't too aggressive. Maybe he had been handled before, and maybe even hand-fed over time. There was a crowd, city cops, state patrol, and a few neighbors. Even a county prison camp truck with a guard and a prisoner showed up. Somebody had managed to tie the bull to a tree to keep him from running any further.

"The trick was gonna be how to get that bull to walk back to that trailer and be convinced to re-enter it. We got a rope halter with a long lead on it and placed it on the bull's head. Then, we took the long lead and advanced to the next tree closest to the trailer and pulled him further toward the trailer. After about ten trees, one by one, we finally ran out of trees and got him close enough to the trailer. Now, it was only a matter of feet to the entrance, and God-willing, the bull would cooperate.

"We tied another rope to the lead, extending the length of it through the back of the horse trailer and out the front window. The state work-camp prisoner with the truck was very cooperative, but his part was tricky. His movements had to be smooth and strategic, lest the rope break or the bull spook and rare up, causing any number of unexpected disasters. We tied the rope to his bumper.

"I spoke clearly and definitively to him, 'You will only hear my voice. You will go when I say go. You will stop when I say stop.' With that, I yelled, 'Go!' The truck advanced slowly, pulling the rope, halter, and bull straight into the trailer. The bull had no choice at this point. When I yelled, 'Stop,' the trailer gates were closed, and ropes removed. The proud prisoner and his truck were released from duty. It was finished, and after some back-slapping and glad-handing, we all waved bye-bye and left."

"So did you talk to your partner and thank him for his generosity in passing the case to you?" I chuckled.

"When I got home after the melee with the bull, I called Dr. Morris to report. 'I only hope you get the next one, and it's in your neighborhood,' I joked."

"And Morris said to me, laughing, 'You know, you really are strong like bull, smart like tractor. I'll gladly defer to you anytime.'"

TODD HOWARD AND DR. WHO

Back in the day when Rick and I first arrived in Newnan and Coweta County, there were lots of dairies that don't exist anymore in 2021. Why? Because of changing demographics in our southern rural area, and the money just wasn't in it anymore for struggling dairy farmers. There was a glut of milk, but dairy consumption had fallen sharply. Matter of fact, there was a government buyout of dairy farms in '86 when ninety-five percent of the dairies in Coweta County closed. In 2021, only one of fourteen large working dairies survives here.

But during their heyday, Rick visited many a dairy to minister to the cows in varying states of health. One of the dairies was owned by Harry Howard whose young son, Todd, was always there when Dr. Berta came to call. For years, Todd observed the goings on as he grew up into adulthood. He sopped up every bit of animal husbandry he could from his daddy and Dr. Rick.

Seemed Todd was always a strange sort, and most anybody who knew him would agree. While we never witnessed it ourselves, we were told that as an adult Todd liked to venture out into the pasture and pretend he was Dr. Who, appearing and disappearing at will in an honest-to-God, full-sized British phone booth. He had either purchased it or constructed it—as if that detail matters. What mattered was—well you know—he was just odd, this boy. This, Rick knew from personal experience.

One day Rick got a phone call.

"Hello, is this Dr. Berta?" said the male voice on the other end of the line.

"It is," Rick said.

"Hi, my name is John Barrow, and I'm a pharmaceutical rep in Florida and Georgia for the Booker Company. I believe we know each other."

"Yes, John, I remember you. What can I do for you?"

"Do you happen to know a Todd Howard?" Mr. Barrow asked.

"Yeah, Harry Howard's son? Howard's Dairy in Newnan?"

"Right. Well, I thought I should call you to let you know what's happening or, should I say, what has already happened. Todd's been down here in Florida using your Georgia state veterinary license number trying to order controlled drugs and claiming he is Dr. Todd

Howard, DVM. He is working for a large dairy as their in-house veterinarian."

"Wow, what?! Are you serious?! Whiskey Tango Foxtrot! How the hell did that happen?"

Rick had no idea what Todd had been doing, and further, was pretty darn sure Todd had never gone to veterinary school or gotten a degree—much less passed a veterinary board or been issued a license. The last Rick knew, Todd had been working as a bovine artificial insemination technician, repping for a semen company in Georgia. He thought about how Todd might have gotten hold of his Georgia veterinary license number. Rick assumed he'd probably taken it off the TB and Brucellosis certification health forms he had filled out for Mr. Howard's dairy. But if Todd was in Florida, it remained a mystery how he could use Rick's Georgia license number and get away with ordering drugs. Perhaps by working for a private farm, Todd had sold the farmer on the fact he was a licensed vet, and they didn't question it? Evidently, nobody else did either, if he ordered uncontrolled drugs like antibiotics, Novocaine, and vaccines.

The rep on the phone told Rick, "I smelled a rat as soon as Todd's purchase order for a controlled drug came across my desk. Todd has no DEA license. It was when he ordered a controlled drug with just a state license that it came to my attention. This guy doesn't have all his marbles."

The drug rep had done business with Rick before, and when Todd's order came in, he researched Rick's license number from past orders. Todd and Rick's license numbers were identical. He reported Todd to the state authorities, the Florida and Georgia state veterinary boards, and the farmer. Suffice it to say, Todd was run out of Florida. Strangely, Todd was never prosecuted. Too bad. He should've been put in jail.

Later, Rick would talk to a retired police officer who had been friends with the Howards. He told Rick what he discovered after the Florida escapade. Evidently, before Todd had even left Georgia, he started advertising himself as a veterinarian. When Rick traded in his old practice truck for a new one, Todd bought it after he saw it sitting on the used car lot in town. Todd dressed in green coveralls, just like Rick's. Todd convinced a cattleman at a bar he was a vet, and the cattleman hired him to do some work. That got the ball rolling. How Todd migrated to Florida is still unknown, but the end of the story is that Todd is not in Florida anymore. We hope not in Georgia either.

Mr. Howard passed away, and the dairy is no more.

Todd's current whereabouts are not known by Rick or anyone else we know. Perhaps, he disappeared one last time into his Dr. Who phone booth and lives happily-ever-after in his Tardis time-machine.

Horses

YOU MUST BE JOKING

Rick and I were about to take a trip to the beach one summer during Rick's large-animal days. It always seemed to happen that somebody had an emergency right before we were to leave. Like Karma saying Rick should earn the trip just a little more before we're allowed to enjoy ourselves. This one June day, a horse owner called the answering service frantic over his colicky stallion. By the time Rick got the message and called him back, the owner had found someone else to take the call. That worked for Rick. And me.

This was a well-known experience with people who had emergencies, by the way. It's the old "Let's call every vet in the phone book and see who shakes out" trick. So an owner would call every vet in the phonebook and leave messages, during which time the vets would all be calling the owner back and getting a busy signal (Remember those?) because the frantic owner was still on the phone calling every other vet and leaving messages.

The advent of call-waiting helped with this problem but not always. There were also times when Rick would call back and there'd be no answer because the owner had left their landline phone to race back outside to their distressed animal. Imagine the consternation this scenario caused all those vets returning all those phone calls.

The concern most vets have for the hurt animals required them to respond—if not by phone, then in person. More than once Rick showed up at a client's home as another vet roared in. They usually worked it out somehow, and one of them was free to go. That very thing is why the advent of cell phones was a game changer. But I digress—this story happened before all that. We barely had electric light bulbs and the wheel, this happened so long ago. Anyway, Rick was relieved when he reached the horse owner and said he didn't have to come.

So, Rick and I resumed packing the family car with everything a young couple with two kids needs to take to the beach. You know, liquor and koozies (priorities), followed by coolers, food, suitcases, and totes filled with beach clothes, sandals, and swimsuits. Then, the board games, reading material, beach towels, beach wagon, beach tent, beach toys, sunscreen, snorkels, masks, and metal detector—basically the entire house. Packing is traditionally an all-day job, and we always fall into bed exhausted every time, wishing we had gone to sleep earlier because the next day would be an early morning and a long six-hour drive—even without fuel stops and potty breaks.

As luck and Rick's charmed life would have it, the horse owner called back at 11:00 p.m. No one had shown up for their emergency—would Rick come?

So duty bound, on a hot, steamy late June night, Rick drove over to Fayetteville—close to an hour away without traffic—to find a young stallion who was sweaty and dehydrated but standing, which meant he was pretty much over his colic.

"The only thing he needs at this point is IV fluids," Rick told the grateful husband and wife, which he administered. The stallion felt so good he got an erection and started thumping his penis on his belly.

After witnessing this, the astonished owner said to Rick who was packing up to leave, "Hey, Doc, you got any more of that fluid?"

The two men were both laughing, and before Rick could respond, the man's wife piped up, totally deadpan and with comedic timing said, "And I'll pay for it."

MYSTERY IN HEARD COUNTY

1982

Rick got a call from Billy Barnes—a good ol' boy farm manager in Heard County. Billy had found a buckskin mare dead in her stall. When Rick arrived an hour later and drove down the long dirt drive, he saw Billy pacing back and forth at the barn. He greeted Rick, and the two went inside.

As Rick entered the stall, the horse was lying on her side, completely still on the thick bed of shavings with her head facing toward the stall door. He saw no sign of trauma to the body on first glance. Was he dealing with deadly colic or a sudden gastric torsion? The mare had no signs she had been sweating or struggling. The shavings were undisturbed.

Whatever it was, the horse had dropped like a rock and died then and there. On closer examination of the body, however, as Rick walked around her, he saw a little trickle of blood from a small hole in the perineal area—just to one side of the anus—below and to the right of the base of the tail. Rick took out his instruments and got to work. He opened the abdominal cavity and found a line of destruction going from the hole forward through the right kidney, into the liver, and then the lungs. He never found a projectile, but here was a dead horse in a stall, a whole lot of blood, damaged interior organs, and an open wound at her rear end.

"What is it, Doc?"

"I know what a bullet track looks like," he said. "This was caused by a low caliber weapon like a .22 handgun or rifle, not a high-powered deer rifle. It would have been silent if pressed directly against the horse's body, as the sound would have dissipated inside the cavity. A good riding horse is gentle and accustomed to being touched and groomed. This mare wouldn't have objected to someone pressing up against her. It doesn't take Sherlock Holmes to know this poor animal died of a gunshot wound. So now, one must ask, why would somebody do this?"

It was a conundrum, for sure. The farm manager and Rick were stumped.

Billy said, "I cain't imagine it, Doc. Had to be pure meanness. Sure ain't for money. This horse ain't even insured."

Rick concurred. He assumed some twisted person just needed to kill a living, breathing, magnificent horse, although he would never understand it. After finishing up, Rick was walking down the barn aisle with Billy and noticed there was another almost identical buckskin looking out at them over the wooden gate in the adjoining stall.

Billy pointed to that one and said, "Now this one, Doc? This one's insured to beat the band. Other one ain't got no value a'tall. Nuts, huh?"

"Well, then, *Hello!*" Rick shouted, slapping his forehead.

"What?" Billy asked.

Rick knew the farm owner, Charlie Grainer. He was a good-looking, high roller who had a winning smile and the gift of gab. Charlie also had the integrity of a weasel and a heart as black as Beelzebub. Rick knew Charlie had been in a great deal of financial trouble of late. Charlie was quite a rascal and had a reputation for being reckless with money—even more famous for doing irrational things to get himself out of deep debt. His solutions were usually the "out of the frying pan into the fire" variety, but Charlie didn't ever look past the frying pan to see how he would burn himself in the ensuing fire. He was a day-to-day kind of idiot. Who goes to a high-end department store, buys expensive furniture on credit, and then holds a yard sale selling the very same furniture to raise money to pay off his debts? Who does that?

Charlie had been out of town when his horse was shot, but when Rick thought about it, Charlie could have easily hired a hit on her. Rick certainly wouldn't have put it past him. Nothing was ever proven. But Rick knew somebody was out for the insurance money. And somebody shot the wrong horse.

"Well, Billy, looks like it was the insured horse that was supposed to die mysteriously and bring some insurance money. Somebody shot the wrong horse. Any idea who?"

Billy was obviously not a suspect in Rick's mind. He wouldn't hurt a horse or a horsefly.

"Oh my Gawd, Doc, that's plum unnnnn . . . unnnfuckin' believable! But what yer sayin' sure makes sense, and then again it don't make any sense a'tall, does it? I feel so sorry for that poor horse," Billy said, removing his ball cap and scratching his forehead, brow furrowed, and face truly perplexed. "That is some scary shit too!"

"I'm calling the Heard County sheriff's office to report the shooting and ask if they want to investigate. I'll also ask them if they would please have some extra drive-by surveillance on the farm for a little while. Just be aware you may have some visitors from time to time," Rick said.

Billy sighed, still in shock, but seemed relieved and grateful.

"Meanwhile, you have a horse to bury, Billy. I'm so sorry."

Because the dead horse was not insured and there was quite literally no smoking gun, there was no further investigation. Whoever the bumbling shooter was and whoever paid him, got off scot-free. Rick still has his suspicions to this day.

Rick had witnessed with his own eyes the evil that lurks in the hearts of men. And once again, reconfirmed his affinity for animals over some of the stupidest, most hateful creatures on God's earth: human beings.

GYPSY

1979

People talk. They confide in Rick as though he were a trusted therapist. In some ways, I guess he is. People unload. He listens. People feel better. Men tell him about their wives, animals, prostates, cars, money, businesses, and share stupid man-jokes. Women talk about their husbands, animals, worries, kids, and sometimes their kids-to-be.

One client told Rick she was pregnant before she told her husband the news. I'm not implying Rick had anything whatsoever to do with any of that, of course. She just needed a sounding board. Who better than your warm, friendly, animal-loving vet? Imagine that. Rick is a big ol' living "Doctor Dan the Band-Aid Man" from their childhood picture books, and people just want to hug him and trust him with their secrets and stories.

Many folks are also happy to share the latest rumor making the rounds. Dr. Berta knows way more about people than he should at this point. He gets around, hears it all, and over the years has always been careful not to put too much stock in rumors. Small towns deal constantly in those, most of which thrive on schadenfreude or stupidity. Rumors and gossip are traps. Somebody could get hurt.

A couple of years after we moved to Newnan, there was a rumor circulating. It was out in the lovely community of Welcome, where farmhouses sit back from the road and long, winding dirt driveways take time to navigate. Hay bales, farm equipment, all manner of animals, outbuildings, silos, paddocks, and horse barns nestle into acres of grassy rolling hills and board-fenced pastures. Rick was making a farm call to see about a lame horse.

The horse owner was standing at the ready, holding a beautiful brown mare named Gypsy by a lead line when Rick arrived.

"Hey, Doc! She was just as sound as she could be yesterday. But not today. I don't know what's wrong," he said, as Rick got out of his truck and approached them.

"Hey, Jimbo. Good to see you. How 'bout walking Gypsy nice and slow over to the fence and back?" Rick said, "I want to see her gait." Rick studied the horse as he watched her limp to the fence and then return. "Looks like she's lame in her left hind," Rick said, thinking aloud.

"Yep," sighed Jimbo, "you do your thing, Doc. Tell me what it is. She's hurtin'."

"I'll do my best," Rick assured him as he gathered some tools from his truck.

"I hear somebody's trappin' house cats, Doc," Jimbo began to chat as Rick started his lameness exam, "and I hear they're sellin' the pelts to a hide-processin' plant over in Griffin. Crazy. You believe that?!"

"Gosh, I hadn't heard that, Jimbo," Rick replied calmly as he bent over, gently following his hand slowly along Gypsy's flank, across her hip, down to her hock, and flexed her hind leg to examine the underside of her foot. "I know folks set out trap lines in this county for wild animals. Maybe they're catching the occasional house cat by accident. It is legal to trap raccoons, foxes, and other wild animals in this state, you know, but it sure would be underhanded to make money off cat pelts, for heaven's sake, intentionally or not. You sure people are doing this?" Rick asked.

"I heard they were sellin' 'em to make fur trim on coats in Siberia er somewhere way far away," Jimbo opined, rolling a toothpick around in his mouth. "And I also heard that Murphy down the road caught a fella trespassin' on his land tryin' to trap some cats to sell."

"Did he actually trap one?" Rick asked, applying the hoof testers with a gentle pressure. Gypsy flinched when he pushed on the frog—the triangle on the bottom of the foot that acts as a shock absorber. She flinched again with pressure just to one side of it on the sole. "Sorry, girl," Rick whispered gently, "a little tender right there, is it, Gypsy?"

"Well, maybe a cat," Jimbo continued, "but coulda been anything for all I know. It sure was somethin' small with fur anyway. Maybe a possum. I dunno. But Murphy caught this guy puttin' traps down on his property without any permission, and he didn't have medallions on his traps like the law says you gotta have. I don't know if Murphy woulda given him permission to trap even if he'd asked—he's been generous like that to a few trappers before—but he didn't get the chance with this guy. So when Murphy caught him red-handed, trespassin' and trappin' on his property, he turned him right in to the DNR."

"Department of Natural Resources wouldn't look too kindly on that, I wouldn't think," Rick replied, still concentrating on his diagnostic exam, feeling with his hand gently along the pastern and cannon bones on the front of Gypsy's leg, her flexor tendons, and the ligaments in the back. "Was there a hearing or anything?" Rick wanted to know.

"Yep. Get this. Hoo, boy, it's a good'un! On the day of, the trespassin' trapper-guy and his wife was in the hall outside the courtroom. Just so happened Murphy came in the hall right then too. The guy's wife went up to Murphy just as brazen as a hussy, grabbed him by the tie, and tried to choke him with it!" Laughing, Jimbo grabbed the toothpick from his lips, then spit a brown stream of tobacco off onto the dirt.

"She succeed?" Rick asked, playfully, grinning as he stood up and brushed his hands together.

"Nope, she let go right quick when she saw the way Murphy's face went all beet red and he gave her a look like she had best reconsider before things got out of hand. I'd say he was a pretty patient man. She's lucky she didn't end up on the floor or standin' up in front of the judge along with her husband. And you know what, Doc? All her sorry husband got was a citation. But he sure got a righteous warning as he and his crazy wife were leavin', and it wasn't from the judge, if you get my drift."

"Jimbo, Gypsy has a foot abscess," Rick said as he made his way over to his truck to gather more tools and supplies. "It's not too bad yet. We caught it early. She'll be ok, but we need to open this abscess and start her on pain medication and antibiotics." Rick grabbed his hoof knife and began carefully paring out the abscess under the sole where Gypsy had been ouchy during his exam. When the pressure was relieved and the fetid fluid drained, he packed it with Ichthammol—a black, gooey coal-tar salve to draw the rest of the abscess out. Then, Rick wrapped the hoof to keep it clean. Drawing up a syringe of penicillin, he popped the needle into her thigh muscle and injected the drug. Another injection followed—this one a Tetanus booster. Finally, handing Jimbo a tube of Bute paste, Rick instructed him to give Gypsy one dose per day for the next five days and to keep her in a dry lot and a clean stall.

Tucking his tools away in a compartment of the veterinary unit in the bed of his truck, Rick then made his way around to the front of the truck and opened the driver's side door. He reached into the front cab, opening the lid on a large, wood document box and retrieved an invoice.

"Is that box what you keep the chickens in?" Jimbo joked.

Rick laughed. He knew what that meant. This wasn't the first time somebody in the countryside had asked him that question. It referred to the custom of bartering. Once upon a time in the country, a nice, fat chicken could be offered and accepted as payment for veterinary services. What better way to transport a man's well-earned chicken home than in a large wood box on the front bench seat of his pickup?

"Nope, not anymore, Jimbo," Rick replied, still laughing. "You know Dorsey Beavers? He told me once about something he learned a long time ago when he started working at Arnall Grocery for Mr. Arnall. A fellow came into the store to buy some feed and supplies, and Dorsey asked him if that would be cash or charge. The man charged it. After he left, Mr. Arnall took Dorsey politely aside and whispered, 'It's cash or check, Dorsey. Make 'em ask for credit.'"

"So no chickens, Jimbo. Those days are long gone," Rick smiled as he handed him his invoice. "I can't deposit feelings, feathers, or fried chicken."

Also smiling, Jimbo replied without missing a beat, "Well, then, can I ask for credit, Doc?"

"Says right there on the invoice, Jimbo, that payment is due within thirty days," Rick laughed.

"You call me if she's not walking normally in a few days," Rick said, as he climbed into the driver's seat, "and call me before that if you hear of another cat pelt going to Siberia." Rick smiled, turned the key in the ignition, backed his F-250 around, and sped down the dirt driveway in a cloud of dust toward the road to another call.

WHEN IT RAINS

1985

In the mid-80s, a monster thunderstorm moved through Newnan, Peachtree City, and then Fayetteville. At the time, Rick got a call from a client who owned a boarding facility over in Fayette County. They said one of their client's horses had died and the insurance company was requiring a vet to come out and do an autopsy to officially declare a cause of death. Right then. As he drove east, Rick stayed with the blinding storm the whole way. When he got to Peachtree City, he couldn't get through because there were trees down in the road, so he blazed a path through Tyrone to get to Fayette County.

When he finally arrived, it was dark. Although it had stopped raining, the skies were still electric and alive with lightning followed by sharp, cracking thunder. The boarding facility owner ushered Rick into the lighted barn where Rick thought he would find his autopsy horse. In there, he presumed he'd be nice and dry with some decent light. Turns out Rick was a little too hopeful. The owner walked all the way through the barn and stopped at the large opening on the far side. Looking out, the woman raised her arm and pointed her finger.

"Out there, Doc," she told him. "Out...there."

The barn light radiated out only a few feet, and Rick couldn't see what she was pointing to. Then, as each lightning strike briefly illuminated the field, Rick could make out a fence; just a foot or so past the barn light he could make out a tree, and a very dead horse lying on the ground at the base of it. It was like seeing an old movie with a strobe light. Rick swallowed hard. The horse was clearly dead, and his job was to determine if it was from lightning. Rick didn't want to join its ranks by trundling his ass out into that field and dying the same way. He waited for the next flash which showed him the tree was split clean in two. Another flash! The horse had on metal shoes, and that rationale was good enough for Rick; it was dead from lightning. Rick intended not to be. End of story. He wrote the papers up right then and there.

Later, the insurance company wrote him back and asked why he hadn't put his hands on the horse and performed a complete autopsy.

Rick wrote back, "I am not some bumbling novice willing to risk his life in an active lightning storm to prove the obvious. I've seen plenty of animals struck and killed by lightning. I saw six cows killed once when lightning struck a barbed wire fence, jumped the gap over to a tree, and laid those bovine out flat and dead as hammers. I've even seen horses bite extension cords and be killed from electricity. I was not going out there to stand under a tree with a metal scalpel in my hand and cut that horse open to prove the obvious. There was a lightning storm. The horse had on metal shoes. The tree was splintered and black. The horse was dead under the tree. If you want to take your fluorocarbon rod and go fishing in a lightning storm, be my guest. Don't ask me to."

Somehow, that seemed to satisfy them.

———

Soon after his set-to with the insurance company and their "lightning police" over the dead horse in Fayette County, Rick was driving up Smokey Road in Coweta County one evening. Another intense thunder and lightning storm was in progress. He had several clients in the area and was hoping they had all brought their horses indoors.

Two weeks later, Rick got a call from one of the horse owners on Smokey telling Rick they did, in fact, have a horse killed in that storm two weeks earlier.

Dead two weeks ago. This is not going to be good.

Turned out, the poor deceased creature had been leased prior to being purchased and there was an insurance policy on the horse that was still in effect. The owner hadn't realized he had the insurance policy until two weeks had elapsed after the horse's death. In order to collect on the policy, it was required that he exhume the body and have Rick examine it to certify it was lightning and not some other means that killed this horse.

On the appointed day, Rick arrived and accompanied the owner to the grave. Rick cussed himself silently for forgetting to bring his Vicks VapoRub to smear on his upper lip, which was an old large-animal veterinary trick. It masks certain offensive fragrances, like, say, the smell of an exhumed horse that's been dead for weeks. So Rick stood by watching, a handkerchief wadded over his nose, as the owner, wearing two bandanas on his face, cranked up his backhoe and dug up that poor dead steed. Rick determined instantly that there was no other evidence of foul play and certified death by lightning strike.

Reinterment was *immediate*.

ARTHUR J

I asked Rick which case in his long and storied career was his most memorable. I know, that's like asking, "Who is your favorite child?" but I was curious if he could come up with the one—the experience that stayed with him and impacted him the most after all his years in practice.

After lowering his head and staring at his lap for a moment, Rick lifted his face and responded with an intensity as though he was recalling yesterday.

"His name was Arthur J. He was a beautiful chestnut, two-year-old Saddlebred horse. It was 1975, and I was fresh out of veterinary school in my first job at the all-equine practice in Virginia. The two senior vets were very skilled, and I was the new guy.

"The horse was a referral from a training stable outside of our practice area. The original veterinarian who attended Arthur J was a general practitioner who saw pocket pets, dogs, cats, livestock, and horses. The case was beyond his ability, and he missed the diagnosis, delaying treatment.

"Arthur J was significantly lame in his left foreleg. He wore the built-up leather pads and horseshoes that give Saddlebreds the exaggerated lift of the forelegs as the horse is ridden. Dr. Kingsbury started the exam. Swelling was evident in Arthur J's left knee down to his coronary band. Dr. Kingsbury instinctively removed the horseshoe and pads. And there it was—a hoof abscess. The pads had obscured the problem, and the infection had gotten into the lymphatic vessels and traveled to the knee. Infection in a joint can progress rapidly to destroy all the cartilage. The result is bone on bone. There is no joint replacement to save a horse. Three-legged horses develop breakdown in the sound limbs from osteo-arthritic founder.

"Arthur J was doomed.

"As a young, newly minted veterinarian, I reflected on the sorry path and horrendous medical failure to which Arthur J had been subjected. We study anatomy on dogs, cats, horses, cows, pigs, and goats. We must learn normal and pathological conditions on all these species. We take exams to graduate and state veterinary medical exams to procure a license to practice in a state. Even so, it's hard to know everything.

"Still, it nagged at me that a proper, basic lameness exam had not been done previously. Richard III came to mind: 'A horse! A horse!

My kingdom for a horse!' And that philosophical nugget from Ben Franklin: 'A little neglect may breed great mischief. For want of a nail the shoe was lost. For want of a shoe the horse was lost. For want of a horse the battle was lost . . .'

"So here I am, forty-six years later, still sad for Arthur J. It surely must have hurt when his shoe was removed, and the abscess and subsequent knee infection were identified. He bore all our poking and prodding with calm acceptance so we could come to a final, terrible diagnosis.

"I can still see it. Feel it. I am at one end of the leather lead line, and at the other is this gracious, gorgeous glistening horse that will not survive the battle. All because of a missed diagnosis by one of the veterinary profession's weakest links. Euthanasia would be his only friend.

"I cannot remember why his death passed to my hands. Probably because I was so green and needed to learn how, but I was the one to inject the solution that would end his life.

"The injection given, Arthur J stumbled a little bit sideways and then collapsed with a thud on to his right side—a once promising life cut short.

"As painful as it was for me to end Arthur J's life, the experience was a glimpse into the difficult life and death decisions I would make in my future career. Since then, it has certainly been borne out in all my years as a vet.

"I must acknowledge the loss and recover on a dime.

"I cannot dwell in such a dark place and keep my sanity.

"There is no time to reflect.

"One after another, there are more patients to see that need me to be present, compassionate, and competent. I must resolve not to fail.

"I must always do my best.

"And I resolve never to be the weakest link."

Epilogue

EPILOGUE 2021

Full-time veterinary work is no longer on Rick's agenda—nor will his tired, aging body, hips, legs, and feet allow it.

In the fall of 2018, after a long, distinguished career—first as an overworked large-animal vet and then an overworked small-animal vet—Rick laid down his sword and shield and partially retired. The man was, as they say, "Rode hard and put up wet." He was exhausted. Every joint ached. His feet were flat from standing all day. His neck, injured from sports, needed surgery. Both of his hands needed carpal tunnel surgery. It was time for Rick to take care of himself.

So, from that day in 2018 to this day in 2021, once a week, Rick has happily strolled into Moreland Animal Hospital—a small-animal practice he adores just a few miles south of town—and does his veterinary thing. He goes just to keep his skills current and his jokes in shape, to stay relevant, to be with and enjoy people, and to help animals.

Also because, Rick quips, he wants to go someplace just one day a week where they do what he tells them.

In a moment of what we can only call grace, after one friend lost his wife suddenly and another lost his to Alzheimer's, Rick realized what was most important in life. It wasn't career anymore. It was family. Us. Me. Our boys. Our grandchildren. The family he had put second for so long was now first. Rick doesn't miss a day without saying, "I love you." Neither do I.

Me? I am retired too. I no longer have the energy nor the desire to constantly run the roads in pursuit of a singing career, education, or anything else. At this point, I'm allergic to traffic. I'm a happy, creative homebody who does quiet things that give me joy. Being the veterinarian's wife is a good and joyful thing but it's only a part of many other things that make up the me I am today. I write. I paint. I decorate. I garden. I babysit and play with my grandchildren. I read. I cook. I connect with old friends and get together with new ones as safely as possible. There's still that goddamn pandemic going on. I'm vaccinated. And boostered. I got my flu shot. I wear a mask.

I share my thoughts freely with my husband, and we talk, joke, laugh, cry, and enjoy spending quality time together. We take the occasional trips to Atlanta for, say, a concert, an art exhibit, or to visit with a friend. Quality not quantity is the byword now. And all of that, including being the veterinarian's wife, is enough.

In our early seventies now, Rick and I are infused with new appreciation and reciprocal admiration for each other. He has delivered his emotional baggage to the universe and freed himself of his grandfather's labored exhortations, his father's shortcomings, and his own demons. The need to compete with ghosts to do better than they did no longer burns in his psyche. The need to get lost in his profession is supplanted by the desire to be present and embrace those pastimes and people he loves.

Rick became Scoutmaster of a Boy Scout Troop. He still goes camping with Scott and our grandchildren. He gives blood. He gardens. He loves a project. He runs our grand-dog in the fields, and they go hunting together. He reads, cooks, and laughs easily. He is happy.

Rick's belief system that "hard work shows love" is now "love shows love." That's not to say a marriage shouldn't include hard work. We worked very hard on ours over the years—his, mine, and our issues.

I survived, living like a single parent over the large part of many years, and a three-year depression. Therapy and pharmaceuticals helped. Rick survived being torn in two directions: work and family. Therapy helped. I learned how to come to terms with having issues with someone everyone else saw as a saint. He learned he wasn't one. I realized I wasn't one either. We both learned how to be present, intentional, considerate, honest, and respectful. We acknowledge and practice the three "A" s: Acceptance, Affirmation, and Affection. Every day.

We are thriving and happier than we have ever been.

Appendices

RECIPES!

THE NOW-FAMOUS CHEESE RING

This appetizer has been a famous family favorite for years. One year we made at least six of them over the span of Thanksgiving and Christmas, during which time Scotty mastered the art. If you ever take it to a party, they will clamor for the recipe:

1 lb. sharp NY cheddar, grated
1 C. pecans, chopped
¾ C. mayo
1 medium Onion, grated or chopped fine
1 clove garlic, pressed
½ t. Tabasco
1 C. strawberry preserves or Polaner All-Fruit

Combine all ingredients except preserves and mix well. Chill. Mold into ring. Fill center with strawberry preserves. Serve with crackers.

ORANGE CRESCENT ROLLS

rind of 1 orange, zested or finely grated
½ C. sugar
3 packages Pillsbury crescent rolls
melted butter

Combine orange rind and sugar. Let sit hours or overnight. When ready to serve, unroll dough from package but do not separate. Brush liberally with melted butter. Measure 1 t. of orange-sugar mixture for each triangle. Brush mixture over surface, one triangle at a time. Cut apart and roll as directed on package for jelly roll. Place on cookie sheets lined with Reynolds Wrap Release non-stick aluminum foil or on Silpat mat. Optional: Brush tops again with butter (Do not brush tops with egg white).

Bake at 375 degrees for 11-15 minutes. Do not over bake!

RICK & SUSIE'S SECRET RICOTTA CHEESE COOKIE RECIPE — A SECRET NO MORE

I've had a change of heart. What the hell. Can't take it with you, so might as well share the love. I'm not babysitting anybody, though. We've tweaked the recipe a bit over the years, and those details are for us to know and everyone else to experiment with. By and large, though, this is the original—the real deal that started it all. Enjoy. You are so welcome.

1 lb. butter
2 C. sugar
3 eggs
1 t. vanilla
1 15 oz. Carton Ricotta cheese
4 C. flour
1 t. baking soda
1 t. salt

Using a large mixing bowl cream butter and sugar together. Add eggs, vanilla, and Ricotta. Mix. In a separate bowl, sift flour, baking soda, and salt together. Add to creamed mixture. Mix well. Drop blobs on cookie sheet.

Bake 350 for 10-12 minutes. Remove cookies to cooling rack or aluminum foil on counter. Makes 85-100. Put icing on when completely cool. Cookies will freeze beautifully.

Icing: Mix 1 lb. confectioner's sugar with 4-5 T. milk.

DR. P'S FIVE SECRETS OF EFFECTIVE COMMUNICATION (EAR)

E = EMPATHY

1. The Disarming Technique (DT): Find some truth in what the other person is saying, even if it seems totally unreasonable or unfair.
2. Empathy: Put yourself in the other person's shoes and try to see the world through his or her eyes.
   - Thought Empathy (TE): Paraphrase the other person's words.
   - Feeling Empathy (FE): Acknowledge how the other person probably is feeling based on what he or she said.
3. Inquiry (IN): Ask gentle, probing questions to learn more about what the other person is thinking and feeling

A = ASSERTIVENESS

4. "I Feel" Statements (IF): Express your own ideas and feelings in a direct, tactful manner. Use "I feel" statements, such as "I feel upset" rather than "you" statements, such as "You're wrong!" or "You're making me furious!"

R = RESPECT

5. Stroking (ST): Convey an attitude of respect, even if you feel frustrated or angry with the other person. Find something genuinely positive to say to the other person, even in the heat of battle.

BIBLIOGRAPHY

Berra, Yogi. The Yogi Book: I Really Didn't Say Everything I Said!. New York: Workman Publishing Company, Inc., 2010.

Brooke, Rupert. "Retrospect." In The Collected Poems of Rupert Brooke, 122-123. New York: Dodd, Mead and Company, 1915.

Dangerfield, Rodney. No Respect. Los Angeles: Casablanca Records, 1980.

Dickinson, Emily. "XV." In Poems, Volume III, edited by Mabel Loomis Todd, 153. Boston: Roberts Brothers, 1896.

Frankl, Viktor E. Man's Search for Meaning. Boston: Beacon Press, 1962.

Franklin, Benjamin. Poor Richard's Almanack. Philadelphia, 1758.

Kipling, Rudyard. "The Power of the Dog." In Rudyard Kipling's Verse, 787. Garden City: Doubleday, Page & Co., 1922.

Rossetti, Christina. "A Christmas Carol." In "Scribner's Monthly" Volume 3 Cover, 287. New York: Scribner & Co., 1871.

Rossetti, Christina. "Love Came Down at Christmas." In Hymns to the Living God, #110. 1885.

Shakespeare, William. Richard III, 5.4. London: 1594.

Shakespeare, William. The Tempest, 4.1.128-158. London: 1611.

BIOGRAPHY

Susie Berta and her husband Rick, a veterinarian, have lived in Newnan, Georgia—a lovely southern town about forty-five miles south of Atlanta—since 1977. They raised two boys and have two grandchildren. As an empty nester, Susie returned to school in 2003 and earned a BFA in art. Retired from a long career as a professional vocalist and performer, Susie writes a regular food column for her local newspaper, blogs, and maintains her website: www.susieberta. com.

The Veterinarian's Wife is her first book. She will never retire from writing.

Made in the USA
Columbia, SC
20 February 2022

56541585R00148